"The pilgrimage to the holy places of Our Lord's Incarnation, Life, Death, Resurrection, and Ascension is an extraordinary font of grace for all Christians, and, in a particular way, for those called to participate in the priesthood of Christ through Holy Orders. Fr. Charles Samson has rendered a great service to priests and seminarians, and to all the faithful, by preparing this pilgrim guide, marked both by his deep faith, his priestly character, and his scholarly expertise. May his outstanding work assist many pilgrims in coming to a deeper knowledge and love of Our Lord Jesus Christ through visiting the places made holy by his Redemptive Incarnation."

—CARDINAL RAYMOND L. BURKE
Archbishop Emeritus of St. Louis

"Fr. Samson's love for the priesthood and for the person of Jesus Christ shines through in this guidebook. His insights are deep and enlightening, and his knowledge of the Holy Land is first-hand and well-studied. He shares these in a manner which reads like a pleasant and focused conversation. Every seminarian making a pilgrimage to the Holy Land will want to be a part of this conversation; it will, in a unique way, bring the seminarian into contact with the reality of our faith in Jesus, to whose heart we priests are called to conform our own in our prayer and ministry."

—ARCHBISHOP ROBERT J. CARLSON
Archbishop of St. Louis

"St. Jerome, the greatest Bible scholar of the early Church, dared to call the Holy Land 'the Fifth Gospel.' Fr. Samson has produced an indispensable commentary on that Gospel—theologically rich, historically grounded, archeologically informed, yet practical in countless ways. A rock-solid and reliable guide. If you're heading for the Holy Land, don't leave home without it."

B

"Today, it is not uncommon for a seminary to include the privilege of partaking in a pilgrimage to the Holy Land as an integral part of its priestly formation. Fr. Samson's Holy Land Guide provides the perfect balance of scriptural, spiritual, and scholarly knowledge that allows a seminarian (or any prayerful pilgrim) to contemplate each Holy Land site."

—VERY REVEREND JAMES MASON
Rector of Kenrick-Glennon Seminary, St. Louis

COME
AND SEE

COME AND SEE

A CATHOLIC GUIDE TO THE HOLY LAND

REV. CHARLES SAMSON, SSL

EMMAUS ROAD
PUBLISHING

Steubenville, Ohio
www.EmmausRoad.org

Emmaus Road Publishing
1468 Parkview Circle
Steubenville, Ohio 43952

Library of Congress Cataloging-in-Publication Data

Names: Samson, Charles K., author.

Title: Come and see : a Catholic guide to the Holy Land / Rev. Charles K. Samson.

Description: Steubenville : Emmaus Road Pub., 2017. | Includes bibliographical references.

Identifiers: LCCN 2017032009 (print) | LCCN 2017032643 (ebook) | ISBN 9781945125676 (ebook) | ISBN 9781945125652 (hardcover) | ISBN 9781945125669 (pbk.)

Subjects: LCSH: Christian antiquities--Palestine. | Christian antiquities--Palestine--Meditations. | Bible. Gospels--Antiquities. | Bible. Gospels--Geography. | Bible. Gospels--Meditations. | Catholic Church--Doctrines.

Classification: LCC BR133.P3 (ebook) | LCC BR133.P3 S26 2017 (print) | DDC 263/.0425694--dc23

LC record available at https://lccn.loc.gov/2017032009

Christian missionary activity.[16] However, the early Byzantine pilgrims do not seem to have paid much attention to Nazareth. In 384, the pilgrim Egeria—more on her later—was shown a "big and very splendid cave"[17] in which Mary lived. After that, there is silence in historically verifiable sources, but many legends sprang up. One such legend, per the sixth-century Pilgrim of Piacenza, was the legend called "St. Mary's Gift," which describes the purported phenomenon that female Jews of Nazareth were better looking than any others in the whole country since they were related to Mary.[18]

Fast-forwarding a bit, a certain Crusader named Tancrid became Prince of Galilee in 1099, and he built a church above the cave in the center of the city. The Russian pilgrim Daniel, visiting Nazareth in 1106, also mentions a second church built above a well and dedicated to the Angel Gabriel; this church is currently operated by the Greek Orthodox, who claim that the Annunciation happened there. Not long after the collapse of the Latin Kingdom of Jerusalem of the Crusaders at the Battle of the Horns of the Hattin in 1187, it became too dangerous for pilgrims to go to Nazareth. The Franciscans received permission to buy the property of the ruined church in 1620 and slowly reestablished a Christian presence, and building, here.[19] This church was dedicated in 1969.

The present Church of the Annunciation was designed by the great Italian architect Antonio Barluzzi, who is responsible for the design of most of the Holy Land shrines. The basilica's form is intended to resemble a giant tent, for here it is that the "Word became flesh, and dwelt"—literally, "pitched his tent" (*eskēnōsen* in the original Greek)—"among us" (Jn 1:14). We shall see that the designs of Barluzzi's Holy Land churches usually have some sort of evangelical inspiration and motivation and, so, help us to evoke and better enter into the mysteries and realities of our faith.

As a dramatic aside, we Americans should feel a bit of pride at this place. On the walk up to the market streets that precede the church, you might notice a large billboard right in front of that Nazareth is mentioned in the Gospels once more after the Infancy Narratives. In Luke 4:16–30, the town does not appear in a very positive light, as its inhabitants reject Jesus and even begin to spurn him.

SCRIPTURE ON SITE:
Luke 1:26-39

This passage contains some serious foreshadowing! Here is a good breakdown of it:

Jesus likens the Nazarenes to those who did not listen to Elijah and Elisha, which angers the Nazarenes; they do not believe in him and so they lead Jesus out of Nazareth to throw him off a cliff to his death. Je-

SCRIPTURE ON SITE:
Luke 4:16-30

sus, Luke says, does not permit this death but, instead, walks through their midst. We have in this one Nazareth story the four elements which outline the program of the rest of the Gospel: At first, Jesus will be marveled at by many, even accepted by many.[12] Second, there will come a time of anger at him and rejection.[13] Third, there will arrive the moment of putting Jesus to death. Finally, there will be his Resurrection, when Jesus escapes the clutches of death.[14]

Archaeological History

Some evidence suggests that a Judeo-Christian community survived in Nazareth during the second and third centuries AD. According to Julius Africanus,[15] the village was a center of Jewish–

---

[12] See John 7:40–41: "Some in the crowd who heard these words said: 'This is truly the Prophet.' Others said, 'This is the Messiah.'" See also John 7:45–46: "So the guards went to the chief priests and Pharisees, who asked them, 'Why did you not bring him?' The guards answered, 'Never before has anyone spoken like this one.'"

[13] See John 7:43: "So a division occurred in the crowd because of him. Some of them even wanted to arrest him."

[14] Kilgallen, *New Testament Guide to Holy Land*, 17.

[15] A Jewish Christian who held a Roman government office with connections to Damascus, Syria (AD 160–240).

I certainly would hesitate to dismiss Luke's witness, much less set one Gospel's account against that of another, and especially not to the effect of insinuating that one is unlikely to be true.[9] What I would say is this: "home" can be spoken of in many ways, as in the place where one was born and the place where one grew up. I have no problem with sustaining that both Matthew and Luke can be correct in calling Bethlehem and Nazareth, respectively, Jesus's home.[10] Jesus was born in Bethlehem and grew up in Nazareth.

Revisiting a point made earlier, it is perhaps surprising that Nazareth is never mentioned in the Old Testament. Given the unimportance of this latecomer in the Old Testament's promises and hopes for salvation, it is not surprising that Nathaniel of Cana retorts to those who spoke of Jesus of Nazareth as the Messiah: "Can anything good come from Nazareth?" (Jn 1:46).[11] Nathaniel's skepticism is echoed later in John when people in Jerusalem questioned whether or not Jesus was the Anointed One, since they knew Jesus's origin to be Nazareth and not Bethlehem, the City of David (Lk 2:11): "Others (in the crowd) said: 'The Messiah will not come from Galilee, will he? Does not scripture say that the Messiah will be of David's family and come from Bethlehem, the village where David lived?'" (Jn 7:41–42).

Moving from incredulity to credulity, we note another—indeed, perhaps the best-known—appearance of Nazareth in the New Testament: the Annunciation, cited in prior pages (Lk 1:26–38). Before going inside the present-day Basilica of the Annunciation, where we are encouraged to stay quiet for the sake of prayer, it would be helpful to read this entire passage aloud.

Finally, moving unfortunately back to incredulity, we note

---

[9] Which insinuation, of course, would imply that one of the Gospels is in error here. A robustly Catholic understanding of the Bible precludes the identification therein of any errors; again, see *Issues Raised* in later pages on biblical inerrancy.

[10] Moreover, this seeming choice between the two candidate cities does no harm to Jesus's Davidic genealogy. Both aptly fit and secure the theme and promises of Davidic, messianic hopes—Bethlehem being, of course, the birthplace of David, and Nazareth being one of the towns in which the line of David, in fact, notably continued after the Babylonian Exile, though without holding any political power. See *Issues Raised*, further on.

[11] John J. Kilgallen, *A New Testament Guide to the Holy Land* (Chicago: Loyola, 1998), 7.

Scripture, it is not allowable to say, The author of this book is mistaken; but either that the manuscript [transmission] is faulty, or the translation is wrong, or you have not understood."[4]

Still, some think that it is "more probable" that Bethlehem, as Matthew has it, was the home of Mary and Joseph before the birth of Jesus, as Murphy-O'Connor writes:

> Joseph belonged to a Judaean family. Were Nazareth their home, it would have been natural to return there when Herod menaced the family, rather than travelling to Egypt.[5] Judaeans, on the other hand, automatically thought of Egypt as a place of refuge.[6] When Archelaus (4 BC–AD 6) showed that he had inherited the murderous unpredictability of his father, Herod the Great, Joseph decided to move his family to the north.[7] Just at that moment Herod Antipas, who had become tetrarch of Galilee, was recruiting artisans for the construction of his capital Sepphoris (today Zippori). Joseph settled at Nazareth 6 km [3.7miles] to the south-east on the Roman road from Sepphoris to Samaria and Jerusalem. All that Luke knew was that the family had lived in Nazareth for so long that it was considered Jesus's "home town" (Mt 13:54; Luke 4:16) and that Jesus had relatives there (Mt 13:55–56). He therefore assumed that Joseph and Mary had been born there.[8]

---

[4] Augustine of Hippo, *Contra Faustum* 11.5, trans. Richard Stothert (1887), rev. and ed. Kevin Knight (2009), accessed June 4, 2017, http://www.newadvent.org/fathers/1406.htm.

[5] Where Joseph, in fact, took the family upon the danger of Herod's threat as revealed by the angel: "The angel of the Lord appeared to Joseph in a dream and said, 'Rise, take the child and his mother, flee to Egypt, and stay there until I tell you. Herod is going to search for the child to destroy him. He stayed there until the death of Herod, so that what the Lord had said through the prophet might be fulfilled, 'Out of Egypt I have called my son'" (Mt 2:13–15).

[6] 1 Kings 11:40: "When Solomon tried to have Jeroboam killed, Jeroboam fled to Shishak, king of Egypt. He remained in Egypt until Solomon's death." See also Jeremiah 26:21.

[7] That is, to Nazareth from Bethlehem, the latter of which is south of Nazareth.

[8] Jerome Murphy-O'Connor, *The Holy Land: An Oxford Archaeological Guide from Earliest Times to 1700*, 5th ed. (Oxford: Oxford University Press, 2008), 423.

Right from the beginning this Lucan tangent confronts us with a crucial question: what do we make of apparent tensions in Scripture, whether between differing Gospel versions or between Scripture and archaeology? To be sure, we should wholeheartedly affirm that none of these geographical disparities between Gospel and "factual" reality threatens Sacred Scripture's *inerrancy*.[2] The holy writers often spoke in general terms, according to the contemporaneous convention available to them. These terms are often less-than-precise, as seems to be the case with Luke's description of the town of Nazareth as a city. The scholarly consternation over Luke's possible exaggeration puzzles me; his description really should not bother us at all.

A similar dynamic is at play in another aspect of biblical Nazareth—that is, the assertion by Luke that Nazareth was the Holy Family's hometown (2:4–5). On this note, the question can arise: wait, which was the Holy Family's hometown—Nazareth, or Bethlehem?

From the outset, we can and should say that when what we encounter might strike us as irreconcilable disparities within the Bible, we should always give to the Word of God the benefit of the doubt and should *never* conclude that the Bible contains any errors![3] Here, a quote from St. Augustine should be emblematic for us: "If we are perplexed by an apparent contradiction in

---

chaeological Discoveries, ed. Rainer Riesner, trans. Keith Myrick and Sam and Miriam Randall (San Francisco: Ignatius, 2010), 428.

[2] See *Issues Raised* below as well as Harrison, "Restricted Inerrancy and the Hermeneutic of Discontinuity," *Letter and Spirit* 6 [*For the Sake of Our Salvation*] (2010): 225–46; and Harrison, "Does Vatican Council II Allow for Errors in Sacred Scripture?" *Living Tradition* nos.145–46 (2010), accessed June 4, 2017, http://www.rtforum.org/lt/lt145-6.html (originally published in *Divinitas* 52, no. 3 [2009]: 279–304).

[3] We are forbidden to entertain the proposition that the Bible contains errors, as §11 of the Second Vatican Council's Dogmatic Constitution on Divine Revelation, *Dei Verbum* (1965), says: "Therefore, since everything asserted by the inspired authors or sacred writers must be held to be asserted by the Holy Spirit, it follows that the books of Scripture must be acknowledged as teaching solidly, faithfully, and without error that truth which God wanted put into sacred writings for the sake of salvation" (accessed June 4, 2017, http://www.vatican.va/archive/hist_councils/ii_vatican_council/documents/vat-ii_const_19651118_dei-verbum_en.html). See *Issues Raised*, on the following pages.

NAZARETH

In the sixth month, the angel Gabriel was sent from God to a town of Galilee called Nazareth, to a virgin betrothed to a man named Joseph, of the house of David, and the virgin's name was Mary.

(Luke 1:26–27)

Scriptural Background

Nazareth has a slightly enigmatic history within the Bible. We read about Nazareth in the Gospels but nowhere else in all of Scripture. Furthermore, the picture of Nazareth that the Gospels paint is not entirely clear. Mark simply states that Jesus came from Nazareth in Galilee (1:9). Matthew and Luke contain many descriptions of and references to Nazareth, but the picture that Luke paints is slightly obscure. How so? Well, archaeology has shown that Nazareth was, at the time of Jesus, no more than a small town that probably belonged to the larger village of Japhia. Luke, though, generously calls it a *polis* (city) (1:26; 2:4, 39). Further, Luke writes that this town was built on a mountain (4:29); Nazareth, however, was situated on a small spur of a mere hill. Based on these and other potentially problematic points, scholars have even surmised that it is likely that Luke lacked local knowledge of Nazareth.[1]

---

[1] Bargil Pixner, *Paths of the Messiah: Sites of the Early Church from Galilee to Jerusalem—Jesus and Jewish Christianity in Light of Ar-*

GALILEE

View of the Sea of Galilee from *Eremos* Hill.

Bible history (Bethany, the Temple Mount, the Siloam Pool, the City of David, etc.). For these items I entrust the reader to my three principal sources.

Discussion about most sites is divided in this way: city (or area) in bold, followed by a Scripture quote featured at the site, and then details pertaining to the following categories:

1. Scriptural Background (a summary of the biblical event at the site with citation);
2. Scripture on Site;[5]
3. Archaeological History (what is seen and/or has been seen here—in particular, the buildings);
4. Issues Raised (what aspects of our faith are relevant to what we experience here);
5. Points of Reflections (in other words, how this spot might speak to you in your spiritual life, with special sections to aid seminarians in their formation to the priesthood).

The reflection questions section could be useful for priest chaperones and pilgrimage leaders in preparing homilies for Masses or talks on site.

I should note that Galilee and Jerusalem will not follow exactly the aforementioned outline, as I found it more convenient to organize those areas in the following way: general introduction, specific sites/churches, and (then) reflection questions and issues raised.

Procedamus in pace! Let us proceed in peace!

---

[5] This step is very important! Pilgrims, especially seminarians, have been told that a journey to and through the Holy Land makes the Scriptures come alive for them. There is no better way to make this happen than to have them read, in full, certain Gospel episodes *where they happened*. Encourage them to bring their Bibles with them and to read the relevant Scripture passage at each site.

accomplishing these tasks, as this faith-filled archaeologist lingers over many topics that extend from the scientifically factual to the spiritually fruitful.[4]

Throughout this guide, I cite the above-mentioned authors frequently. An exegete by training, and still young in my priesthood, I am no archaeologist or spiritual master, and so I rely on the contributions of those so competent! Nevertheless, I have taken it upon myself to adjudicate between their contributions, placing in the body of my text the particular information about a given site that I deem most likely valuable and enlightening to a seminarian or cleric. When the facts—scriptural or historical—of a given place are uncertain, I will share my thoughts based on my own experiences in the Holy Land on any issue that is raised by the presentation of a given site's history, reality, and significance. The material in the footnotes covers aspects of the above considerations that the reader—seminarians in particular—could consult on their own for further investigation.

That which I could call specifically my own about this project is the choice of what pieces of information to present at a given site, reflection questions, and issues raised at individual sites.

I have endeavored to create a book that one can conveniently carry and consult and from which leaders could read aloud. It will be most effective if the guide reads, beforehand, the material relevant to a day's visits, indicating in his own copy of the book the relevant pieces of information that he will want to convey vocally to the group. In this way, the leader will be able, while on site, to consult with relative facility the appropriate material. The faithful and seminarians alike, then, would be encouraged to read—on site, or perhaps later, in prayer—the theological issues raised and the points of reflection offered.

It has been necessary to exclude some interesting sites from

Archaeological Discoveries, ed. Rainer Riesner, trans. Keith Myrick and Sam and Miriam Randall (San Francisco: Ignatius, 2010).

[4] However, there are a few factors of Pixner's book which work to this source's detriment: (1) Pixner at times dwells upon and strongly proposes items which are at best hypothetical, even exaggerating, in my opinion, some elements of the dynamic of the early Church's life in the Holy Land, such as the Essenes's influence on early Christianity; (2) his book is a bit cumbersome to carry; (3) the volume details a bit more archaeology than could be retained on a week or two's pilgrimage to the Holy Land on the part of a budding theologian and future priest.

HOW TO USE
THIS GUIDE

I have attempted to provide what I have noted to be somewhat lacking among guidebooks to the Holy Land—that is, a study that balances Scripture, history, archaeology, architecture, and prayer to meet the needs of a reader either educated or interested in theology, and in particular those men who are in formation for the Holy Priesthood. I have indeed found guidebooks that excelled in one or two of these categories: the volume of Jerome Murphy-O'Connor, O.P.,[1] is far and away the best available source of archaeological (and quite practical travel) information, and the work of John J. Kilgallen, S.J.,[2] offers excellent scriptural and spiritual explanations of the major New Testament events organized by site and area. Nevertheless, I have searched in vain for a work that attempts to cover all—or, better, as much as satisfyingly possible for the audience in mind—such areas. The substantial work of Bargil Pixner, O.S.B.,[3] comes closest to

---

[1]   Jerome Murphy-O'Connor, *The Holy Land: An Oxford Archaeological Guide from Earliest Times to 1700*, 5th ed. (Oxford: Oxford University Press, 2008).

[2]   John J. Kilgallen, *A New Testament Guide to the Holy Land* (Chicago: Loyola, 1998).

[3]   Bargil Pixner, *Paths of the Messiah: Sites of the Early Church from Galilee to Jerusalem—Jesus and Jewish Christianity in Light of*

maus Road Publishing and the St. Paul Center of Biblical Theology, who graciously accepted this project and brought it to a wonderful completion, in particular through the careful revision of their copy editors Kathryn Hogan and Brett Kendall. I thank Fr. Brendan Hurley, S.J., who led me on my first pilgrimage to the Holy Land during my time at the Pontifical North American College, for his many years of service in this capacity and for his inspiring, priestly example that caused the Scriptures to come alive before my eyes (Lk 24:32). I appreciate as well the hospitality, fraternity, and wise instruction of the Jesuits of the Pontifical Biblical Institute in Jerusalem, where I spent a semester studying at the Hebrew University of Jerusalem. I am most grateful, too, for Raymond Leo Cardinal Burke, who sent me as a seminarian to Rome to study theology, and for Archbishop Robert Carlson, who encouraged me to pursue my License in Sacred Scripture at the Pontifical Biblical Institute and my (forthcoming) Doctorate in Sacred Theology at the Pontifical Gregorian University. To those who have served as my "guinea pigs" in the testing out of my notes—my mother; the then–St. Louis seminarians Fr. Zac Povis, Dcn. Clark Philip, and in particular Andrew Auer; and, finally, the Scharmer family and my friend Alli—thank you for your encouragement, contributions, advice, photo ops, and patience! Fr. Michael Rubeling of Baltimore deserves more than a nod for his excellent photography. I would also be remiss not to thank Marsha Feingold for her superb proofreading and extensive, incredibly helpful comments, as well as John Noronha for his assistance. Lastly, I express my heartfelt gratitude to my family for supporting me in my first foray into the world of publishing, which I pray greatly benefits not only the seminarians of Kenrick-Glennon Seminary (St. Louis) whom I will lead to the Holy Land but also, in a special way, the men of the Latin Patriarchate Seminary in Beit Jala, Palestine, to which institute I happily donate the entirety of the proceeds that I will receive from the sale of this book. Thank you, my brothers in the Middle East, for answering the call to discern the priesthood! May we be, as your motto has it, one in faith—*una fides*—in our work in the Lord's vineyard for the salvation of souls.

know the Word who became flesh and made his dwelling among us (Jn 1:14).

In order to facilitate such an encounter, especially on the part of those who are in formation toward sacramental configuration to Christ the priest in Holy Orders, I have composed this guidebook to the Holy Land. On your pilgrimage, the Lord is inviting you, as he invited me, to "'come and see' . . . where he was staying" and to "stay with him" (Jn 1:39). Of this land, indeed, we are neither the master nor the owner, but rather mere sojourners—passers-through—for the Holy Land belongs, in a singular way through the Incarnation, to God. So, truly, this land is yours, O pilgrim, insofar as the Lord shares it with you because he wants you to know him more fully and intimately, and inasmuch as your faith is in a *real*, even sensorial way, connected to these very places, as you will discover during your days in ancient Israel. It is this *tactility* of our faith that has deeply moved me in my own relationship with Jesus Christ and that I want to share with you. In this light, I make my own the words of John and I hope that you will be able to do the same:

> What was from the beginning,
> what we have heard,
> what we have seen with our eyes,
> what we looked upon
> and touched with our hands
> concerns the Word of life—
> for the life was made visible;
> we have seen it and testify to it
> and proclaim to you the eternal life
> that was with the Father and was made visible to us—
> what we have seen and heard
> we proclaim now to you,
> so that you too may have fellowship with us;
> for our fellowship is with the Father
> and with his Son, Jesus Christ.
> We are writing this so that our joy may be complete.
> (1 Jn: 1–4)

At the outset, I must extend a word of gratitude to all of those who contributed to the realization of this project. Firstly, I thank the eminently professional, kind, and helpful staff of Em-

INTRODUCTION

For the land is mine, for you are strangers and sojourners with me.

(Leviticus 25:23)

I will never forget the blossoming of friendships that I forged with two families—one Dutch, the other Italian—over the course of my years of study for the priesthood. I met both before moving across the Atlantic and got to know especially the former quite well within youth ministry, but it was not until I went to visit them in their homelands that I felt I really got to know them. Through hearing their languages and observing how they naturally expressed themselves (the first with many traditional, joyful songs around a table ever devoid of napkins, the latter with abundant hand gestures and more-than-extended family time around the best of kitchen tables!), and in seeing and walking the places dear to them in their childhoods and current lives, I was given a uniquely revealing glimpse into who they were.

Such an analogy came to be, for me, the best way that I could capture the essence of the mix of emotions, graces, growth, and spiritual eye-openers that characterized my own time in the Holy Land. I came to see my pilgrimages there as occasions in which the Lord shared himself with me in a special way—that is, by sharing the special part of himself that is his homeland. By getting to better know his *landscape*—cultural, linguistic, historical, topographical—I strongly believe that I got to better

FOREWORD

Most first-time pilgrims to the Holy Land will usually search for a helpful guidebook, and there are dozens of them, many very good.

This one, *Come and See: A Catholic Guide to the Holy Land* by Rev. Charles Samson, will prove uniquely helpful even to a seasoned pilgrim. Father Samson is a biblical scholar who has lived in the land of Christ's life and death. His familiarity with its history and culture, its stones and sites, is unmistakable. His fascination with and love for the mysteries of the Holy Land shine forth on every colorfully crafted page.

Of unique value is this compact volume's scriptural commentary offering moments to pause, reflect, and pray along every step of the pilgrim's journey. Galilee, Jerusalem, and the Dead Sea come alive, surely throughout Old and New Testament reflections, but also through the observations of early Roman and Christian witnesses, not to mention the spiritual and theological insights of this modern Scripture scholar.

Individual pilgrims will surely benefit from this *Guide to the Holy Land*. But its stimulating and inspiring style will be especially enriching for groups of believers before, during, and after a singular and grace-filled pilgrimage to the land loved by Jesus.

As one who encourages the thousands of our members of the Equestrian Order of the Holy Sepulchre to pilgrimages there, I am especially pleased to recommend this fine resource.

Edwin Cardinal O'Brien
Grand Master
Equestrian Order of the Holy Sepulchre of Jerusalem

To my family,
In great gratitude (Col 3:15)

Table of Contents

Imprimatur: Bishop-Elect Mark S. Rivituso
Auxiliary Bishop-Elect of St. Louis
April 10, 2017

Maps and Illustrations used with permission:

Cover design and layout by Margaret Ryland

the view of the church tower. This advertisement boldly cites the Qur'an to the effect that Islam is the only true faith and that all believers in other religions will be lost in the end. Unfortunately,

The exterior and dome of the Church of the Annunciation, which was built in the shape of a tent in reference to the literal meaning of the Greek of John 1:14.

in Nazareth some Christian–Muslim tension has built up over the long years. In fact, toward the end of the last century, the city of Nazareth was considering building a large mosque right next to the basilica, which the mosque would overshadow not only by its size but also by its loud calls to prayer. However, President George W. Bush urged Ariel Sharon, then–Prime Minister of Israel, to pressure the city of Nazareth not to build this mosque. The city backed down, thus preserving the peacefulness of this shrine. *God bless America*!

Going inside the church from the entrance gate, we come upon the lower level of the basilica. There you can, from above, look down into the middle and see Byzantine remains conserved in a large, almost cylindrical-looking floor section in the center of the Crusader-church floor. The Byzantine apse belonged to a small, eighteen-meter-long church of the mid-fifth century which was built over what might have been a synagogue—which happens to align, to the left, to the Cave of the Annunciation. Various graffiti—such as *chaire maria*, "Hail, Mary," from the lips of Gabriel the Archangel (Lk 1:28)—that has been incised into the plaster covering of the seven descending steps has convinced excavators that the cylindrical space was a pre-Constantinian baptistery. A mosaic panel contains a motif of a victory crown with trailing ribbons surrounding a monogram cross, which could be dated to the third century AD.[20]

The main attraction of this lower-basilica is the Cave of the Annunciation. It consists of two parts. The smaller part was dedicated to Conon, who was a deacon of Jerusalem martyred in Asia Minor during the reign of Decius (AD 249–251) and whose early cult is evidenced by the floor mosaic. At his trial, he professed to the court: "I am of Nazareth in Galilee, I am of the family of Christ to whom I offer a cult from the time of my ancestors."[21] The larger part of the cave is the site where tradition holds that

The cave in which the Angel Gabriel appeared to Mary at the Annunciation. The altar's inscription reads: "And the Word here was made flesh," a reference to John 1:14.

---

[20] Ibid., 424.
[21] Ibid.

the Archangel Gabriel appeared to Mary, telling her that she will be the mother of the Lord (Lk 1:26–38). The altar in the cave contains a very powerful inscription that poignantly inserts—by means not of dogma but of devotion—a word into the third antiphonal line of the Angelus, so as to say: "And the Word *here* was made flesh." Wow! This is the space and place where the infinite became finite, the eternal entered time, God became man! Truly, we are standing on "holy ground" (Ex 3:5).

Ascending the stairs, we arrive in the upper, and much more modern, basilica. Through the left side exit, we enter a large courtyard that overlooks many first-century remains from Nazareth at the time of Jesus: silos, oil presses, house foundations. Before we move on past the courtyard up to the church dedicated to St. Joseph, the synagogue ruins from the lower basilica merit further comment, in light of these ruins below our feet. Jesus visited a synagogue similar to the one whose ruins we saw in Luke 4:16–30. Jesus was handed the scroll of the prophet Isaiah and, having read it aloud ("the Spirit of the Lord is upon me"), applied it to himself ("this passage is fulfilled in your hearing"), to the amazement and dismay of the congregation ("is this not Joseph's son?"). Matthew appraises the crowd more negatively than Luke does:

> He came to his native place and taught the people in their synagogue. They were astonished and said: "Where did this man get such wisdom and mighty deeds? Is he not the carpenter's son? Is not his mother named Mary and his brothers James, Joseph, Simon, and Judas? Are not his sisters all with us? Where did this man get this?" And they took offense at him. But Jesus said to them: "A prophet is not without honor except in his native place and in his own house." (Mt 13:54–57)

These episodes of the adult Jesus in Nazareth reveal a few aspects of our Lord's life:

1. Jesus is clearly known to the community as a faithful Jew who frequented the synagogue and who even took it upon himself to act like a teacher;
2. Jesus knew and spoke both Hebrew and Aramaic, since the synagogue service would have consisted of

a recitation of the *Shema Yisra'el* ("Hear, O Israel" [Deut 6:4]), a reading of the Torah (in Hebrew), a reading from the Prophets (again in Hebrew), a translation of the Torah into Aramaic (the *targum*), and then a homily (in Aramaic);

3. Joseph is identified as a *tektonos*, which many believe refers simply to an "artisan," not specifically to a "worker in wood"; O'Connor thinks it would be more realistic to think of him in terms of an all-purpose village builder, like a smith or stonecutter, than to think of him as a carpenter.[22]

I, for one, would like to believe that Joseph was a carpenter. Firstly, tradition has so identified him, and I hesitate to easily jettison either tradition or the memory of the early Christian communities. To me, those important witnesses are innocent until proven unfounded. However, to many critical scholars, such testimonies are doubted until verified by "fact." The former approach, I believe, is more respectful of our faith and history and, frankly, fosters a better pilgrimage attitude.[23] Secondly, Joseph's being a carpenter would line up well with something we read in the Jerusalem Talmud, as Bargil Pixner quite wonderfully writes:

Jesus originated from a very pious family. His foster father Joseph is called a "just man" (Mt 1:19). A *zaddik* ("just man") is one within the Jewish community who is considered a diligent, faithful observer of the law. Joseph the carpenter (Mt 13:55) and Jesus, who learned this craft from him (Mk 6:3), remind us of a story recorded in the Jerusalem Talmud (*Jebamoth* 8 [9b]): A man comes into a village and seeks someone who could help him

---

[22] Ibid., 427.

[23] Indeed, to quote our Lord and apply his words to our situation of pilgrimage to the Holy Land, I think that when we are evaluating the credibility of some historical or topographical claim, we need to be both "wise as serpents and innocent as doves" (Mt 10:16). I simply believe that, on a pilgrimage to the Holy Land, one will spiritually profit all the more if, at the outset, he leans toward the latter half of this balance, giving to the enduring witness of the local Christian community the benefit of the doubt.

solve a problem. He first asks the people of the village whether there is a rabbi present. On receiving a negative answer, he asks: "Is there a carpenter or the son of a carpenter, who can give me a solution?" This seems to suggest that in a small village (like Nazareth), the carpenter was the best informed for *halakhic*, or morality-related,[24] questions. The *zaddik* carpenter Joseph and the *zaddik* carpenter Jesus might have been such men. It would not have been unusual, then, that Jesus went regularly to Nazareth to the synagogue (Lk 4:16). The fact that the Nazarenes had their own synagogue, despite the small size of their settlement (and despite a synagogue close at Japhia), could be because they had a different understanding of *halakha* from their neighbors.[25]

A final word on the Holy Family's trade, as it sheds further light on Jesus the God-man: it is likely that Joseph and Jesus either worked in or took their trade products to the nearby city of Sepphoris, also known as Zippori, in order to sell their handiwork. This city's history reveals something fascinating about Jesus and the languages that he spoke.

The Roman governor of Syria declared Sepphoris the capital of Galilee in 55 BC. Jews rebelled there, but Rome quelled

A statue of St. Joseph the Worker and the child Jesus inside the Church of St. Joseph. The inscription on the pages of the book that is being held by Jesus reads: "Go to Joseph," in reference to Genesis 41:55.

---

[24] A word which refers to "moral"—literally, in the Hebrew, "ways of walking," or "ways of living a holy life."

[25] Pixner, *Paths of the Messiah*, 381–82.

the uprising and burned the city. Herod Antipas rebuilt it, and the Sanhedrin remained there until the second half of the third century. At the time of Jesus, this city was an epicenter of both Judaism and building trades—carpentry, for example. As such, the city also witnessed a daily confluence of spoken languages. Because of the Sanhedrin's presence there, Hebrew was common-ly spoken in Sepphoris, and because the language of commerce in the Roman Empire of the time was Greek, the Hellenistic tongue was often heard throughout this city's streets.

So, at Sepphoris, Jesus would have encountered both *spoken* Hebrew and Greek. Setting aside for now the theological question of the knowledge of Jesus with regard to language, we can at least say that from a young age, based on the Holy Family's trade, Jesus would frequently have encountered He-brew and Greek in speech, in which he surely participated. That Jesus spoke Hebrew, few doubt; he was able to read aloud (and interpret) the text of Isaiah 61:1–2 in Luke 4:16–21. We can see that Jesus spoke some Greek from his use of such words as "hypocrite" (Mt 23:13), which was a technical term of the theater—a small one of which, moreover, has been found at Sep-phoris near the marketplace where Jesus would have worked and sold goods. It seems clear, then, that Jesus spoke Hebrew and at least some Greek.[26] Lastly, wrapping up this brief tan-gent on the languages of Jesus, we can presume that Jesus spoke with a distinct accent[27] and even in a unique dialect of Aramaic called Galilean.[28]

With all of this in mind, we move on up the street to the Church of St. Joseph, whose house and/or workshop is supposed to be underneath it. This area is accessible from the church's inside without disrupting any service in the upper, main part of the church.

---

[26] There is no biblical evidence that Jesus spoke any Latin, although he surely could have heard some of it here and, later, during his trial, since Latin was the language of courts and justice at the time.

[27] Recognized also in Peter during Jesus's trial (Mt 26:73), as he, too, was from Galilee.

[28] Consult Steven Fassberg, "Which Semitic Language Did Jesus and Other Contemporary Jews Speak?" *Catholic Biblical Quarterly* 74 (2012): 263–80 (the conclusion will suffice), as well as the last entry in *Issues Raised*, further on.

Some doubt the reliability of this supposition.[29] However, I would simply say that whether or not this location's identification is credible does not impact the significance of this space. Going down to the level of Joseph's house/workshop, you will notice in front of the altar opposite the excavations a small disk of porphyry,[30] around which run the words: *hic erat subditus illis*—here he (Jesus) was submissive to them (his parents), when they went down to Nazareth after the Finding in the Temple (Lk 2:51).

This whole space speaks to the harmony of family life: the solicitous care and provision of a good, gentle father; the warm, nourishing presence of a mother; and especially the deference of a child to his parents. In other words, the Holy Family here shows us the beauty of the Fourth Commandment: "Honor your father and mother, that you might have long life in the land that I am giving you" (Ex 20:12). To quote Pope Paul VI in his homily at Nazareth in 1964—a homily found in the Office of Readings—Nazareth can teach us a lesson of domestic life:

The inscription indicates that here, in the house of azareth, the child Jesus was obedient to his parents, in reference to Luke 2:51.

> May Nazareth serve as a model of what the family should be. May it show us the family's holy and enduring character and exemplify its basic function in society: a com-

---

[29] Murphy-O'Connor, *The Holy Land*, 426. Murphy-O'Connor notes that this tradition only goes back to the seventeenth century, though there have been found in this area fragments of pottery which date to the Roman and Byzantine period. Moreover, why would the floor below the main altar be decorated with mosaics unless it were venerated as a sacred spot?

[30] Porphyry is precious purple stone reserved for monuments and royal projects in Rome. In St. Peter's Basilica in Rome, Italy, this stone functions prominently.

munity of love and sharing, beautiful for the problems it poses and the rewards it brings, in sum the perfect setting for rearing children—and for this there is no substitute.[31]

This place is meant to be a prayerful place of understanding, appreciating, and giving thanks for the gift of family. O Holy Family, pray for us!

A statue of the Holy Family on the outside of the Church of St. Joseph.

Issues Raised

Issue 1

Many scholars interpret *Dei Verbum* §11 as claiming that the Word of God is *inerrant* only in matters that regard strictly our salvation. Such an interpretation suggests that the Bible can contain errors in things that are not directly relevant to our salvation—for example, historical or scientific facts. Interpretation allowing for errors is known as "limited inerrancy" or "restricted

---

[31] Paul VI, *Homily at Nazareth* (January 5, 1964), accessed June 4, 2017, https://www.crossroadsinitiative.com/media/articles/lessons-of-nazareth/.

inerrancy." It is widely used by scholars to reconcile[32] some parts of the Bible that seem to contradict the "truths" of science.[33] One need simply read the text of *Dei Verbum* in the Latin to see that limited or restricted inerrancy is an aberrant approach to Scripture that has no basis in the text of *Dei Verbum* or in our Tradition from biblical to conciliar times.[34]

In short, we believe that, though the human authors of Scripture were "true authors," the ultimate author of Sacred Scripture is God, the Holy Spirit,[35] who, as Vatican I puts it, "cannot deceive or be deceived."[36] Hence, according to the mind of the

---

[32] Actually, "explain away" may be a more adequate term. This really amounts to little more than academic *blushing* at certain biblical passages, like Leviticus 11:20–23 (which seems to claim that insects of six legs actually have four), Matthew 13:32 (in which Jesus claims that the mustard seed is the smallest of seeds, though the orchid seed is smaller), 1 Kings 7:23–26 (which seems to paint the picture of a circle whose dimensions would make *pi* equal simply to 3), etc. These and other passages did not phase the Church Fathers at all, who, in carrying out biblical exegesis, recognized two very important realities: (1) at times, the sacred writers spoke generally and generically—with approximation and according to the advances in knowledge available to each in his own time—about the world around them; (2) some statements in the Bible which seem to be statements of fact are, to be sure, operating according to a literary genre different than that of a post-Enlightenment, positivistic *report*. For example, Jesus was not making a botanical pronouncement in Matthew 13:32, but rather a moral one, appraising not the size but the worth of the smallest among us. To see in such citations a contradiction between the Bible and science is to misread the Bible.

[33] I put this term in quotes without any reserve. Far too often, when biblical scholars make use of certain kinds of science (archaeology and form-critical theory, in particular) in their explanations and reasoning, they commit gross, though basic, errors in logic. The most common error is the attempt to pronounce as definitive something which is properly only possible (meaning undetermined). In other words, one all too often finds deductive statements which are nothing more than inductive hypotheses. One need only to read a few pages of a proponent of Wellhausen's Documentary Hypothesis (Old Testament, Pentateuch) or the infamous Q-source theory (New Testament, Gospels) for manifest examples of this error of logic.

[34] For a thorough treatment of inspiration and inerrancy, see Lawrence Feingold, *Faith Comes from What is Heard: An Introduction to Fundamental Theology* (Steubenville, OH: Emmaus Academic, 2016), 279–31.

[35] Vatican II, *Dei Verbum*, §11.

[36] First Vatican Council, Dogmatic Constitution *Dei Filius* (1870), ch. III.

Church, Sacred Scripture can contain no error (read: is *inerrant*), because even though its true human authors were imperfect, God—the ultimate author of Scripture—is perfect and cannot err.

In light of this, be careful when you read *Dei Verbum* §11, as some renditions of this text imply or build-in a limited-inerrancy narrative into the wording of their translation. For example, some translations of this paragraph run like this: "Therefore, since everything asserted by the inspired authors or sacred writers must be held to be asserted by the Holy Spirit, it follows that the books of Scripture must be acknowledged as teaching solidly, faithfully and without error that truth that God wanted put *into* sacred writings *for the sake of our salvation.*"[37] Let us critically break down this translation, specifically examining the two phrases italicized above.

Working backwards, let us begin with the phrase "for the sake of our salvation." This phrase[38] should *not* be read (as the Pontifical Biblical Commission unfortunately claims that it *should* be read)[39] like an adjectival clause modifying/specifying "truth."[40] Rather, it is to be read as an adverbial clause modifying "wanted." This proper reading does not in any way qualify—or restrict—the kind of truth that is protected from error in the Bible, but instead simply describes *why* God wanted the Bible composed: that is, for the sake of our salvation![41] The improper rendition of this phrase suggests that some of the Bible's content is not inspired by God *for the sake of our salvation*, but rather is

---

[37] Taken from the Vatican's website cited above.

[38] In the official Latin text, with the emphasis being mine: "Cum ergo omne id, quod auctores inspirati seu hagiographi asserunt, retineri debeat assertum a Spiritu Sancto, *inde Scripturae libri veritatem, quam Deus nostrae salutis causa Litteris Sacris consignari voluit, firmiter, fideliter, et sine errore docere profitendi sunt.*"

[39] Pontifical Biblical Commission, *The Inspiration and Truth of Sacred Scripture* (2014), §63. Unfortunately for English speakers, the Vatican initially published this text only in Italian, French, German, and Spanish. However, in those versions, the identification that I am critiquing is clearly noticeable here in §63. The text has, however, been published in an English translation in America: trans. Thomas Esposito, O.Cist., and Stephen Gregg, O.Cist. (Collegeville, MN: Liturgical Press, 2014), 71.

[40] With the cash value being that *only* the truth necessary for our salvation is protected from error.

[41] Harrison, "Restricted Inerrancy and the Hermeneutic of Discontinuity," 233.

the exclusive product of limited human authors. The limited-in-errancy interpretation fails simply in this: there is nothing in the Bible that is not somehow salvific, since "*all* of Scripture is inspired by God and useful for teaching" (2 Tim 3:16). Therefore, there is nothing in Scripture that is for the sake of our salvation *to the exclusion of other parts*. How could God inspire a part of Scripture if the content of that part errs in truth? That is impossible—but such is precisely what the theory of limited inerrancy does, instantiated in an improper translation of the phrase *causa nostrae salutis* in *Dei Verbum* §11.[42]

Moreover, the preposition *into* is also poorly rendered in the earlier-cited, official English text from the Latin of *Dei Verbum* §11, to the effect of advancing, again, the theory of limited inerrancy. This translation treats "sacred writings" (*litteris sacris*) like a phrase in the dative case (the Latin case ending used for nouns—or here, a phrase consisting of noun and adjective—when they are the indirect object of a verb, usually translated into English by adding "to" or "for" before the noun/phrase), as if the sacred writings were some kind of depository into which truth is placed. The problem with this rendition is that the Latin verb *consegnare* ("to put," as above) *never* takes a dative case; rather, it takes an ablative case, which connotes not place but *means* and would render a proper translation of *litteris sacris* as such: ". . . the truth which God wanted put *by means of sacred writings*."

Pointing out this syntactical flub might seem like an irrelevant fuss, but it is far from it, for this error of improperly interpreting this phrase as a dative gives the limited-inerrancy scholars ammunition for advancing their case. When the Bible is understood as a kind of depository *into* which truth is placed, then it becomes possible to insinuate, as these scholars do, a distinction in the *types* of truth that are found within the Bible. In other words, it becomes possible for scholars to claim that, in the Bible, there are to be found both some truths that are salvific/for the sake of our salvation, and so are inerrant, and some truths

---

[42] It is my personal contention that such an aberrant interpretation is the result of over-emphasizing the role of the human authors of Scripture in the composition of Holy Writ. The Bible is *both* of the divine and of the human, insofar as it is the Word of God in the words of men. Some biblical interpretations (such as that of limited inerrancy) focus on simply the human component of this process, to the effective exclusion of the divine element thereof.

that are *not* salvific/for the sake of our salvation, and so are *not* inerrant. This argument, though, is built on compromised syntactical footing and so does not, cannot, stand. Hence, in this way, *Dei Verbum* §11 likewise resists interpretations that would limit the truth of the Bible to matters purportedly exclusively geared towards our salvation.[43]

Rather, *Dei Verbum* §11 should be translated along these lines: "Therefore, since everything asserted by the inspired authors or sacred writers must be held to be asserted by the Holy Spirit, it follows that the books of Scripture must be acknowledged as teaching solidly, faithfully and without error that truth that God wanted, for the sake of our salvation, put down by means of the sacred writings." While all of this might seem like a nitpicky distinction or two to make, it is in fact foundational, as it affects our understanding of the nature and utility of one of the primary expressions of divine revelation—Sacred Scripture. The inerrancy of Scripture is, of course, crucial to apologetics, as well.

Now, this explanation might strike some scholars as a kind of erudite fundamentalism, according to which the human-author side of the equation in the writing of Scripture would get overlooked in favor of highlighting the divine-author part of the picture. I, though, think that it does not transgress, but rather properly places the human component within the authorship of the Bible. Moreover, I lament this straw man argument, which is so often erected in order to caricaturize, and so discredit, this traditionally Catholic hermeneutic without seriously engaging in it. A reading of the Bible to the exclusion of errors therein is decisively *not* a "fundamentalist" reading of Scriptures; rather, it is a reading that is faithful and faith-filled,[44] one that seeks the truth

---

[43] Harrison, "Does Vatican Council II Allow for Errors in Sacred Scripture?" 1.1.2. Harrison later notes (in 2.2.4) that Pope Paul VI even *personally* intervened in the drafting of *Dei Verbum* §11 and was keen to make sure that its wording would exclude the possibility of a restricted-inerrancy theory being derived from this paragraph.

[44] That is, consonant with a Patristic reading (see above) and with St. John Paul II's vision of faith and reason as being two, cooperative wings by means of which "the human spirit rises to the contemplation of truth"; see the opening paragraph of Pope John Paul II, Encyclical Letter *Fides et Ratio* (September 14, 1998), accessed June 4, 2017, http://w2.vatican.va/content/john-paul-ii/en/encyclicals/documents/hf_jp-ii_enc_14091998_fides-et-ratio.html.

of the Bible according to the way in which that truth, in its many instances, is expressed in the literary genres of respective books.[45]

Issue 2

Throughout his book, Pixner treats the Davidic *roots* (pardon the Is 11:1 pun!) of Jesus of *Nazareth*. We see throughout the New Testament instances in which, in Jesus, the town of Nazareth and the Davidic dynasty are linked. In Luke 18:38, the blind beggar, having been told that "Jesus the Nazarean" was passing by, burst out spontaneously: "Jesus, *Son of David*, have mercy on me!" In Romans 1:1–3, Paul writes about Jesus descending from David according to the flesh. Moreover, we see that, outside of the Bible, Nazareth and the family of David were identified after the time of Jesus. Pixner explains that Julius Africanus had once journeyed into the region of Batanea, where he made several inquiries. The Church historian Eusebius quotes from a script (ca. AD 250) by Julius that, in the Jewish villages of Cochaba and Nazareth, there lived blood relatives of the Lord Jesus who had kept the genealogies of the Davidian family.[46] Moreover, the Egyptian monk Hegesippos (AD 160) reports that many relatives of Jesus—Nazareans living in Nazareth and elsewhere—were persecuted for being descendents of David while under the Roman Emperors Vespasian, Domitian, and Trajan.[47]

How, you might ask, did Nazareth and David's line become connected *before* the time of Jesus? The history is fascinating. From the Old Testament, we know that, at the end of the Babylonian Exile, the Davidic clan was found in Babylon. In the thirty-seventh year of their exile, King Jehoiachin of Judah was released from prison and was given to eat "for the rest of his days" from the King of Babylon's table (2 Kings 25:27–30). The line of David, then, was not exterminated at the conquering of Jerusalem in 587 BC. Then we read that the house of David, represented in the "head of the ancestral house" of Hattush, eventually settled back in Jerusalem (Ezra 8:1–2, 23). Finally, as Pixner claims, it seems very possible that a group of these descendants could have emigrated into the region of Batanea in the second to first centuries BC and, from this base, established other settlements such

---

[45] An emphasis of *Dei Verbum* §12.

[46] Pixner, *Paths of the Messiah*, 173; *Historia Ecclesiae* 1.7.14.

[47] Ibid., 26.

as nearby Nazareth close to the large city of Japhia. Pixner notes that archaeological records of settlement plans support this interpretation.[48] So, too, I might add, does the fact that the name of the town of Nazareth does not appear in the Hebrew Bible, which makes it seem that this town's existence as such a Jewish settlement was a recent phenomenon. What seems to have happened is that those of the kingly line of David named their town "Nazareth" after the word *nezer* in Isaiah 11:1, which prophecy they applied to themselves in the hope that, one day, God would raise up from among their kingly kin a successor-*shoot* to the throne of their forefather, David, of Jesse's fallen stump.

Such historical background explains why we Catholics read Isaiah 11:1 so often in Advent (e.g., Second Sunday, Year A), as we believe that the *nezer*-shoot of Jesse's lineage to which this prophecy fully applies is none other than Jesus of *Nazareth*, about whom it was foretold to Mary by the Archangel Gabriel that: "He will be great and will be called Son of the Most High, and the Lord God will give him the throne of David, his father, and he will rule over the house of Jacob forever, and of his kingdom there will be no end" (Lk 1:32–33). Appropriate here, as well, are the also-Advent-worthy words of inspired Zechariah: "Blessed be the Lord, the God of Israel, for he has visited and brought redemption to his people. He has raised up a horn for our salvation within the house of David his servant, *even as he promised through the mouth of his holy prophets of old: salvation*[49] *from our enemies*" (Lk 1:68–71; emphasis added).

Another merit of mapping out this historical background is that it reveals an incredible, yet subtle, irony expressed by the *patibulum* that hung above the Cross. Recalling that most truly Hebrew words were of a tri-literal, consonantal root, we can picture the "written charge against him" (Mt 27:37) hanging above Jesus on the Cross, written in Hebrew, Latin, and Greek: "Jesus the Nazorean, King of the Jews" (Jn 19:19–20). The word "Nazorean" would have been written with its consonants *n-z-r*, which is of course the same root as the "shoot" (*nezer*) which was prophesied would "sprout from the stump of Jesse" (Is 11:1). The irony could not be thicker! There, on his wooden

---

[48] Ibid., 173.

[49] Which word in Hebrew is, of course, *yeshua*—from which is derived the name of Jesus, who saved us from our sins!

throne, bearing a mock crown of thorns, Jesus was proclaimed by the pagan Romans to be the Messiah, in fulfillment of the prophecy of Isaiah 11:1—and also its conclusion in verse 10: "On *that day*,[50] the root of Jesse, *set up as a signal for the nations, the Gentiles will seek out. His dwelling shall be glorious.*" Not even the Jewish leaders picked up on this subtle, but strong, irony; they quibbled with Pilate that he had written "king" (Jn 19:21–22). What should have really scandalized them, blinded as they were by their murderous rage, was the mention of Jesus's provenance which linked him to the family of David.

Issue 3

The idea of Jesus learning languages, and even a trade, touch upon the disputed question of the knowledge of Jesus. Theologians will differ in the degree of their gnoseology (the study of Jesus's knowledge, *gnōsis* in Greek), but from my understanding of the debate, the question hinges on this issue: did Jesus, who at every moment enjoyed the beatific vision, ever gain any experiential knowledge? To me, it seems so. Perhaps, however, it is best to avoid phrasing the question in terms of "did Jesus ever *learn* how to make a table, or *learn* languages, etc.," and rather simply speak of how he *encountered* such things. This would leave the mechanisms of his knowledge the rightful mystery that they are.

Issue 4

In John 20:11–18, we read the incredibly rich account of Jesus revealing himself to Mary Magdalene at the empty tomb. Putting ourselves in Mary's shoes, we can feel how touching it must have been to hear Jesus call her by her own name. What a heartwarming and earth-shattering realization on her part: "He knows my name! He called me by name. He *knows* me . . . *I* know him." That Jesus addressed her by name must have made that moment so tender and precious a moment. However, there was at play another factor that made the moment even *more* intimate. Jesus not only spoke Mary's name; he also said it with the same accent with which Mary herself spoke.[51] Such a tone of voice and inflec-

---

[50] That is, in a Christian reading, Good Friday.

[51] Since Nazareth is near the Sea of Galilee, and Magdala is a town on the sea itself, Jesus and Mary both spoke the Galilean dialect of Aramaic. See Fassberg, "Which Semitic Language," 280.

tion of word would have made that revelatory encounter all the more dear to Mary, who in turn addresses Jesus not in Hebrew (*rabbi*), but in their shared Aramaic (*rabbouni*). How truly sweet to realize that Jesus is here with you, that he knows you by name and even speaks that name like you hear and once heard it at home, spoken with truly familiar love!

Issue 5

A final issue that should be discussed at Nazareth is the proper way for a Catholic to read Old Testament prophecies. As a case in point, let us consider the appearance of the Lord's angel to Joseph in a dream (Mt 1:20–24). The angel explains to this righteous man, about to divorce Mary quietly so as to keep her from public shame (Mt 1:19), that Mary would bear a son and that he was to name the child Jesus. Matthew comments that all of this took place to fulfill what the Lord had said through the prophet Isaiah: "Behold, the virgin shall be with child and bear a son, and they shall name him Emmanuel" (Mt 1:22–23).

It is common for scholars to say something along these lines: Isaiah did not "actually foresee this birth of Jesus around 6 BC," since "Isaiah was speaking about another child of his own time," that is, the time of the Syro-Ephraimite War. This child, they say, "would be an instrument of God for the peace and protection of Israel." Having said this, those scholars go on to say that, hence, the case is closed. It would be improper, they assert, for a Christian to claim that the *literal sense* of these Old Testament prophecies is anything other than what the original author intended to convey to his original, intended audience. It would be a perversion, some would even go so far as to claim, of the meaning of this text for our brothers and sisters of Jewish faith to claim that such a *fulfillment-in-Christ* reading of the Old Testament text is the truest, fullest reading of that prophetic word.

Fortunately, not all Catholic scholars put it that way. Some look at it in this way:

> Isaiah's words are, as Sacred Scripture, the words of God; Matthew knew this, and understood that God was speaking about Jesus, even if God's prophet Isaiah did not understand the words to refer to Jesus. Since Matthew knows how truly God is with us through Jesus, he took God's words, which Isaiah spoke and understood

in one way, and indicated that these words of God were truer than Isaiah ever expected: they were really speaking about Jesus. It is this truth that Matthew affirms when he writes that Jesus is the fulfillment of Isaiah's ancient words about a wonderful child.[52]

Here we behold a truly Catholic understanding of the inspiration of Sacred Scripture. Although the human authors of the sacred books are true authors,[53] nevertheless, the ultimate author of Scripture is God, whose Spirit inspired those authors to write that and only that which he wanted them to write. Therefore, God, whose knowledge and plans far surpass any of our understanding,[54] can use the words of the human authors to refer to things that those human authors did not have primarily in mind while writing them. John J. Kilgallen argues that, in light of Matthew 1:22–23, Isaiah's words about Emmanuel-God (7:14) *were truer than Isaiah ever expected*, insofar as they were *really* speaking about Jesus all along![55] To adapt the wording of St. Thomas Aquinas, this kind of instrumentality does not diminish, as so many scholars misguidedly posit, but rather enhances the human authorship of the hagiographer. In this way, with St. Thomas, we can sum it all up by saying: "It is to be known that, in the Old Testament, some passages refer to Christ and are [properly] said of him alone, as 'Behold, a virgin shall conceive and bring forth a son' (Is 7:14)."[56]

---

[52] Kilgallen, *New Testament Guide*, 12.

[53] *Dei Verbum*, §12.

[54] See Psalm 139:6 (NABRE):

> Such knowledge is too wonderful for me,
> far too lofty for me to reach.

[55] Such is the gist of Hebrews 11:13, which, speaking about the patriarchs and holy ones of the Old Testament, says: "All these died in faith. They did not receive what had been promised but saw it and greeted it from afar." The author here is of course referring to Jesus and the fulfilling, in him, of all of the promises of old.

[56] In his commentary on Matthew, Thomas Aquinas states that Theodore Mopsuestia is in error to say that nothing in the Old Testament is said literally of Christ, but is adapted. "Against this," Thomas writes, "is the final chapter of Luke: 'It is necessary that all that was written about me in the law of Moses, in the prophets, and in the psalms be fulfilled'" (*Super Evangelium Sancti Matthaei lectura* 1, lec. 5, ed. R. Cai [Turin: Marietti, 1951]; translation mine).

POINTS FOR REFLECTION

- Do you believe that the Bible is the inspired Word of God? How do you understand the nature of Scripture, which the Church has described as the Word of God in the words of men? Do you believe that, since the Holy Spirit is its author, there can be contained therein no error—even though the hagiographers, who were true authors as well, were fallen, imperfect human beings? As a Catholic, it is important to believe not only in Scripture's power (Rom 1:16–17) through which God speaks, but also in the characteristics consequent to its power: its inspiration and inerrancy.

- Conon the Martyr professed to be of the same family of Christ. We, too, by our baptism, are incorporated into the family of the Church; at that moment, we can call Jesus our brother. Do you see Jesus as your brother? Surely you know him as your Lord and Redeemer, but do you know his fraternity?

Especially for Seminarians

- You will one day be preaching on the Word of God; it behooves you to believe especially in the power of Scripture (Rom 1:16–17) through which God speaks to you and to your congregation, and in the Scripture's inspiration and inerrancy, which come necessarily from its unique power.

- The brotherhood of Christ takes on a new and deeper character for those who have received Holy Orders. As a priest, you will be even more closely conformed to him than as a member of the baptized and, so, will be able to call your fellow priests "brother priests."

- How supportive of your vocation to the priesthood have your family and relatives been? If supportive, this would be a good place to give thanks for them; if not very supportive, this would be a very good place to pray for them: may the Lord open them to the grace of conversion of heart.

THE SEA OF GALILEE

Jesus withdrew toward the sea with his disciples. A large number of people [followed] from Galilee and Judea.

(Mark 3:7)

The Sea and Its Way

The heart-shaped Sea of Galilee is about eleven miles long at its longest and seven miles wide at its widest. It is called the Sea of *Galilee* because it forms the northeastern part of the territory of Galilee. But this is not its only name; this body of water is also called the Sea of Gennesaret and the Sea of Tiberias. The name Gennesaret comes from the Hebrew word for "harp," which shape the sea resembles. The name Tiberias comes, in New Testament times, from the name of the Roman Emperor Tiberias, who ruled the Roman world during the public life of Jesus (Lk 3:1). Herod Antipas, the son of Herod the Great and stepfather of Salome, whose dancing won the head of John the Baptist (Mk 6:21–29), named a large, prominent sea town after the emperor, and made it the capital of Galilee.[1]

At the beginning of his public ministry, Matthew tells us that Jesus left to live in Capernaum by the sea (Mt 4:12–13). Situated on the northwest corner of the lake, this area around Caper-

---

[1] Kilgallen, *New Testament Guide* 28.

naum was ideal for Jesus to meet the "large crowds" (Jn 6:2–5) that would come out to meet him, as this area was characterized by a good network of roads leading to and from faraway lands.[2] Perhaps for this reason our Lord even chose this area as a "hub" for his preaching and healing activity!

The region of the Sea of Galilee known generally as Tabgha, just south of the town of Capernaum.

The most important road in this region was the great overland highway from Egypt to Syria, which was called the *Via Maris*, or "Way of the Sea." This road led from the Nile Delta along the northern coast of the Sinai Peninsula, past Caesarea on the Mediterranean Sea, and all the way north to Damascus (in modern-day Syria) via Galilee. A part of this road, the Roman historian Flavius Josephus tells us, was used by pilgrims en route to sacrifice in Jerusalem.[3] Evidence of this road was found in Capernaum, where a Roman milestone from the days of the emperor Hadrian (AD 117–138) was discovered.[4] Jesus would have used this road himself when travelling from Galilee to Jerusalem for the feasts (Jn 2:13).

Not only, though, did Jesus use this road to travel *away from* Galilee; he also used it to travel *within* Galilee. This might seem like a minor point to make, but it is, on the contrary, *very* significant. Let me explain. The Romans called this overland highway

2   Pixner, *Paths of the Messiah*, 54.
3   In *The Antiquities of the Jews* 17.26, in *The Works of Josephus: Complete and Unabridged*, trans. William Whitson (Peabody, MA: Hendrickson, 1987), 452.
4   Pixner, *Paths of the Messiah*, 55–56.

the *Via Maris* because it went by the Mediterranean Sea, and the Latin word for "sea" is *maris*. The people of the time of Jesus would hardly have called this road the "Sea Way" (or, literally the "Way of the Sea"), as such was its Roman appellation. However, Matthew in fact *does* just that, applying this Latin name to the section of this road that runs along the Sea of *Galilee*. Citing the prophet Isaiah, Matthew writes:

> When [Jesus] heard that John had been arrested, he withdrew to Galilee. He left Nazareth and went to live in Capernaum by the sea, in the region of Zebulun and Naphtali, that what had been said through Isaiah the prophet might by fulfilled:
>
> > "Land of Zebulun and land of Napthali,
> > the way to the sea, beyond the Jordan,
> > Galilee of the Gentiles,
> >
> > the people who sit in darkness
> > have seen a great light,
> > on those dwelling in a land overshadowed by death
> > light has arisen." (Mt 4:12–16, NABRE)

It is remarkable to note that the Greek of Matthew 4:15 (*hodos thalassēs*) matches the Hebrew of Isaiah 8:23 (*derek hayyom*). Further, both *happen* to have the same meaning as this road's later, Latin name: *Via Maris*, the Way of the Sea.[5] Talk about Providence! All of this is to say, per Matthew, that the engineering feat of this Roman road[6] in fact worked to fulfill this prophecy of Isaiah. Jesus, walking on the "Way of the Sea," is the one who brings light to those dwelling, in this region, in the darkness of unbelief in him who is God. It is as if this prophetic word "were perfectly tailored to the needs of the evangelist for describing the physical and spiritual landscape in which the principal ministry of the Messiah was to unfold."[7] Wow!

---

[5] Ibid., 61–62.

[6] Or, better, Jesus's *walking* along this Roman road into the area of Capernaum, which was known in Old Testament times as the region of the tribes of Zebulun and Napthali.

[7] Pixner, *Paths of the Messiah*, 62. For a related matter of significance, see *Issues Raised*, further on, at the "fullness of time."

Jesus's Missionary Tours

It might surprise us to realize that, according to the organization provided by Mark's exposition, Jesus embarked on three self-contained "preaching tours," or "missionary journeys,"[8] in and around the Sea of Galilee region. I say that this might surprise us because sometimes, when we read about Jesus's early preaching, we have this sort of nebulous idea about Jesus being

Kingdom of Herod the Great (Copyright 2007 by Faithlife Corporation, makers of Logos Bible Software, www.logos.com).

---

[8] Much like Paul himself did, the apostle was ever conformed to Christ (Gal 6:17).

somewhere near the sea but are not really aware of where, exactly, he was when he was saying certain things. From my studies, I have learned that we skip over such seemingly passing details to the detriment of our understanding of the Gospels and the meaning of Jesus's messages. Let us unpack this a little bit.

Having made Capernaum his home base, Jesus set out from, and returned to, this town a full three times. The first journey (Mk 1:5–20) consisted of a round trip across the lake, touching the roadways only in one corner of the Decapolis, in the land of the Gerasenes. Though he certainly traveled often by foot, Jesus would also have taken a boat from the sea's northern to southern shores on his pilgrimages to Jerusalem.[9] The second journey (Mk 5:21–8:10) took the form of a long, horseshoe-shaped walking tour from the feeding of the 5,000 on the west shore of the lake, across the territory of Tyre and the Decapolis, to the feeding of the 4,000 on a hill in the eastern shore's wilderness.[10] Lastly, a return to the villages of Caesarea Philippi comprised Jesus's third trip (Mk 8:11–9:33).[11]

Geographically organizing Jesus's work into these three journeys not only helps us to orient ourselves when we read the Gospels, but also allows for an enhanced reading of them. We shall see that location and topography not only likely determined when he said what he did, but also brought his message home, in a uniquely decisive way, to the people living there. Let us examine a few highlights from Jesus's second and third missionary journeys.

Feedings of the Five Thousand and the Four Thousand
The first topography-informed story and message consists in the miraculous feedings by Jesus of the crowds following him. A reader of Mark and Matthew will see that two such feedings occurred: one of the 5,000 (Mk 6:34–44; Mt 14:13-21) and one of the 4,000 (Mk 8:1–10; Mt 15:32-39). A reader of the other Gospels, however, might notice that Luke and John record only one such feeding. Why, we might ask? How many times did Jesus actually break and multiply bread: once or twice?

---

[9] From 1986–1987, when the sea's water level was historically low, a boat from Jesus's time was discovered. It was found to be able to easily hold 13 people—such as Jesus and the Twelve! See Pixner, *Paths of the Messiah*, 63–64.

[10] Ibid., 64.

[11] Ibid., 72.

Most critical scholars suppose that, in Matthew and in Mark, we are dealing with a doublet—that is, that these evangelists, or a later editor of them, *wrote up* a second feeding—whereas only one feeding, as Luke and John have it, actually happened.[12]

SCRIPTURE ON SITE:
Mark 6:34-44
Matthew 8:1-10

I, however, do not think we have good reason to see here a doublet. These twin stories in Matthew and in Mark are marked by very intentional details—*suited perfectly to topography*—that are appropriate to the specific account in which they occur. More likely, I think, is a summarizing of the feedings into one episode in Luke and John,[13] who perhaps blended some details of the two events as they are contained in the other Gospels.

Let us take Mark as the basis of our examination. We shall see that, within Jesus's second journey from Capernaum, it is important to note *where* Jesus is when he feeds the crowds: first the five thousand at the region of Tabgha, *southwest of Capernaum*, with the five loaves and two fish; and second the four thousand in the area closer to Bethsaida, *northeast of Capernaum*, with seven loaves. Topography helps us make sense of details that differ between these two accounts,[14] as well as the similar-yet-different messages that these stories convey about Jesus's actions.

To begin, we should note that, at Tabgha (Mk 6) during the time of Jesus, there were various farms and villages, where the multitude following Christ could have bought something to eat. By contrast, the northeastern shore region of Bethsaida (Mk 8) is sparsely populated.[15] Such explains why, at the feeding of the

---

[12] It is a fairly standard criterion of textual criticism that, when trying to decide which of two disputed versions, or readings, of a text is older or more original (and, hence, to be preferred), one should choose the shorter version, as it is supposedly easier to foresee a successive lengthening of a given text than a successive abbreviating of a given text. This principle, of course, is far from inherently decisive, though many scholars treat it as such.

[13] Pixner, *Paths of the Messiah*, 71.

[14] Ibid., 69.

[15] This region is described as *eremeia*, the Greek word for "deserted place" (Mk 6:35).

5,000, the disciples protest: "Are we to buy two hundred days' wages worth of food and give it to them to eat?" (Mk 6:37), as there were food venues in the region. In contrast, the disciples make a different protest in the sparsely populated Decapolis area: "Where can anyone get enough bread to satisfy them here in this deserted place?" (Mk 8:4).[16]

Moreover, we need to realize that Tabgha was located in the Jewish region (ruled by Herod the Great) of the Sea of Galilee, while Bethsaida and its environs were located in the Gentile region (the Decapolis, ruled by the peace-loving tetrarch Philip).[17] This topographical fact explains the differing number of baskets of leftovers after Jesus's miracles were complete.

On the one hand, after the feeding of the five thousand at Jewish Tabgha, there advanced twelve wicker baskets (Mk 6:43). This number, of course, symbolized the twelve tribes of Israel and, so, casts Jesus as the Messiah for the Jews, whose scattered tribes he was reuniting into one people.[18] In this way, Mark touches on the theme of feeding God's people under the Mosaic covenant.[19]

On the other hand, after the feeding of the four thousand near Gentile Bethsaida, there were left behind seven wicker baskets (Mk 8:8). This number indicates the seven Gentile peoples[20] whom the Lord *removed* from the Promised Land at their expulsion by the twelve tribes of Israel. Those who had been excluded from the Lord's covenant in former times Jesus was now

---

[16] A potential confusion of terms could arise here. I will treat further on (in the chapter on Tabgha) a certain part of the region of Tabgha known as *Eremos* Hill—which is the solitary, *deserted* place where our Lord would retreat to pray. The point made earlier is that the region of Bethsaida, not that of Tabgha, was quite *deserted* and sparsely populated in the time of Jesus. Here, one might ask: "Ok, so which one of those two—Tabgha or Bethsaida—is actually *hermitic*?" The answer is, for the sake of the multiplication of the loaves, Bethsaida (see the successive paragraph in the text above), though there is, indeed, a small part of the region of Tabgha which is, in contrast to the rest of the well-populated region, quite deserted: *Eremos* Hill.

[17] More on this in the next item covered further on.

[18] Making this imagery even more explicit is the comment that the people sat before Jesus in groups of hundreds and fifties (Mk 6:40), which is exactly the same organization to which the Israelites were accustomed during the wilderness wanderings under Moses (Ex 18:25).

[19] Pixner, *Paths of the Messiah*, 64.

[20] "Hittites, Girgashites, Hivites, and Jebusites, seven nations more numerous and powerful than you . . . " (Deut 7:1).

symbolically bringing back by offering to them the "Bread of Life"[21] and including them into the one people of God, heirs of the promises alongside those of Hebrew origin.

In light of topography, therefore, we can understand in Mark and Matthew the two feedings of the crowds not as a *doublet* presentation of the same event, but rather as the intentional presentation of two events that were known by the authors to be separate events, each with its own unique significance.

Jesus's Border Crossing in Mark 6

The second point of topography's influence on Jesus's actions can be seen in the haste and direction of Jesus's movements during his second journey from Capernaum. In response to the Pharisees's threat—"Go away, leave this area because Herod wants to kill you" (Lk 13:31)—Jesus retorted: "Go and tell that fox [Herod] I must continue my way today, tomorrow, and the following day, for it is impossible that a prophet should die outside of Jerusalem" (Lk 13:32–33). But then Jesus, urging his disciples to travel by boat right away to Bethsaida (Mk 6:45),[22] immediately withdrew from the area where he was preaching and ministering.

Here, again, we find a detail—that is, Jesus's physical transposition—over which we often skip when we read the Gospels or hear them proclaimed. That is really too bad, because a careful consideration of topography not only can account for Jesus's motivation for moving to another region, but also can provide us a chance to come to know better the God-man by getting, as it were, *inside his own head*, understanding how and why he thought and acted as he did. The goal of such an enterprise is an ever-closer drawing near to Jesus, whose mind, Paul says, we have (1 Cor 2:16). When we come to know how Jesus likely thought, we come to know better Jesus himself, who is the "king and center"[23] of every heart.

Let us examine the matter at hand. When Jesus responded to the Pharisees, he was standing in an area within the Jewish region of the Sea of Galilee which was ruled by Herod Antipas.

---

[21] Pixner, *Paths of the Messiah*, 69.

[22] I know that I am here mixing Mark and Luke, but these two Gospels do, at these points, match each other, insofar as both Mark 6 and Luke 13 treat Herod's reaction to Jesus's ministry.

[23] A phrase of the Litany to the Sacred Heart of Jesus.

Herod, per the Pharisees, was seeking his life (Lk 13:31). Being so under threat, Jesus moved away from that land, passing into an area within the Gentilic Decapolis region of the Sea of Galilee that was ruled by Philip. Unlike Herod, Philip was a peace-loving, permissive, and stable ruler.[24] So, there, in that region north and east of Capernaum, Jesus could exercise his ministry and carry out his mission freely and effectively with his life in no danger.

What exactly was the reason for Jesus's being under threat? In other words, why was Herod seeking Jesus's life? The answer is that Herod, who had felt threatened by John, now felt threatened by Jesus, whom he took to be John risen from the dead, saying: "It is John whom I beheaded. He has been raised up" (Mk 6:16).

In order to understand why Jesus was a threat to Herod, we must first ask: why was John a threat to Herod? We might be inclined to sustain that it was the Baptist's preaching against Herod's adultery that Herod saw as a threat.[25] Josephus, though, details how Herod in fact feared an uprising from John's followers, as the historian writes:

> Now, when [many] others came in crowds about him, for they were greatly moved [or pleased] by hearing his words, Herod, who feared lest the great influence John had over the people might put it into his power and inclination to raise a rebellion (for they seemed ready to do anything he should advise), thought it best, by putting him to death, to prevent any mischief he might cause, and not bring himself into difficulties, by sparing a man who might make him repent of it when it should be too late.[26]

---

[24] "He had shown himself a person of moderation and quietness in the conduct of his life and government" (*Antiquities* 18.106 [Whitson, *Works*, 483]).

[25] Herod was the one who had John arrested and bound in prison on account of Herodias, his brother Philip's wife, whom he had married. John had said to Herod, "It is not lawful for you to have your brother's wife. . . . Herod feared John, knowing him to be a righteous and holy man, and kept him in custody" (Mk 6:17–18, 20a).

[26] *Antiquities* 18.116–118 (Whitson, *Works*, 484). Josephus's account here of the reason for John's beheading notably differs from the reason provided by Mark—that is, the Baptist's preaching against Herod's adultery (Mk 6:18). I, though, think that Josephus is per-

So, Herod feared a revolt on the part of John's followers. What seems to have happened, then, with regard to Jesus, is this: Herod, who confused Jesus with John (Mk 6:16, above), transferred his revolt fears about John onto Jesus. Such a transfer is, indeed, understandable, considering the fact that Jesus's feeding of the 5,000 awakened messianic enthusiasm in the crowd.[27] Herod thus feared a destabilizing revolt[28] on the part of Jesus's followers and, so, sought Jesus's life (Lk 13:31). Immediately after this menace was made known to him by the Pharisees, Jesus moved into a region outside of the jurisdiction of Herod. This historical danger, generated by Herod's fear of the followers of John the Baptist, hence most satisfactorily explains why Jesus, having brusquely responded to the Pharisees (Lk 13:31), immediately crossed over to the Decapolis region of the Sea of Galilee.

Jesus's Discussion about Jewish Dietary Laws in Mark 7

Thirdly, knowing that there lived, in these regions in and around the north of the Sea of Galilee, religious and political Zealots opens up a new perspective into Jesus's statements in Mark 7 about Jewish dietary laws. Note, coincidentally, that it is *here*, where there lived Jews *zealous* for Israel's laws, that Jesus discusses and abolishes the Jewish dietary laws by taking a decided stand against a rigorous interpretation of these laws: "You disregard God's commandment but cling to human tradition. . . . You nullify the word of God in favor of your tradition that you have handed on. . . . Hear me, all of you, and understand. Nothing that enters one from outside can defile that person; but the things that come out from within are what defile" (Mk 7:8, 14–15).

Jesus is here placing his finger on the *zeal* of the people for

---

fectly reconcilable with Mark in the latter's attribution of motive for John's beheading, as Herod could have used John's condemnatory preaching as an alibi.

[27] See John 6:15: "Since Jesus knew that they were going to come and carry him off to make him king, he withdrew."

[28] This fear, on Herod's part, was stoked by the presence and activity, in those regions, of radical Zealots. Herod always had to keep a close watch on the Zealots, whose belligerent messianic expectations he feared could trigger a violent revolt against Rome (Josephus, *Wars of the Jews* 4.84–86, 92–97 [Whitson, *Works*, 668]).

their religious laws and, thereby, attempting to redirect their zeal by expanding it into a more perfect law, much like he did in the famous antitheses in Matthew's sermon on the Mount (Mt 5). Again in this instance, topography matters! It is not random happenstance—as a listless, inattentive reading of Scripture might suppose—that Jesus makes this plea in an area filled with Zealots. By knowing his surroundings and his audience, Jesus makes a plug that packs a poignant and powerful punch.

Jesus Compliments the Syro-Phoenician Woman's Faith in Mark 7

Fourthly, the fact that mostly Gentiles lived in the areas in which Jesus ministered from Mark 7 and on explains Jesus's words and preaching at this point in the Gospel. Here, Jesus tested and then complimented the faith of a Syro-Phoenician woman who was Greek by birth:

> She begged him to drive the demon out of her daughter. He said to her, "Let the children be fed first. For it is not right to take the food of the children and throw it to the dogs." She replied and said to him, "Lord, even the dogs under the table eat the children's scraps." Then he said to her, "For saying this, you may go. The demon has gone out of your daughter." (Mk 7:26–29)

Many readers balk a little bit at the almost derogatory tone of Jesus's first response to the woman's cry for help. He almost seems elitist, cold, and a bit crass. How are we to interpret Jesus's words in this episode?

I believe that Jesus raised this "Hebrews first" principle as a bit of a façade in order to elicit the faith of those non-Jews in whose presence he found himself at that time, in that area of Tyre. Such would accord with the prophecy about the royal servant in Isaiah's second Servant Song:

> It is too little, he says, for you to be my servant,
> to raise up the tribes of Jacob,
> and restore the survivors of Israel;
> I will make you a light to the nations,
> that my salvation may reach to the ends of the earth.
> (Is 49:6, NABRE).

We find a similar sentiment in Simeon's prophecy that this child, Jesus, was a light both for revelation to the Gentiles and for the glory of God's people Israel (Lk 2:30–32). It is no mistake that Jesus's preaching and miracle working that expanded the perceived boundaries of God's people to include *the nations* happened *here*, in distinctly Gentile territory.[29] Topographically, it was fitting!

Markan Secrecy and the Rebuking of Peter

Fifthly, a topographical consideration seen already in the second journey is important to make, by way of context, in understanding Jesus's third journey from Capernaum. After Peter's confession of faith in Jesus as the Messiah (Mk 8:29), the disciples were surprised by Jesus's peculiar order to "tell no one about him" (Mk 8:30). This command can confuse us readers of Mark's Gospel, too! Why would Jesus insist that the disciples keep quiet about his identity as Messiah? Is not this the very message of which he convinced them, and of which he wanted them to convince others?

Theologians throughout the centuries have offered, for this infamous, so-called "Markan Secrecy," many possible theological motivations: the disciples's lack of faith, a criticism of faith motivated only by miracles, the fact that his hour had not yet come (see Jn 2:4), and so on. Thanks to topography, we could add to these possibilities a very practical motivation. Jesus ordered the disciples to be silent because, in that area, there lived many Zealots, whose headquarters was the nearby town of Gamla and to whose idea of Messiah Jesus neither himself subscribed nor wanted his disciples to subscribe. As Pixner writes:

> With its patriotic ideas, [Gamla] influenced a large portion of the Jewish population around Lake Gennesaret. Judas of Gamla, probably a Pharisee scribe, together with Rabbi Zadok (also a Pharisee), had called the movement of the Zealots into being in AD 6 (*Ant.* 18.4–10, 23, 24). His family was from Gamla, and it developed into a dynasty that controlled the Zealots until their demise at

---

[29] A fact attested by the presence of swine (Mk 5:11), which were, to the Jews, unclean animals.

Masada[30] (AD 73/4). Judas' father, Ezechias, had been a patriot before him and had been leader of a guerilla gang that rose up against Romans and their friends in Trachonitis (*War* 1.204, 256). The youthful Herod the Great had taken him prisoner and executed him in short order, which caused an outcry among the Jews. Judas of Gamla taught a radical theocracy, i.e., God alone is the ruler of Israel, not the Roman emperor. Therefore, it was wrong to pay him taxes (cf. Mk 12:13–17[31]). . . . Two of Judas's sons, James and Simon, were crucified under procurator Tiberius Alexander (AD 46–48; *Ant.* 20.102), while another son, Menahem, took possession of weapons after an attack on Masada in AD 66, [and] entered Jerusalem as if he were the messianic king and seizing control of the insurgents (*War* 2.433–49).[32]

The rebellious Zealots's stronghold of Gamla, perched above the Sea of Galilee.

---

[30] Which fell, along with almost all of ancient Israel, to Rome's Tenth Legion.

[31] Especially v. 17a: "Give to Caesar what belongs to Caesar."

[32] Pixner, *Paths of the Messiah*, 73.

In all, then, we see that the Zealot movement was strongly motivated by expectations that a political Messiah would lead his troops in victorious battle over Rome. Such could explain why Jesus hushed the disciples when Peter called him "Messiah," as Jesus did not want them to think of him as the nearby Zealots thought about the Messiah. It also surely paints in different light the statement of Andrew[33] when he told his brother Simon Peter: "We have found the Messiah" (Jn 1:41). Andrew might very well have been thinking in Gamla terms! Moreover, the possibility that the thinking of the Zealots might have infiltrated Jesus's chosen band is supported by the presence therein of the apostle Simon, who was called "the Zealot" (Mk 3:18).[34]

In Mark and John we see that Jesus needed to retrain[35] the Twelve, indeed, likely away from any kind of Zealot messianism. After Peter's confession of faith, Jesus immediately sought to re-form his disciples: "He began to teach them that the Son of Man must suffer greatly and be rejected by the elders, the chief priests, and the scribes, and be killed, and rise after three days" (Mk 8:31). He then even had to correct Peter for his potentially improper image of Messiah: "Get behind me, Satan. You are thinking not as God does, but as human beings do" (Mk 8:33). Only in light of the "zealous" topography of Jesus's third missionary journey do his perplexing statements therein make sense!

All of this is to say that *where Jesus was* (that is, who lived there, who ruled there) when he said what he did *matters*! Such topographical considerations help to make sense of otherwise seemingly random or puzzling things that Jesus speaks or that the Gospels say about Jesus and his disciples. As a final, perhaps recapitulating example, we could ask: "Why would Jesus mention, while in the region of Batanea east of the Sea of Galilee, those who are eunuchs for the sake of the kingdom of heaven" (Mt 19:12)? The answer: because there lived in that region the Essenes,[36] some of whom practiced celibacy; so, the people to whom Jesus preached about "eunuchs for the sake of the kingdom" already had in their mind some experience with which to

---

[33] Who was from Bethsaida, which town was in the area of the Zealots (ibid.).

[34] Ibid.

[35] Ibid., 74.

[36] Ibid., 190.

relate Jesus's words, which therefore struck the people more intimately and could thereby more likely win their hearts to Jesus's
message. *Place* matters!

Issues Raised

Speaking about the *Via Maris* would provide us another instance
by means of which we can seek to better understand the "fullness of time" of which Paul spoke in reference to the historical

timing of the Incarna-
tion (Gal 4:4). In his
infinite Wisdom, God
chose, from among
all the ages of man-
kind's history, none
other than the time
in which Rome ruled
the world[37] as the
time in which to come
and dwell among us
(Jn 1:14). From this
fact, we can suppose
that there must have
been, about this era,
something eminent-
ly *fitting*—or, better,
fitted—to the Jesus
event. Instances of
this fittingness could

The Corinthian capital of a column found in
Cesarea Maritime. One notes how the Christian
imagery of the Cross is literally grafted onto
this piece of Greco-Roman art, which thereby
shows itself—and by extension the culture that it
represents—to be most befitting to the message
of the Gospel and its proclamation.

include the following: the best of Greco-Roman philosophy pen-
etrating deeply into the heart of reality (especially the nature of
man), the natural law, and virtue; the "confluence," to quote Pope
Benedict XVI, of Greek and Hebrew thought in the Septuagint

---

[37] A touching reference to which reality we find in the Roman Marty-
rology's *Nativity of our Lord Jesus Christ*, which chant is sung at
the Christmas Vigil Mass: "In the forty-second year of the reign of
Caesar Octavian Augustus, the whole world being at peace"—a reference to the *Pax Romana*—"Jesus Christ, eternal God and Son of
the eternal Father, desiring to consecrate the world by his most loving
presence, was conceived by the Holy Spirit, and when nine months
had passed since his conception, was born of the Virgin Mary in Bethlehem of Judah, and was made man."

translation of the Hebrew Scriptures, which corpus set so many stages for the fulfillment, on the part of Jesus, of the Old Testament and its various prophecies;[38] and lastly and most relevant to the present discussion, Rome's vast network of roads connected the various parts of the empire, literally *paving the way* for the spread of the Gospel, the proclamation of which was greatly facilitated by both the peace of Rome's rule and the vast system of roads that led to almost all of the then-known world.

In like manner that we can say that all roads lead to Rome, we can also say that Rome gave the Gospel uniquely effective "inroads" to and for peoples and cultures near and far. Indeed, it is no accident that, as the conclusion of the Pontifical Biblical Commission's 1993 document *The Interpretation of the Bible in the Church* points out, "the eternal Word became incarnate at a precise period of history, within a clearly defined cultural and so-

[38] Benedict XVI, "Faith, Reason, and the University: Memories and Reflections" ("The Regensburg Address"), September 12, 2006, accessed June 4, 2017, https://w2.vatican.va/content/benedict-xvi/en/speeches/2006/september/documents/hf_ben-xvi_spe_20060912_university-regensburg.html. See the sixth paragraph from the top. For official, German citation, see the bibliography.

cial environment."[39] That which we find in the Book of Wisdom could not be truer: God's wisdom "spans the world from end to end mightily and governs all things well" (Wis 8:1).

POINTS FOR REFLECTION

• From the above observations, one reason as to why our Lord was so captivating a speaker becomes clear—that is, he knew his surroundings, so he could reach best the audience before which he found himself in specific locations. How important it is for a preacher to have such presence of mind—so flexible, observant, and dynamic a delivery! Take a moment to think of some of the best sermons you have ever heard. Pray for those priests who delivered those homilies, and pray for all priests—especially young priests—that they might be effective preachers of the Word of God.

Especially for Seminarians

• When you preach, imitate Jesus and speak to the people not only on their own turf, but even about their own turf—make cultural references to the area in which your people live (e.g., the local sports team, the new store that opened up down the street, even the best ice cream venue nearby!), for those references will help make immediately relevant the specific message of the Good News that you seek to convey.

---

[39] Pontifical Biblical Commission, *The Interpretation of the Bible in the Church* (Boston: St. Paul Books and Media, 1993), 133.

CAPERNAUM

When Jesus returned to Capernaum after some days, it became known that he was at home.

(Mark 2:1)

Scriptural Background

As noted earlier, Jesus made Capernaum his "home base" from which he set out upon his missionary journeys around Galilee. Jesus spoke and did some famous things here in this town. After calling his disciples, Jesus entered the synagogue of Capernaum and, on the Sabbath, taught "with authority" those present (Mk 1:21–22). Therein, he also cast out the unclean spirit who knew that he was the Holy One of God (Mk 1:24). Leaving the synagogue, he entered the house of Simon and Andrew and healed Simon's mother-in-law of her fever (Mk 1:30–31). Mark concludes with Jesus healing *many*[1] sick and possessed persons (1:34). After this, Jesus "went out along the sea" and called Levi (Matthew), who was sitting near the custom's post (Mk 2:13–14). When Jesus returned to Capernaum after a journey, he forgave and healed the paralytic man who, on a mat, had been lowered by his friends down through a roof, which sign revealed the power and authority that he had from being the Son of God (Mk

---

[1] A classic "Markan hyperbole," such as "the *whole*" town gathering at the door in 1:33.

2:2–12).[2] After another journey, Jesus told the disciples, who had been discussing amongst themselves along the way who was the greatest, that "if anyone wishes to be first, he shall be the last of all and the servant of all." He then placed a child in their midst and, "putting his arms around it, said to them: 'Whoever receives one child such as this in my name, receives me . . . and the One who sent me'" (Mk 9:36–37). Luke relates the episode of the centurion sending the elders of the town to beseech Jesus to heal his servant; Jesus praises the faith of the centurion, the likes of whose faith he had not seen in all of Israel (Lk 7:1–10).[3] Matthew records Jesus's rebuke of Capernaum for its lack of faith despite the miracles done in its midst (Mt 11:23). His Gospel also contains the bizarre episode of Peter, at our Lord's behest, finding a coin for the Temple tax in the mouth of a fish (Mt 17:24–27). Lastly, Jesus's famous "Bread of Life" discourse was spoken in the synagogue here (Jn 6:22–71).

Archaeological History

Capernaum, which means "town of Nahum," sits on the north-northwest shore of the Sea of Galilee. Just over two miles east of Capernaum, the Jordan River runs into the sea, down from its origin in Mount Hermon further north. Capernaum was a tax outpost along the *Via Maris*.[4] Traces of occupation in the thirteenth century BC have been discovered there, though the immediately relevant history of the town begins, for us, in the second century BC. Jerome Murphy-O'Connor provides us with a helpful breakdown of the historical dynamics of this town and its buildings:

> When Herod's kingdom was divided after his death, it fell to the lot of Herod Antipas. As the first town encoun-

---

[2]   The word for "power" and "authority" is, in Greek, *exousia*, which is composed of the prefix *ex*, meaning "from" or "out of," and the noun *ousia*, meaning "being."

[3]   We ourselves take up the faith-filled words of the centurion when we, knowing ourselves, too, to be unworthy of the Lord's presence, proclaim at Mass immediately before receiving the Eucharist: "Lord, I am not worthy to have you enter my roof, but say the word and let my servant be healed" (Lk 7:6–7).

[4]   See *Issues Raised*, further on, for Pixner's discussion on Matthew's tax-collecting work.

tered by travelers coming from his brother Philip's territory on the other side of the Jordan, it was equipped with a custom's office (Mt 9:9) and a small garrison under a centurion. The poverty of the inhabitants can be inferred from the fact that the latter, a Gentile, had to build them a synagogue (Lk 7:5). No unique advantages induced Jesus to settle there; it offered nothing that could not be found in other lakeside towns. He probably chose it because his first converts, the fishermen Peter and Andrew, lived there (Mk 1:21.29). This initial success was not maintained; Jesus's preaching had no more impact here (Lk 10:23–24) than at Nazareth.

Nevertheless, some of Jesus's converts either lived or settled down there, because a continuing Christian presence is attested both archaeologically and textually. Writing in 374, Epiphanius says that Capernaum was one of the towns in which Jews forbade Gentiles, Samaritans, and Christians to live. Moreover, rabbinic texts imply that relations between the communities were marked by considerable tension. Both had their own religious centers, as Egeria noted on her visit there between 381 and 384: "In Capernaum, the house of the prince of the apostles has been made into a church, with its original walls still standing. . . . There also is the synagogue where the Lord cured a man possessed by the devil. The way in is up many stairs, and it is made of dressed stone." The [current] synagogue was erected in the Byzantine period and, given the rivalries between the two communities, it is not improbable that its construction inspired the transformation of the house-church of St. Peter.[5]

As can be seen, there are two important buildings about which to speak here in Capernaum: the House of Peter and the synagogue. Each will be treated here below.

Looking straight ahead through the entrance to Capernaum, we see an oddly shaped construction standing atop some ruins. This edifice is a church, built by Antonio Barluzzi in the shape of a boat, as it rests above the remains of the house of Peter who was a fisherman—hence the boat design of the church. From in-

---

[5] Murphy-O'Connor, *The Holy Land*, 251.

side the church, you can peer through the glass floor down to the excavations carried out by the Franciscans, who care for and oversee this ancient site.

The Church of St. Peter, built over his house in Capernaum.

Before going into the church, turn and look left towards the synagogue. You will see in front of the synagogue the ruins of a neighborhood of what archaeologists call *insula* houses. These houses were little "islands" placed next to each other along a common road. The houses had walls of basalt but were of weak structure; the walls could hold up only a fragile roof made up of a network of light branches covered with straw and earth. Here, and in light of these considerations, we "automatically think of the cure of the paralytic in Mark 2:1–12,"[6] in which passage the man's friends remove the simple roof and lower the sick man on a mat through it.

Now, going into the church, look down through the glass floor before the altar. There, you will see ruins that are not unlike those in front of the synagogue. The ruins below your feet, though, do have unique and significant qualities. To begin,

The houses of ancient Capernaum, which dwellings consisted of basalt walls and fragile, thatched roofs.

6   Ibid., 252.

unlike all the other rooms in the area of Capernaum, this special room below us had walls that were *plastered*. Furthermore, we can note a shift in the use to which this special room was put: "Prior to the mid-1st century AD, the broken pottery found in the floor revealed normal family use; thereafter, only storage jars and lamps were found. Despite our ignorance regarding the contents of the jars, the hint that the room was put to some type of public use is confirmed by the great number of graffiti scratched in the plaster walls," some of which proclaim Jesus Lord and Christ.[7] Such findings suggest that this space was at first used as

a home/living space, and then used as a public space—specifically, as a place of worship. Egeria saw the original walls of the house of Peter,[8] which became a kind of *domus ecclesia*, where early Christians met in the house of Peter to pray. Confirmation of the public, liturgical use of this space consists in an octagon-shaped structure that encircles this innermost building layer (dating to the fifth century) in which a church was built around the house of Peter.

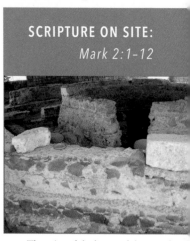

SCRIPTURE ON SITE:
Mark 2:1–12

The ruins of the house of the apostle Peter, and the successive churches built around it, underneath the present-day Church of St. Peter.

Stepping outside of the church and turning right, we can see what is indeed the most visually impressive ruin at Capernaum: the synagogue, dated to the fifth century AD by the coins and pottery found at the floor level of its walls. Its elevated position, the quality of the external decoration, and the brilliance of the white limestone against the surrounding black basalt houses give this edifice "exceptional status."[9] Many scholars agree that this synagogue stands on top of a basalt synagogue that goes back to the first century AD. It is almost certain that this earlier

---

[7]   Ibid.

[8]   Pixner, *Paths of the Messiah*, 125.

[9]   Murphy-O'Connor, *The Holy Land*, 254.

synagogue was the very synagogue that Jesus and his friends attended, and the one where our Lord spoke about himself as the bread of life (Jn 6:59).[10] But consensus on how all of the various

The synagogue of Capernaum.

pieces of this edifice fit together does not exist in scholarly circles, within which there continues a "lively, ongoing debate" about the dating of the structure.[11]

Egeria writes that she was shown a limestone synagogue atop of a basalt one. This limestone synagogue was based on the Byzantine foot (approximately 12.5 in.) and three triangles of 3:4:5 proportion (i.e., Pythagorean), which features suggest that the structure could have been built in the Constantinian period at the earliest. Moreover, this limestone structure was built in stages and then repaired over the later decades of that fourth century.[12]

A unique phenomenon is presented by one of the four lime-

---

[10] Kilgallen, *New Testament Guide*, 32.
[11] Murphy-O'Connor, *The Holy Land*, 255. I like Pixner's solution and so I present it here.
[12] Pixner, *Paths of the Messiah*, 117.

stone steps that led Egeria, as they lead us, to the Byzantine synagogue entrance: "It was specially hollowed out, apparently to
make it unnecessary to destroy the basalt step protruding into
it. The beautiful limestone ashlar blocks were mercilessly cut to
fit over the not-completely-horizontal basalt wall of the earlier
synagogue, probably in order to preserve the older wall."[13] For
this reason, this white limestone building seems to be what has
been called a "demonstrative synagogue," or rather, a memorial
synagogue, that was built over, *so as to preserve*, the original
basalt synagogue in which Jesus worked and taught.[14] Look to
the left of the first limestone (white) step, and you will see that it
has been made to fit *on top of* a smaller, basalt step, almost so as
to conserve that earlier step, up which Jesus would have himself
walked in order to enter the earlier, basalt-walled synagogue to
pray and to preach.

    This limestone synagogue was a hallowed place to the Jewish
Christians of the town, who likely built it up as a place of worship for themselves, while the
Byzantine Christians, whose
relationship with their counterpart Christians was marked
by much tension, built up the
House of Peter not far away.[15]
This memorial synagogue was
probably built with the aid of
imperial subsidies, perhaps in
the reign of Theodosius (AD
379–395), who was favorable
to the Jews by emphasizing,
in his laws, that Judaism was
a *religio licita* [allowed reli-

The interior of the synagogue

gion] in the Roman empire, thereby making it forbidden to destroy synagogues.[16]

---

[13] Ibid., 124.

[14] Ibid.

[15] It might seem odd to us to hear that there was such infighting between
Jewish Christians and Gentile Christians. It is true, though, that there
was—and for a long time! It was not until just before the year 400
that the two groups were officially reconciled. See *Issues Raised* in the
chapter on Mount Zion, further on.

[16] Pixner, *Paths of the Messiah*, 127.

SCRIPTURE ON SITE:
Luke 7:1–10
John 6:22–71

POINTS FOR REFLECTION

- How gentle and endearing is our Lord's embrace of the child while teaching his disciples about true humility! Jesus loved children, of whom he, placing his hands on them, said is the Kingdom of heaven (Mt 19:14–15). Though they can sometimes test our patience, children—

A statue of the apostle Peter in his home town of Capernaum.

whether your own, members of your family, or children of friends—can show us much about what faith in God should look like.

- Look toward the sea and notice the impressive bronze statue of the Apostle Peter, holding a bishop's staff. This catcher of fish became a catcher of men (Mt 4:19) who would later write:

  > I exhort the presbyters among you, as a fellow presbyter and witness to the sufferings of Christ, and one who has a share in the glory to be revealed, tend the flock of God in your midst, overseeing not by constraint but willingly, as God would have it, not for shameful profit but eagerly. Do not lord it over those assigned to you, but be examples to the flock. And when the chief Shepherd is revealed, you will receive the unfading crown of glory. (1 Pet 5:1–4)

These would be good words over which to pray here in Peter's town, where he learned, by sharing a home with the Good Shepherd (Jn 10:11), to be like him who was meek and humble of heart (Mt 11:19), who lays down his life for his sheep (10:11), and who serves as an example for us (Jn 13:15).

Especially for Seminarians

- Ministering to children—in the back of Church at Sunday Mass, in the classrooms, lunchroom, and playground at school, and in their various clubs or organizations—is one of the most joy-filled aspects of our priestly ministry. As one brother priest told me: "If you are having a bad day in the rectory, go over to the school and make a visit, in your collar or cassock, to the Kindergarten class!" Though we have no children of our own, we priests need to foster a love for God's littlest ones, who have much to teach us about faith.

- Pray over the Scripture passage from the First Letter of Peter, above, reflecting on it and asking Peter to help you become a good, generous, and gentle priest.

TABGHA

*After this, Jesus revealed himself again to his disciples at
the Sea of Tiberias.*

(John 21:1)

About two miles west of Capernaum lies an area named, in
Greek, *Heptapegon* (pronounced *hep-TAH-peh-gone*). This
name comes from the Greek *hepta* ("seven") and *pege* ("spring");
the area was named after the "seven springs" of water that run
together here and empty into the Sea of Galilee. The name *Heptapegon* merged into the Arabic *ettabgha* (pronounced *et-TAB-
gah*), from the last two syllables of which comes the current-day
name *Tabgha*.

Within this area are several sites of interest to our pilgrimage:
the Church of the Multiplication of Loaves, the Church of Peter's
Primacy, *Eremos* Hill, and the Mount of Beatitudes. Each will be
treated further on individually. Rather than organizing the information concerning Tabgha along the usual categories—scriptural background, archaeological history, Scripture on site, issues
raised, points for reflection—I will simply fold such details into
the descriptions of those individual sites, so as to avoid a stilted
presentation. However, a final section of reflection questions and
considerations will be provided at the end.

Firstly, before examining each unique site, it would be good
to consider the history, and even plausibility, of locating within
this area (Tabgha) the places where all the events that happened
here actually or at least seem most likely to have happened.

Throughout your time in the Holy Land, something or some things will make you wonder whether or not we can really say that *this* happened *here* and *that* occurred over *there*. It could be very easy to grow skeptical about whether or not any given place or monument can, with reliability, be attributed to a given event in the life of Jesus and the early Church. How should we adjudicate in such a situation?

The best answer that I can provide is in light of the exhortation that our Lord gives his disciples in Matthew 10:6, when he tasked them to be *both* "cunning as serpents" and "meek as doves." Adapting this phrase to our historical-reliability crossroads with regard to the places commemorating moments in the life of Christ and the Church, we could say we should want to be, on the one hand, critical[1] (informed archaeologically and realistic), while at the same time, on the other hand, giving the benefit of reasonable doubt to the witness of tradition and to the trustworthiness of the memory of the early Christians.[2] In this way, we should strive to avoid both naïveté and cold skepticism.[3]

One way that we can do that is by taking seriously the memory of local, early Christians, buttressing their witness with historical sources, especially the witness of Egeria. This early pilgrim from Gaul made a trip to the Holy Land in the early 380s AD and left behind a diary that has become very important in the retelling of the history of Christianity in ancient Israel. Egeria took assiduous notes, especially on things liturgical, and so provides a unique and bona fide testimony of the reality of life in the early days of the Christian faith in ancient Israel.

---

[1]   That is, in the proper sense of the word, rational and careful.

[2]   This cannot be overstated! It makes sense that the early, local Church, so on fire with love for the Lord whom they knew, even at times personally, would remember with accuracy where he was when he did certain things, especially when they involved miracles!

[3]   Murphy-O'Connor, unfortunately, falls over again into the latter camp. Here is what he has to say with regard to the area at hand of Tabgha: "It was perhaps inevitable that this well-watered area with its shade trees on the shore of the Sea of Galilee, where Byzantine pilgrims ate their picnics, should have been identified as the location of two gospel episodes involving the consumption of food: the multiplication of the loaves and fishes (Mark 6:30–34) and the conferral on Peter of the responsibility of leadership after a fish breakfast (John 21). Then it became convenient to localize the Sermon on the Mount (Mt 5–7) on the small hill nearby" (*The Holy Land*, 314–16). I imagine that most pilgrims would find such a presentation less than edifying.

With regards to Tabgha, we note that Egeria saw three churches here: one over the seven springs, one over the cave in which Jesus spent the night in prayer, and one on the seven stone steps where Jesus fed his disciples after the Resurrection.[4] Rubble from the ruins of two of these can be seen still today: on the hillside above the road practically across the street from the Church of the Multiplication of the Loaves, and just outside of the chapel of Peter's Primacy alongside the outer wall that faces the sea, respectively.[5] How and why did these buildings get to where they were at the time of Egeria? They did so by the historical memory of the local Jewish Christians, who lived in this area from the time of Jesus until the fifth century, and who passed on these traditions from generation to generation. In my opinion, it makes sense to trust the memory of these early followers of Jesus, who understandably retained the places where God-made-man did and said what he did. How could they forget?!

The ruins of one of the churches that Egeria saw on her pilgrimage to the Holy Land in the late fourth century.

As a final aside, this area is also called *Magadan* (Mt 15:39) and *Dalmanutha* (Mk 8:10, the parallel passage). *Magadan* probably comes from the Hebrew *migdal* ("tower"); there seems to have been in this area an ancient Hebrew tower, which here would fit in well with the other ancient fortification structures that have been found in this area. *Dalmanutha* might be an Aramaic combination of *dal* ("of") and *manutho* ("his residence"), which would make reference to the town and region of Capernaum, which Jesus made his home base (see Mt 9:1, as earlier in the chapter on Capernaum).

---

[4] Pixner, *Paths of the Messiah*, 80.

[5] See treatment further on.

Church of the Multiplication of the Loaves

If you were to read Luke's account of the multiplication of the loaves and fish (9:10–17), you would find that this passage is immediately followed by Jesus's asking his disciples: "Who do the crowds say that I am?" The disciples respond: "John the Baptist, others Elijah, still others 'one of the ancient prophets has arisen.'" And then Jesus asks them: "But who do you say that I am?" To which Peter responds with "the Messiah of God" (Lk 9:18–21).

The juxtaposition of these two episodes is fascinating. In this way, Luke seems to be implying that Jesus was seeking an answer that would be influenced by his multiplication of the loaves and fish. It is perhaps not surprising that some of the people thought that Jesus was Elijah, as Elijah was involved in providing food miraculously for a large number of people.[6]

SCRIPTURE ON SITE:
Mark 6:34-44

Jesus was, indeed, often thought to be Elijah. The crowds told Herod as much in Mark 6:15, when they were trying to come up with the identity of Jesus. Elijah, of course, was expected to come again in the messianic days, as we read in Malachi 4:5–6: "Behold, I will send you Elijah the prophet before the great and terrible day of the Lord comes. And he will turn the hearts of fathers to their children and the hearts of children to their fathers, lest I come and smite the land with a curse."[7] Hence, it is understandable that the people wondered whether Jesus, who was working such miracles, was the one who would realize these anticipations.[8] Luke, for his part, utilized this con-

---

[6] "You will eat and have some left over" (2 Kings 4:42–44). See Kilgallen, *New Testament Guide*, 44–45.

[7] We find the same expectation in Mark 9:11–12, in which our Lord responds to his disciples's questioning him about why the Scribes believe that Elijah will come before the resurrection of the dead with: "Elijah will indeed come first and restore all things."

[8] Moreover, it was not only the crowds of Galilee who confused Jesus with Elijah, but also those who stood at the foot of the Cross. From the Cross, Jesus's shriek in a loud voice to God (*Elōi, Elōi, lema sabachthani* [Mk 15:34]) was misheard by the bystanders, who thought that Jesus was calling on Elijah to take him down from the Cross (Mk 15:35–36). Jesus, it turns out in Mark's Gospel, was praying this Psalm not in Hebrew (as he did in Matthew's Gospel, which has

fusion with Elijah in order to cast Jesus in a distinctly messianic light—or, in other words, as yet another way in which to show that Jesus was the Messiah.

Pursuant to these Scripture considerations, let us make our way towards the courtyard of the church, so that we can prepare ourselves for what we will see within the actual church. In this Benedictine church is contained what pilgrims venerate as the limestone rock on which Jesus placed the loaves when he fed the 5,000-strong crowd. Is it actually *the* rock? I do not see why we should doubt it! After all, the fourth-century church, seen by Egeria, lies beneath the present floor, and so we can be sure that the tradition of this rock is very, very old, which boosts its credibility. That church was much smaller (15.5 x 9.5 meters), and the two sections that are left exposed show that the orientation was slightly differently angled.[9]

Walking toward the front of the present-day church, you can see the famous mosaic of the basket of five loaves flanked by two fish. In the two transepts and in the intervals between the pillars, you can observe some very fanciful floor mosaics. The oldest among them date from the second half of the fifth century. One of their craftsmen drew extensively from Egyptian motifs for the charming flower called the *lotus*,[10] as well as from fauna that are not found in Palestine. Another mosaic mentions "to the memory and repose of the sponsor, the holy patriarch Martyrios." This patriarch of Jerusalem donated and blessed the church, built just after he died in AD 486. It is known that this patriarch lived in Egypt when he was a young monk; Pixner muses that he might have brought a prominent Egyptian mosaicist with him to Tabgha, which would explain the motifs of the Nile landscape,[11] as well as the architectural presence of transepts, which were not seen in Palestinian churches at that time.[12]

---

the Hebrew spelling of "My God" as *Eli* [27:46]), but in his native, Galilean Aramaic, the accent of which made all "o"s sound like "a"s such that a call for *Elohi* (my God) sounded to the bystanders like *El-yah* (which would have sounded just like "Elijah").

[9] Murphy-O'Connor, *The Holy Land*, 317.
[10] Which design also adorned the columns in the Temple of Jerusalem.
[11] The non-Galilean birds perched on stylized papyrus, the Nilometer, etc.
[12] Pixner, *Paths of the Messiah*, 106.

The famous "Loaves and Fishes" mosaic beneath the main altar of the
monastery at Tabgha.

Church of Peter's Primacy

At this place,[13] there occurred four particularly noteworthy
events. The first two come from the part of John's Gospel after
the Resurrection and involve especially Peter. The next two come
from early on into Mark's Gospel and involve Peter and Andrew (first of these latter two events) and James and John (second event), whom Jesus called personally to follow him. Each of
these four events will be covered further on.

Firstly, at least from the days of the travels of Egeria, who
mentioned the rock contained within the Franciscan chapel that
was later built here in 1933, this has been venerated as the place
where Jesus, after his Resurrection, offered his disciples breakfast
after their miraculous catch: "When they climbed out on shore,
they saw a charcoal fire with fish on it and some bread. . . . Jesus said to them: 'Come, have breakfast'" (Jn 21:9, 12). At the
base of the walls furthest from the chapel's altar, the walls of a
late fourth-century building are visible on three sides. This early
building already enclosed the flat rock projecting in front of the

---

[13] By "primacy" is meant the unique importance, and hence authority
within the Church, that Peter had in relationship to Jesus.

present altar. Outside of the church on its lake-facing side, you can see the rock-cut steps that Egeria mentions.[14]

You might be wondering: what was Jesus's purpose in eating breakfast with his apostles? The simple answer is that Jesus wanted to demonstrate to his disciples that he had truly and physically risen from the dead. The word "simple," though, is a bit deceiving, as the corporeal reality of resurrection was far from an easy and widely accepted concept in the earliest days of the Church. In fact, though it might surprise us to hear, we can see, even from the many New Testament efforts to affirm it, how the bodily resurrection of Jesus "was a concept that had to be struggled for in the first century."[15] Luke 24:36–43 has Jesus appearing to the disciples behind a locked door and eating a piece of baked fish in front of them so as to assuage the wonder of the disciples, who, terrified, thought they were seeing a ghost. John 20:27–28 has Jesus inviting Thomas to touch his scarred hands, feet, and side—in short, the crucified body in which Jesus resurrected—so that he would no longer be unbelieving, but believe. Moreover, we can note how, in Matthew 28:17, the disciples worshipped Jesus about to ascend, "but they doubted." This doubt "seems centered about the reality of the resurrection of the body of Jesus."[16]

> **SCRIPTURE ON SITE:**
> *John 21:1-14*

The rock on which, per Egeria, Jesus fed his disciples breakfast in John 21.

Faithful Christians offered three arguments for the bodily resurrection of Jesus: the empty tomb, which did not prove that Jesus rose, but which surely did support it; Psalm 15, which indicated that a descendant of David would die but not stay dead, escaping permanent death in body and soul:

---

[14] Murphy-O'Connor, *The Holy Land*, 319.

[15] Kilgallen, *New Testament Guide*, 48.

[16] Ibid.

because you will not abandon my soul to the nether
   world,
nor will you suffer your holy one to see corruption.
   (see Acts 2:25–31);

and Jesus's very physical, post-Resurrection appearances to his
disciples, such as in John 21.[17]

Emphasizing Jesus's corporeal resurrection is of utmost importance for our faith, as it informs what has been called the
Catholic "habit of being"[18]—that is, the way of seeing the world
through a sacramental lens. Within this "sacramental imagination," which notices that "God saves and sanctifies the world
through the materials of the world," we come to understand an
important truth about our faith: matter *matters*, "stuff counts."[19]
The "ordinary stuff of the world," such as bread and wine, water, oil, and so on, is "the [very] material God uses to bring us
into communion with the truly extraordinary—with God himself."[20] Hence, for those with eyes to see (Mt 13:16), the physical
world can become not only a conduit of grace in the sacraments,
but can also otherwise serve to point our minds and hearts to invisible, spiritual realities. To a Christian, who believes in Jesus's
bodily resurrection from the dead, matter *matters*.[21]

Secondly, going back both to John 21 and the name of this
site, we note that this place derives its name from the pastoral
mission and authority that Jesus entrusted to Peter alone—hence
the name of the place: "Peter's *Primacy*." Simon's post-prandi-
al, triple profession of love for Jesus was met with the divine

---

[17] Ibid.

[18] George Weigel, *Letters to a Young Catholic* (New York: Basic Books,
2015), 17.

[19] Ibid., 86.

[20] Ibid., 87.

[21] This statement makes me think back to Adam and Eve. Jesus, the
New Adam, in taking on and redeeming flesh, reversed the curse
which God uttered on the ground itself at the sin of Adam and Eve
(Gen 3:17), thereby reverting the material world from being a re-
minder and occasion of our sin, toward being an opportunity for
and "means of" our salvation, as Preface III of Ordinary Time in the
3rd edition of the Roman Missal puts it. It is such a vision which a
pilgrimage to the Holy Land seeks to foster within the heart of each
one who comes into contact with the very places where God walked
this earth 2,000 years ago. "Lord, that I may see" (Mk 10:51)!

commands: *feed* my lambs, *tend* my sheep (Jn 21:15–19).

A few things about John 21:15–25 stick out. To begin, Jesus's semantic descent from *agapaō* to *phileō*, in the third question raised to Peter, is well known and often interpreted as an indication of the imperfection of Peter's love for Jesus, as well as of the latter's *condescending*—in the word's positive sense of stepping down to our level, as in Philippians 2:6–7—love for Peter. However, this exchange can also be read so as to put Peter in a good light:

> SCRIPTURE ON SITE:
> *John 21:15-25*

> Before Jesus, the Good Shepherd, left earth definitively, he took the opportunity to give Peter the responsibility of tending [his] flock, the flock of the new people of God. This responsibility was based on the fact that Peter truly loved the Shepherd and therefore could be entrusted with the care of Jesus's own flock; Jesus was going to entrust his loved ones only to someone who, he knew, loved him above all else. It is love for Jesus that will keep Peter faithful to the flock.[22]

Indeed, this interaction between Jesus and Peter bespeaks not only Jesus's giving Peter a chance to profess and perfect his love for the Lord, whom he had betrayed three times,[23] but also our Lord's trust of Peter—that is, his positive appraisal, and reception, of Peter's love. It is on the basis of Peter's love for the Lord, and his solicitous love for God's entire flock, that the third successor to the See of Peter, St. Clement of Rome, could write a letter to the Corinthians, thereby demonstrating that the Bishop

---

[22] Kilgallen, *New Testament Guide*, 50.

[23] The number three here is significant. In many Semitic languages, there is no *superlative* form of the adjective (e.g., "holi*est*"). The way that these languages express a superlative adjective is by repeating the adjective three times. So, in order to convey the meaning of "holiest," a language like Hebrew would say: "holy, holy, holy"—which we find in Isaiah 6:3 and Revelation 4:8. So, by having Peter say that he loves Jesus three times, John's Gospel is showing *just how much* Peter loved Jesus: Peter loved him *most, greatly, exceedingly.*

of Rome presides over all the other Churches in charity.[24]

The fact of the matter is that, here, on this shore, the God who once observed and rejected the utterly selfish as unfit shepherds of his people, and so had taken the reins up and vowed that he, himself, would shepherd his people (Ezek 34:1–16), now gives those very reins to another shepherd—to Peter. This fisherman is imperfect indeed, yet, trustworthy, since he was full of selfless love in imitation of his Master, whose love he personally

A fishing boat on the Sea of Galilee.

felt and which prompted him to write: "So I exhort the presbyters among you, as a fellow presbyter and witness to the sufferings of Christ and one who has a share in the glory to be revealed. Tend[25] the flock of God in your midst, overseeing not by constraint but willingly, as God would have it, not for shameful profit but ea-

---

[24]　Pope Benedict XVI once said that Clement's Letter to the Corinthians "is all the more meaningful since it represents, from the first century, the concern of the Church of Rome which presides in charity over all the other Churches" (General Audience, March 7, 2007, accessed June 4, 2017, https://w2.vatican.va/content/benedict-xvi/en/audienc es/2007/documents/hf_ben-xvi_aud_20070307.html).

[25]　The Greek verb used by Peter here in his letter is *poimanō*—the same Greek verb that Jesus uses in John 21:16!

gerly . . . be examples to the flock" (1 Pet 5:1–3, NABRE).

Thirdly, we should note that Peter and Andrew were *called* by our Lord not far from this shoreline.

How can we know that, somewhere nearby, these two fishermen were invited by the Lord to be his disciples? A detail within this passage gives us a clue:

> **SCRIPTURE ON SITE:**
> *Mark 1:16-18*

The bay at Seven Springs was one of the most sought-after spots for fishermen in Jesus's time, just as it is today. Especially in winter and spring, the warm springs that pour into the lake attract the tilapia fish, known as "St. Peter's Fish," which prefers tropical temperatures. . . . Capharnaum's fishermen had their place of work here in a small harbor just north of Dalmanutha and of the Mensa Domini—which [workplace has been called] "Peter's harbor." Fish like to stay among the reeds that grow plentifully along the shores west of the springs. Peter and Andrew stood in the shallow water where they were fishing with a casting net, just as men do today. The manner in which Mark describes them handling[26] [their nets] indicates exactly this kind of fishing near the lakeshore.[27]

All of this is to say that Peter and Andrew must have been called somewhere nearby, where the water was shallow enough to net fish among the rocks and reeds. Where exactly were they called? We are not sure. Based on the progression of the first chapter of Mark, which moves from the call of Peter and Andrew to the call of James and John (see further on) to Capernaum, I would suspect that the former pair were called not far south from Peter's Primacy.

Fourthly, just a bit north along the Sea of Galilee, we see that a strong waterfall pours out of the earth and into the lake. The voluminous waterfall is the result of the confluence of the seven springs for which Tabgha is named. In this waterfall, which spills

---

[26] The noun that Mark uses for "fishing net" is *amphiblestron* (1:16), which root this participial form, *amphiballontes*, echoes (4:18).

[27] Pixner, *Paths of the Messiah*, 82–83.

The waterfall formed by the confluence of the Seven Springs, where Jesus likely called James and John.

into a wide expanse of shallow water running through the rocks and into the Sea of Galilee, fishermen even to this day wash their nets and get them ready to be used again. We think that Jesus, who "walked along a little further" from where he called Peter and Andrew, saw and met here James and John, who were doing this kind of work of "mending[28] their nets," and he called them (Mk 1:19).[29] They "left their father Zebedee in the boat along with the hired men and followed him" (Mk 1:20).

This waterfall, called Ein Eyov, is certainly worth seeing and visiting. You can hop across the rocks and even feel the spring water below the fall! To get there from Peter's Primacy, climb back up to the main road that leads to and from Capernaum, and take it a short distance. You will see, on the right hand side of the road after the bend, through a fence, a path that leads down toward the water. Take this path all the way down to the shore, and look right: you will hear the waterfall before you see it; it rushes out of a large pipe or two protruding from the fauna. This pipe funnels into the sea the water from all seven of Tabgha's springs.

Eremos Hill

Just up the hill and across the road past the seaside sites,[30] we find a cave that, affectionately called the "Jesus Cave," offers a wonderful venue for quiet prayer overlooking the sea. Above it, we see a grassy plain that extends to the distant complex of the

---

28 In Greek, *katartizontes*.
29 Ibid., 82.
30 You will see a path, with a short metal staircase at the path's uphill starting point. This point is almost directly across the street from the path which descends to the waterfall.

Church of the Beatitudes. Egeria identifies this place as the traditional location of the Sermon on the Mount. This is probably the
"deserted place"[31] to which Jesus would retreat in order to pray
(Mk 1:35 and Lk 5:16). At the top of this hillside was possibly
the "mountain" to which Jesus departed to spend the night in
prayer to God before choosing the Twelve from among his larger
group of disciples (Lk 6:12–16).

The cave in the deserted place where Jesus would go and pray through the
night at times

It is well known that, while Matthew depicts Jesus climbing a
mountain or hill (*oros*; 5:1) to deliver his Sermon on the Mount,
which begins with the Beati-
tudes (5:3–12), Luke has Jesus
coming down from the mountain to a level place (6:17) to
deliver his so-called "Sermon
on the Plain" (6:20–49). How-

SCRIPTURE ON SITE:
Matthew 5–6 and 8:1

---

[31] In Greek, *tais eremois*, from which root word (*eremos*) we get the
English word "hermit," who is a person who lives in a lonely, or
"eremitic," place, to which Jesus would retreat in order to pray (Mk
1:35 and Lk 5:16).

The elevated plane on which Jesus delivered the Sermon on the Mount.

ever, you can see that this elevated, yet fairly flat, space fits both Gospels's account very well.[32]

I have found a lovely description of the topographical context of Jesus's famous sermon:

> In the spring, the hill is a magnificent flower garden filled with anemones and irises, the "lilies of the field" (Mt 6:28), and chirping "birds of the air" (Mt 6:26) hop from limb to limb in the prickly sidr trees. The words about the "city set on a hill" (Mt 5:14) were put into the Lord's mouth by the splendorous Decapolis city of Hippos, which in those days beamed from a rocky vantage point across the lake. Towering above the northeast corner of the lake was the rock fortress of the Jews—Gamla, the Zealots' place of origin with their militant messianism that in forty years would plunge all Israel into ruin. This moved Jesus to bless the peacemakers and the meek, "for

---

[32] Pixner, *Paths of the Messiah*, 84. Hence, rather than setting these two Gospels against each other on this account, we can use topography to reconcile what many scholars stumble over as a purported "difference" or contradiction between these two Synoptic Gospels.

they shall be called sons of God" and "inherit the earth"
(Mt 5:5, 9).[33]

Here, we note that Jesus was always aware of *where* he was
when he said what he said. While preaching, he used topography
and geography to his advantage, so as to advance more effectively his message. On this hillside, which has been intentionally
kept without buildings so as to resemble what it would have
looked like at the time, Jesus taught the crowds what exactly the
Kingdom of God looked like here on earth in the hearts of all
who believe in him.

Lastly, if you again descend the hill back towards the road,
and then take the road about five hundred meters towards Capernaum, you will find a small, well-formed bay surrounded by an
essentially theater-like terrain that slopes down to the shore. This
is very possibly the place where Jesus spoke from a boat to the
crowd assembled there at the water's edge (Mk 4:1). This "Bay
of Parables," as it
is called, contains
excellent, scientifi-
cally tested acous-
tics that would
have amplified the
voice of Jesus who,
being in the boat
not far from the
shore, would have
been standing at
the focal point of
the convex curve
formed by the wa-
terside.

The bay from which Jesus likely preached while
standing on a boat (Mk 4).

Mount of Beatitudes

The grounds of this shrine are very tranquil and peaceful. The
shaded groves provide a perfect place to discuss an overview of
Jesus's work around the lake, since, from this spot, we can see
almost every place where Jesus spoke and performed miracles.

---

[33] Ibid., 85–86.

Here, we can think about the spiritual aspects behind all of Jesus's words and deeds in Galilee.[34]

The Church of the Beatitudes and its peaceful grounds.

You will note that the present church is in the shape of an octagon. This form commemorates, of course, the Eight Beatitudes. It has been noted that the Beatitudes bear the marks of "clarity, simplicity, and memorability."[35] In Matthew, they indicate the kinds of virtues or ways of living that characterize a follower of Jesus: "humble and not proud or haughty, seeking justice as God defines it, being single-minded, that is, set on God, able to suffer persecution for Jesus's sake . . . [and] having a concern for those who are simply poor, humiliated, sorrowing."[36]

SCRIPTURE ON SITE:
Matthew 5:3-10

---

[34] Murphy-O'Connor, *The Holy Land*, 318.
[35] Kilgallen, *New Testament Guide*, 55.
[36] Ibid., 56.

Caesarea Philippi

This area is named Banyas, which is an Arabic corruption of "Paneas."[37] The name refers to the Temple of Pan that was built here after the conquests of Alexander the Great in 332 BC. It is a nicely wooded area full of pastures, which environs prompted the building here of the temple to Pan, who was the god of woodlands and pastures. His name originally derived from the Greek word *paien*, which means "to pasture," though an ancient pun linked his name to the Greek word for "all"—*pan*.[38]

Caesar Augustus Octavian gave the ancient shrine and its surrounding town to Herod the Great, who, in gratitude, dedicated to his patron a temple of white marble located near a spring. His son Philip inherited Paneas from his father, and in 2 BC, here gloriously built up the capital of his territory, which eventually included the entire northern region of then-Palestine. He named this territory Caesarea to honor the emperor. To distinguish this place from the coastal Caesarea, where Herod the Great had built the known world's largest port,[39] Philip joined his own name to this capital, calling it Caesarea Philippi. More accurately, this should be called "The Caesar city of Philip," as the latter noun is recorded in the genitive case in the Gospels (Mt 16:13).[40]

Jesus here healed the woman who had been suffering from a hemorrhage (Mk 5:25). The great Church historian Eusebius (265–340) saw her house on a visit and observed, on a column at the house's entrance, a bronze statue of a woman kneeling and pleading, with hands outstretched toward a young man (Jesus).[41]

SCRIPTURE ON SITE:
Mark 5:25-34

---

[37] Native speakers of Arabic have difficulty in pronouncing the plosive letter *p*.

[38] Apparently, there were widespread rumors about the circumstances of his mythical birth. It was said that Penelope, in Odysseus's absence, slept with *all* 108 of her suitors and gave birth, at the end of it, to *Pan*.

[39] From where Paul, having appealed his case to Caesar, shipped off for Rome (Acts 26:32; 27:1–2).

[40] Kilgallen, *New Testament Guide*, 67.

[41] Pixner, *Paths of the Messiah*, 88.

Also here, significantly for us Latin Catholics,[42] Jesus asked the disciples, "Who do people say that I am?" (Mt 16:15), and Peter famously responded, "You are the Messiah, the Son of the living God" (Mt 16:16). Jesus replied: "Blessed are you, Simon son of Jonah. For flesh and blood has not revealed this to you, but my heavenly Father. And so I say to you, you are Peter, and upon this rock I will build my church, and the gates of the netherworld shall not prevail against it. I will give you the keys to the kingdom of heaven. Whatever you bind on earth shall be bound in heaven, and whatever you loose on earth shall be loosed in heaven" (Mt 16:17–9).

SCRIPTURE ON SITE:
Matthew 16:13-20

It is supposed that Jesus chose just such a location as this for such an encounter—or, at least, that he used the geography of the place, which contains a *huge* rock outcrop, to his catechetical advantage. The Greek, as well as its Latin translation,[43] contains a clever play on words between the new name that Jesus gives Simon (that is, *Petros*) and the "rock" (that is, *petra*) upon which Jesus says he will build his Church. Tradition has interpreted this wordplay so as to highlight the confession of faith made by St. Peter, with the result being that we are given to understand that Jesus hereby placed Peter—and, by extension, his successors after him—at the head of the Church community that Jesus wanted to establish on earth.

The massive rock outcrop above the Temple of Pan at Cesarea Philippi, where Jesus declared Peter to be the rock on which he would build his Church (Mt 16:18).

Another reason why Jesus likely found this location most

---

[42] In the Holy Land, Roman Catholics are called either "Latins" or "Christians." As it is, the latter almost exclusively refers to Catholics.

[43] "Tu es *Petru*s et super hanc *petra*m aedificabo ecclesiam meam."

appropriate to the message that he wanted to convey has to do with his promise to Peter that the "gates of the netherworld" will not prevail against the Church (Mt 16:18), which is built on the apostle's confession of faith. Look again at the bottom-left-hand section of the rock outcrop, and you will see a large cave. It is well known that the Greco-Roman pagans of this area believed that this cave constituted a gate to the underworld, where the supposed fertility gods lived during the winter, which season was thought to be caused by their retreat underground via the spring of water that used to bubble out of this cave. These gods, it was believed, would return to earth each spring from this cave, bringing with them the sprouting of new life in that season. In order to allure the return of their god, Pan, out of his winter hiding each year, the pagans of this region took part in terrible deeds that included prostitution and other sexual indecencies. By evoking the horrific evils that took place here at Paneas and the tremendous power supposedly wielded here over the earth in its changing seasons, Jesus sought to reassure the disciples that this divinely inspired and divinely instituted enterprise, which he called the Church (Mt 16:18), is utterly impregnable—that is, that no wave, however powerful and terrifying, will ever sink the Barque[44] of Peter. Or, better, Jesus wanted to make it clear to his disciples that whatever power that the pagans believed to be wielded here at Paneas utterly pales in comparison to the real power bestowed upon Peter in his being handed the keys to the kingdom of heaven by Jesus (*Issue 4*, further on).

Immediately after this Petrine profession of faith, we hear Jesus strictly warn Peter and the others not to speak of this exchange to anyone (Mt 16:20). This brings us back to the issue of Markan Secrecy, described earlier. John Kilgallen posits that it was a concern for *faith at the foot of the Cross* that prompted Mark repeatedly, and Matthew occasionally, to convey the theme of messianic secret: "[They were] most precisely concerned with what his disciples would call Jesus when they see him hanging in pain and humiliation and failure on a cross until his life oozes out of him. Would they still call him Messiah, the only one who

---

[44] A word that means "ship," deriving from the Latin *barca*. It is based on this passage and its imagery of an unassailable, unsinkable ship that the architecture of the ceilings of the main aisle—also known as the "nave," from the Latin *navis* for "ship"—in many churches looks like the bottom of a large wooden boat upside-down.

will fulfill all the hopes of our hearts?"[45] By relaying often Jesus's insistence on silence with regards to his messianic nature and mission, the evangelists want the reader to realize, alongside and with the twelve disciples, that the Cross is an essential part of "the meaning of Jesus."[46]

Issues Raised

Issue 1

Given the above discussion of Jesus's cry, in Aramaic, "My God, my God, why have you abandoned me?" (Mk 15:43), we should recognize that the citation of this Psalm, on the lips of our cruci-fied Lord, does *not* express—as many take it to convey—a faith-*less* cry of despair. Rather, it constitutes a faith-*filled* expression of trust in God, despite the pangs of trial. Evidence of this is twofold.

Firstly, consider verse 25 of Psalm 22 (NABRE), which Jesus began to cite when he cried out to his Father:

> For he has not spurned or disdained
> the misery of this poor wretch,
> Did not turn away from me,
> but heard me when I cried out.

Such words are certainly not expressions despairing of God's Providence. Moreover, according to the method of prayer of the Hebrews of Jesus's time, the quoting of even (and only) the first line of a given Psalm in fact evoked the *entirety* of the rest of the Psalm, whose later themes, hence, would be *already expressed* by such an abbreviated citation of the Psalm's opening line. Hence, I do not understand how scholars claim that Jesus, from the Cross, was raising his voice out of some kind of personally felt despair as if he were experiencing the "absence of God." He was *praying*! If nothing else, he was thereby taking on all of our own distress and sorrow, just as he took on himself all of our sin, and presenting it to the Father so as to plead for relief in our suffer-ings. Or, perhaps he was giving us an example, so that what he has done in professing trust in God, we should also do in times of personal distress (see Jn 13:15).

---

[45] Kilgallen, *New Testament Guide*, 69.

[46] Ibid., 70.

Secondly, it was impossible that Jesus could have experienced despair because he, in a Thomistic Christology, never had "faith" in God. Enjoying the beatific vision in his humanity through the privilege of the hypostatic union, Jesus did not need "evidence of things not seen" (Heb 11:1), and so he could never have doubted God whom he *knew*, not in whom he *believed*. ,

Thirdly, lastly, there was no way that Jesus was doubting the presence of God, because he even had, at that moment on the Cross, proof that God *was* still with him. The proof was his mother, whom the Father gave him—and, by extension, whom God gives us—for such a moment, to remind us that we are not alone in our suffering and that we have a Sorrowful Mother "next to" (Jn 19:25) us in our crosses, too, to encourage us and have God tell us, through her: "It is going to be all right. *I* am here."

Issue 2

Many commentators on the Scriptures frequently succumb to a certain kind of historical-critical skepticism that has become regnant in many scholarly circles. We see this often in regard to the biblical account of the multiplication of the loaves. Consider the following comment:

> Since the Eucharist of bread and wine was celebrated at least every Sunday from the earliest times of Christianity to the period when Mark was writing, about AD 70, it would not be surprising to find a miracle of Jesus written up to support this Eucharistic practice without any distortion of the basic intention of Jesus to feed a hungry crowd before him. Therefore, many scholars suggest that Mark described this miracle of the bread not only to underline the wonder Jesus worked, but also to link it specifically with the Eucharist by which hungry Christians of every time can share in the food provided by Christ.[47]

Did you catch the problem? It lies in the assertion that this episode was "written up" by Mark "to support this Eucharistic practice."[48] Firstly, on a level of science—or, better, a method

---

[47] Ibid., 42.

[48] I bother even to bring this up because it is representative of an illogical method and problematic position that too many scholars adopt

of science—there is no way to prove this suggestion of "many scholars." Such a hypothesis is purely speculative and is sheer induction, which itself forbids—or, rather, should forbid—any scholar from presumptuously using positive language in expounding therefrom a deductive conclusion (such as: "Mark *described* this miracle"). Rather, it should be conveyed in conditional language (as in: "Mark *might have described* this miracle"). Read biblical scholarship with this critical eye, and you will unfortunately see this fallacy committed frequently. Moreover, for all our concern to be "scientific," it should be said that in *no other science* would adroit scholars draw this kind of conclusion, much less build entire systems of thought, around so mere a hypothesis; rather, they examine and depend on data and objective evidence, neither of which, for this suggestion of many scholars, can or will be found.

Secondly, such a hypothesis cannot be reconciled with *Dei Verbum* §19, which states: "Holy Mother Church has firmly and with absolute constancy held, and continues to hold, that the four Gospels, whose historical character the Church unhesitatingly asserts, faithfully hand on what Jesus Christ, while living among men, really did and taught for their eternal salvation until the day he was taken up into heaven (see Acts 1:1)." Within the faith of the Church, a Catholic scholar really cannot submit that the Evangelists *created*[49] the happenings and doings of Jesus; rather, they faithfully passed on what Jesus Christ really "did and taught" (Acts 1:1). To suggest otherwise is to interpret the Gospels in a way foreign to the vision of the Second Vatican Council in its Dogmatic Constitution on Revelation, and so it should not have a place in *Catholic* biblical scholarship—not least since Cardinal Ratzinger, in his Erasmus Lecture of 1988, lifted this Bultmannian veil off of scholarly eyes opaqued by Kantian positivism and Heideggerian hermeneutics.[50]

---

and from which I urge future priests and budding theologians to stay far away.

[49] Though, to be sure, the evangelists surely *colored* the details of the events of Jesus's life. In their accounts, the hagiographers emphasized and/or excluded, etc., some details, according to their theological interests. They crafted, but did *not* create or conjure up.

[50] Joseph Ratzinger, "Biblical Interpretation in Crisis: The 1988 Erasmus Lecture," *First Things*, April 26, 2008, accessed June 4, 2017, https://www.firstthings.com/web-exclusives/2008/04/biblical-interpretation-in-cri.

Issue 3

It has been noted that, in the Sermon on the Mount, Matthew seems to be presenting Jesus in parallel to Moses as a kind of "new Moses," delivering a "new Law"—of love—that goes beyond the demands of the Torah.

For one, when Moses went up the mountain to receive the tablets of stone, he "remained" on the mountain for forty days (Deut 9:9). The verb *yshb* is ambiguous here and has been read by some early rabbis as meaning "to sit" rather than "to remain," which, of course, syncs with Jesus's seated position (Mt 5:1) when he delivered his sermon, especially given Matthew's knowledge of the Hebrew text of the Old Testament and its Jewish exegetical tradition.[51]

Secondly, Matthew 1–2 lines up the events of Jesus's life with those of Moses's life: some rulers, learning from sacred scribes of a birth of the future liberator, order a slaughter of male infants, which leads to the liberator's being taken into safety in a foreign land, from which he returns at the divine prompting, and so on. Moreover, on this note, Matthew 3–4 can be seen as presenting a new Exodus—as Jesus emerges from the waters to enter the wilderness—with Matthew 5–7 then describing how Jesus immediately thereafter goes up on a mountain and speaks of the Law.[52] In other words: "Every major event in Matthew 1–5 apparently has its counterpart in the events surrounding Israel's exodus from Egypt." Thus, we can say that: "When Jesus goes up the mountain to utter the Sermon on the Mount, he is speaking as the mosaic Messiah and delivering messianic Torah."[53]

Beyond these observations of William Davies and Dale Allison, we could point to the legal language of the antitheses spoken by Jesus in Matthew 5 and see therein a connection between Moses and Jesus that makes the latter out to be the fulfillment of the promise that Israel's lawgiver made to the people on Mount Horeb:[54]

[51] William D. Davies and Dale C. Allison, *The Gospel According to Saint Matthew: I–VII*, International Critical Commentary (Edinburgh: Bloomsbury T & T Clark, 1997), 424. This is an excellent commentary!
[52] Davies and Allison, *Matthew*, 424.
[53] Ibid., 427.
[54] Which many consider to be a different name for Sinai.

A prophet like me will the Lord, your God, raise up for you from among your own kindred; that is the one to whom you shall listen. . . . The Lord said to me . . . "I will raise up for you a prophet like you from among their kindred, and will put my words into the mouth of the prophet; the prophet shall tell them all that I command. Anyone who will not listen to my words which the prophet speaks in my name, I myself will hold accountable for it." (Deut 18:15–19)[55]

Issue 4

What exactly do the "keys of the kingdom," which Jesus promised to give to Peter, mean? The idea expressed here is based on the Old Testament image of the special and only person assigned by the king to have all the keys that open and close all the doors of the palace (see Judg 3:25). This imagery, then, indicates that it is Peter who will open and shut the doors of heaven—effectively, by forgiving or retaining one's sin. To make this idea clearer, we look to Matthew 23:13, where Jesus "excoriates" the scribes and Pharisees because they "shut up the kingdom of heaven in men's faces, neither going in [them]selves or allowing others to go in who want to." Though these people "had the power to understand the teaching of God that would allow them and others to enter or to be kept out of the kingdom, . . . They failed to use this potential for themselves and others . . . because they so often wrongly interpreted the will of God. Peter, rock and keeper of the keys of Jesus's community, will teach correctly, so that people can rightly enter, or be kept from entering, the kingdom."[56]

POINTS FOR REFLECTION

- The Nile motifs in the mosaic of the Church of the Multiplication of the Loaves bring to mind a divine command—to plunder the Egyptians (see Ex 12:36)—that became dear to the Church Fathers, who used it to argue

---

[55] For a further, excellent treatment of the Jesus–Moses parallels, see Lawrence Feingold, *The Mystery of Israel and the Church: Things Old and New*, vol. 2 (St. Louis, MO: Miriam Press), ch. 2 (127–45; "Jesus as the New Moses").

[56] Kilgallen, *New Testament Guide*, 73.

that we should look around into the secular, surrounding world and, seeing good therein, affirm it as good and use it to preach the Gospel. Justin the Martyr called such truths *logoi spermatikoi*, or "Seeds of the Word," as they essentially were evangelical elements latent within popular culture, just waiting to be expounded upon with great effectiveness by a skilled teacher—like Paul, who seized upon the occasion in Acts 17 to use the religiosity underneath the Athenians' altar to the unknown god so as to preach Jesus Christ. We have all heard dynamic preachers who execute this technique so well. Let us pray for the ability to receive messages of grace even from unexpected sources, and for the spiritual sensitivity to turn those encounters with the wisdom of God into a prayerful moment of wonder and awe.

- Before you make any big decision, do you retreat first to silent prayer, just as our Lord himself did? If you have a tendency toward impulsiveness, especially in decision making, pray with Jesus's example and seek to imitate him who "has given [us] an example, that what [he] ha[s] done, [we] also should do" (Jn 13:15).

- Jesus's command to Peter to tend and feed the flock is seen by many scholars as pertaining to two distinct and essential elements of Christian life: teaching the will of God and providing the Eucharistic food. Priests do this in Mass by preaching and consecrating the Eucharist, and often  we call priests our "spiritual fathers." What is your understanding of this phrase? Is there a priest whose spiritual fatherhood has influenced your life?

- In light of the Crucial (Cross) mechanism behind the so-called "Markan secrecy," we should consider the possibility that, as God asked the cross of Jesus, something no one expected of the Messiah, so God may ask me to follow Jesus with my own cross, which I would not have expected to have to carry.[57] What are the big crosses that you have had to carry in your life? Have any of them come as a surprise to you, as Jesus's Cross came as completely unexpected to many of his contemporaries? Are you able to see the hand of the Messiah in and on your crosses? Some writer once said that Jesus's Passion, by turning our sufferings into crosses, made them bearable for us—for, without his sufferings, our own would be meaningless, places not of hope but of despair. *Hail, O Cross, our only hope!*

Especially for Seminarians

- Pray for the grace to have eyes to see and ears to hear (Mt 13:16) opportunities to "baptize the culture" and to affirm the good in the secular when you recognize it as a priest. The effectiveness of your preaching will thereby be greatly enhanced.

- Before you make any big decision as a priest, do you follow our Lord's example and turn first to silent prayer?

A frescoed cross on an ancient Roman wall at Beth Shean.

This meditative contemplation is especially important for the life of a priest. If you tend to make decisions impulsively, pray with Jesus's example and seek to imitate him who would go up on the mountain to pray alone during the evening (Mt 14:23), early in the morning in a lonely place (Mk 1:35), and during the day by withdrawing to the wilderness (Lk 5:16).

---

[57] Ibid., 70.

- At the place where Jesus called James and John, it would be good to go back over, in prayer, your own vocation story. How did our Lord call you? Where did he call you? Where he called the Apostles was something that Jesus used to reveal to them the heart of their commission, to be fishers of men (Lk 5:10). Where our Lord called me— that is, at the altar and in the grade school—spoke, I later learned, to the heart of what kind of priest he wanted me to be—a parish priest and teacher.

- So much of my priesthood—daily Mass, in particular!— has revolved around the two tasks that Jesus commanded of Peter: teach and feed. In the priesthood, these manifest themselves as teaching the will of God and providing the Eucharistic food.[58] When I do these two things, I feel like a real, spiritual father. What do you understand by the phrase "spiritual father?" How does a priest manifest his paternity? Take our Lord's yoke upon you and learn from him (Mt 11:20); teach and feed, like Jesus did.

- What are the crosses that you have had to carry specifically pertaining to your vocational discernment? Have you seen the work of God in your crosses? Take a moment to contemplate Christ's suffering, and how it can sanctify your own suffering, both now and in the future.

---

[58] Ibid., 51.

MOUNT TABOR

After six days, Jesus took Peter, James, and John his brother, and he led them up a high mountain by themselves. And he was transfigured before them; his face shone like the sun and his clothes became white as light. And behold, Moses and Elijah appeared to them, conversing with him. Then Peter said to Jesus in reply: "Lord, it is good that we are here. If you wish, I will make three tents here: one for you, one for Moses, and one for Elijah."

(Matthew 17:1–4)

Scriptural Background

The localization of the Transfiguration has shifted a bit throughout the early Church's history. Three candidate mountains were nominated by various figures: Mount Hermon (north of the Sea of Galilee), Mount Tabor, and the Mount of Olives. Eusebius (AD 340) hesitates between the former two, while the Pilgrim of Bordeaux (AD 333) chooses the third. In AD 348, Cyril of Jerusalem decided on Tabor, and the support of Epiphanius and Jerome established the tradition firmly.[1] Many exegetes believe that Mount Hermon or a nearby peak would do better justice to the Gospel accounts and to the history of Mount Tabor, which, in the time before, during, and after Jesus's life, was a mountain

---

[1] Murphy-O'Connor, *The Holy Land*, 413.

inhabited and fortified by Hasmoneans, then by Romans, and then by Jewish rebels.[2] The notes in the New American Bible Revised Edition (NABRE) contend that the anonymity of this mountain in the Synoptic Gospels shows that the meaning of the "high mountain" is theological rather than geographical, possibly recalling the revelation to Moses on Mount Sinai (Ex 24:12–18) and to Elijah at that same place (1 Kings 19:8–18).[3]

The sight of this lonely mountain is very impressive. The power that it evokes explains why one of the early names for God used by the Hebrews is *el-shadday* (Ex 6:3), which has been translated as "God *Almighty*," but which many think originally meant "God of the mountain." The mountain is first mentioned in the Bible in connection with the defeat of the army of the king of Hazor by Deborah and Barak in 1125 BC. The 900 Canaanite chariots swept across the plain of Jezreel from near Megiddo,

SCRIPTURE ON SITE:
Matthew 17:1-8

The apse mosaic above the main altar in the Basilica of the Transfiguration.

---

[2] Pixner, *Paths of the Messiah*, 74.
[3] NABRE 2010 edition (Washington, DC: Confraternity of Christian Doctrine). Mount Horeb and Mount Sinai are often thought to be difference appellations of the same mountain.

but God threw the troops into a panic near the foot of Tabor, which disruption slowed them down enough for the Israelite charge from the mountain to overtake them (Judg 4:4–16). Heterodox Jewish worship on Tabor is condemned by Hosea (5:1), and it symbolized the might of Nebuchadnezzer of Babylon for Jeremiah (46:18).

Lastly, of course, we note the occurrence of the Transfiguration of Jesus here.

Archaeological History

Here at Tabor, from 80000 to 15000 BC, Neanderthals came to make flint tools.[4] In 218 BC, Antiochus III of Syria, by feigning retreat, enticed the Egyptian garrison from their position on the summit and slaughtered them in the plain, and the same stratagem enabled the Roman general Placidus to defeat the Zealot Jews who, under the future historian Flavius Josephus, had built a wall around the summit in forty days (AD 67). The text[5] describing this event "incidentally suggests that a village existed on the summit in the first century AD, possibly inhabited by the descendants of a garrison left behind by Alexander Jannaeus (103–76 BC) when he consolidated Jewish control over the center and north of the country."[6]

The date of the first religious constructions on Tabor is uncertain. The anonymous Pilgrim of Piacenza saw three basilicas here in AD 570. Willibaldus, on the contrary, in 723 mentions only one church dedicated to Jesus, Moses, and Elijah. The apparent contradiction disappears, though, if we assume three chapels architecturally linked, as in the present church.[7] Tancred, the ruling Crusader, installed Benedictine monks on Tabor in 1099. They were massacred and their buildings destroyed by a Turkish attack in 1113. The caliph al-Malik al-Adil fortified the mountain against the threat of the fourth crusade (1202–1204); the ruins of these fortifications are still visible around and behind the church, on the left side.[8]

---

[4] Murphy-O'Connor, *The Holy Land*, 412.

[5] Josephus, *Wars of the Jews* 4:54–61 (Whitson, *Works*, 666–67).

[6] Murphy-O'Connor, *The Holy Land*, 413.

[7] Ibid.

[8] Ibid., 414.

Go around either side of the basilica and take in the view of the incredible, sweeping panorama of the valley and countryside. Look left and you can see the mountains of Upper Galilee, with the mass of Mount Hermon in the distance slightly to the east. There you can see the infamous valley called the Horns of the Hattin, where the Crusaders were decisively defeated by the Muslims under Saladin. Further east, you can see the depression containing the Sea of Galilee. If the weather is good, to the west you can see Nazareth. Throughout history the entire plain, known as Jezreel, has "resounded to the tramp of the armies of all the great generals who campaigned in the Middle East, from Thut-mose III (ancient Egypt) to Alexander the Great (Greece), Napoleon (France), and Allenby (British)."[9] It is fitting, then, that because this area (known also as Armageddon [Rev 16:16], which is Hebrew for "Mountain of Megiddo") was the scene of many decisive battles in antiquity (Judg 4–5; 2 Kings 9:27; 2 Chr 35:20–24), it became the symbol of the final disastrous rout of the forces of evil in the apocalyptic age.

The view of the Valley of Armegeddon from behind the Basilica of the Transfiguration.

9   Ibid., 415.

The basilica was built between 1921 and 1924, in the style called Roman-Syrian, which represents the splendor of the fifth–sixth centuries.[10] Upon entering, if you turn around so that your back is to the main altar, you can see two chapels—on the right, one dedicated to Moses, and on the left, one dedicated to Elijiah—much older than the current basilica. As seen from the outside, the roofs above these side chapels and the main chapel are shaped in the form of a tent, which recalls Peter's question in

The Basilica of the Transfiguration.

response to the dazzling transfiguration: "Rabbi, it is good that we are here! Let us make three tents: one for you, one for Moses, and one for Elijiah" (Mk 9:5).[11] The alabaster windows of the basilica enhance the sense of mystery and glory that is associated with the Transfiguration of Jesus. On the lower level, there are mosaics of the four "transfigurations," in the sense of revelation of Jesus: the Nativity, the Eucharist, the Passion, and the Resurrection.[12]

Issues Raised

This episode in the Gospels could contain an allusion to the Jewish liturgical custom of the Feast of Tabernacles, which lends to the Transfiguration a rather strong, messianic message. This celebration is also called the Feast of Booths (in Hebrew, *Sukkot*), which recalls the Israelites's dwelling in tents during the journey from Egypt to the Promised Land (Lev 23:39–42). The roots of this feast, as is the case for all of the Hebrews's feasts, are agricultural. While harvesting in ancient times, the workers often stayed in booths in the field rather than go all the way home. Of course,

---

[10] Kilgallen, *New Testament Guide*, 80.

[11] Mitch Pacwa, *Holy Land Prayer Book* (San Francisco: Ignatius, 2004), 89.

[12] Kilgallen, *New Testament Guide*, 81.

the meaning of this feast's celebration developed over time and shifted from an agricultural to a religious tone, and (moreover,) within the latter, it took on more than merely a recollection of the saving acts of God for the ancients; the celebration came to be a foretaste of messianic times, when God's "people will abide in a peaceful habitation, in secure *dwellings*, and in quiet resting places" (Is 32:18).

On a Christian reading, then, of the event of the Transfiguration in light of those passages, we hear in Peter's inquiry about building tents (*skēne*) a resonance with John 1:14 ("The Word became flesh and *dwelt*[13] among us"). These lexical gymnastics reveal to us that the Evangelist's point in painting the Transfiguration in the colors of the Jewish feast of *Sukkot* is this: we do not need booths anymore because we are no longer on a journey either to the Promised Land of Canaan or to the promised messianic place of peace. No, *already now*, in the presence of Jesus, who is the fulfillment of the Law (Moses) and the Prophets (Elijah), we are indeed *home*. With Jesus in our midst, we "hear a loud voice from the throne saying: 'Behold, God's dwelling is with the human race. He will dwell with them and they will be his people, and God himself will always be with them as their God. He will wipe every tear from their eyes, and there shall be no more death or mourning, wailing or pain, for the old order has passed away'" (Rev 21:3-4). At the voice of God the Father on Mount Tabor, where he identifies Jesus as his own Son, we realize that in the incarnated, second person of the Trinity, Ezekiel 27:27, with all its benefits, finally comes to pass: "My *dwelling* shall be with them; I will be their God, and they will be my people."

POINTS FOR REFLECTION

- Have you ever shared, or heard others share, a "glory story"? That is, a joy-and-awe-filled encounter with the true, the good, and the beautiful, which heavenly contact brings individuals to experience the bounty of the God who is rich in mercy and gracious beyond all telling (Ex 34:6-7) in giving gifts to his children. Here on this mountain, where we can even physically feel closer to the God

---

[13] In Greek, *episkēne*, which is the word for "booth" in the Septuagint of Leviticus and in the text of Matthew!

above (Ps 115:3), it would be good now to recall to your own mind and heart—and even to share with others, if you feel so called—the various, wonderful ways in which the Lord has given you to see a glimpse of the full weight of glory that awaits you in heaven, beyond the sufferings and trials of this life (2 Cor 4:17).

- While there are many glorious moments in life, there are sure also to be battles. Foremost among these is what the Catechism of the Catholic Church calls the "struggle," or "battle" (2520), for purity, to which we as Catholics are all called.[14] How are you doing in this arena? Are you able to keep custody of the eyes in public and in private on your devices (phone, computer, TV)? Are you able to think of friends of the opposite sex as brothers and sisters in Christ, so as not to lust in your heart—which Jesus condemns as adulterous (Mt 5:27–28)? Have you been able already to live successfully a chaste life, whatever your vocation? Either way, poorly or well, turn to the Lord and rely on his strength (Ps 18:2). Beseech, especially if you do not already do so explicitly, the Lord's grace, which was indeed "sufficient" for St. Paul, tormented as he was by the infamous "thorn in the flesh" (2 Cor 12:9)—the Greek word for which quality of grace (*arkei*) is the same word used to describe the protective action of a fortified city wall, which imagery of impenetrable strength this fortress-like church evokes. In moments of temptation, invoke the Lord and both trust in and be comforted by the strength of his grace, which will protect and encourage/empower your heart—just as the glorious light radiating from the face of Jesus fortified the faith of the disciples to accept the inevitability of the Lord's coming sufferings, so as not to be completely scandalized by those terrible moments.

---

[14] Catechism of the Catholic Church, 2nd ed. (Washington, DC: United States Catholic Conference, 2000), §2520. In the official Latin text, the word used here for "struggle" is *certamen*, which means "contest."

Especially for Seminarians

- You will certainly have, in your priesthood, mountain-top experiences! You can be assured that many of them will come to you from such places as these: in the confessional when, through you, one more soul—especially, in the words of St. John Vianney, a "big fish"[15]—is won back for God from sin; in the classroom, when a child, to whom belongs the kingdom of heaven (Lk 18:16), shares with you a keen, yet simple, knowledge of or insight into the faith, one that blows you away and deeply edifies you; in the front pews when you behold in the open casket before the altar an old, fellow priest, vested in the chasuble in which he was ordained (as will be you), and that is now, like his skin, worn down from a lifetime of faithful service in the Lord's vineyard . . . and then you feel the rush of the throng of your brother priests attending his funeral and singing, after the Final Commendation, the Salve Regina, to which sweet, deep melody you lift your own voice and priestly heart. In these moments, you will say, with Peter: "Lord, it is good that I am here." It is good to be a priest! Fitting here would be an inclusion of the famous words of Jean-Baptiste Henri Lacordaire, O.P.: "To live in the midst of the world with no desire for its pleasures; to be a member of every family, yet belonging to none; to share all sufferings; to penetrate all secrets, to heal all wounds; to daily go from men to God to offer him their homage and petitions; to return from God to men to bring them his pardon and hope; to have a heart of fire for charity and a heart of bronze for chastity; to bless and to be blest forever. O God, what a life, and it is yours, O Priest of Jesus Christ!"

- Speaking of a "heart of bronze for chastity," this virtue can be a fitting object of your prayer here on Mount Tabor. The ways in which you have exercised well, or not, this priestly virtue would be a good thing to bring to Jesus, beseeching him for the strength of mind, will, and

---

[15] Abbé François Trochu, *The Curé d'Ars*, trans. Dom Ernest Graf (Charlotte: TAN Books, 2007), 264.

spirit to live out the ideals of priestly celibacy. Ask the Lord who died on the Cross as a virgin, stretching his arms out wide so as to embrace *all* of God's people, to give you the magnanimity of heart that is part and parcel of celibate, priestly love. May your love for all of the people of God be both intense and yet detached. May it also be an effective sign for others of the Kingdom of God that awaits us (see Mt 19:12); after all, as the Catechism points out so well, "priestly celibacy, accepted with a joyous heart, radiantly proclaims the Kingdom of God" (1579). Pray here for the grace to claim with good cheer this priestly discipline.

• Almighty God has bestowed real power to the priesthood. By your outstretched hands (see Ex 6:6) and clear voice, you will confect the Eucharist, turning bread and wine into the very Body and Blood of Jesus. By your words, you will bind and loose (Mt 18:18) in Confession, and in pastoral counseling you will "break asunder bonds"

Fresco of Elijah in the dome above the basilica's side chapel dedicated to Elijah. He is depicted praying to God to send down fire upon the offering on his altar so as to prove to the prophets of Ba'al, who was indeed the real God: the Lord of the Israelites (1 Kings 18:17-40). This image conveys well the power of priestly prayer and intercession since the supposed god of Ba'al failed to bring fire.

(Ps 2:3) of guilt, shame, grief, and regret. All of this authority, like that of our Lord's (Mk 2:10), will be yours *ex-ousia*—literally, "from [your very] being," conformed ontologically to Jesus as an *alter Christus*. How awesome is the power of the priesthood! And yet, aware of your many weaknesses that make you "unworthy" of so great a power, you will know the humility with which Paul wrote that we hold this treasure in earthen vessels, so that the surpassing power may be of God, and not of us (2 Cor 4:7). Let this prayer often be on your lips as a priest: "Not to us, Lord, not to us, but to your name give the glory" (Ps 115:1).

Fresco of Moses in the dome above the basilica's side chapel dedicated to Moses. He is depicted holding the Ten Commandments (Ex 20:1–20; also Ex 34:28) with the glory of the Lord shining off of his face (Ex 34:29–35) and with Mount Sinai and the burning bush (Ex 3:1–6) in the background. Moses appeared at the Transfiguration so that Jesus could be seen to be the fulfillment of the Old Law. The bush which burned but was not consumed (Ex 3:2–3) has been interpreted by many as an image of celibacy.

THE DEAD SEA

An eastward view of the Dead Sea from atop the hike through Ein Gedi.

JERICHO

*Now Jericho was in a state of siege because of the presence
of the Israelites. And to Joshua the Lord said: "I have delivered Jericho, its king, and its warriors into your power.
Have all the soldiers circle the city, marching once around
it. Do this for six days, with seven priests carrying ram's
horns ahead of the ark. On the seventh day, march around
the city seven times, and have the priests blow horns.
When they give a long blast on the ram's horn, all the
people shall shout aloud. The wall of the city will collapse,
and the people shall attack."*

(Joshua 6:1–5)

Scriptural Background

Four episodes most famously characterize biblical Jericho. The
best known is that of Joshua and the Battle of Jericho, when the
Hebrews, having just crossed the Jordan into the Promised Land,
paraded around the city, the walls of which fell upon the shouts
(Josh 6). This event was intended to convey that it was God,
not human strength or feats, who secured victory for his people (v. 2). The next-best-known episodes involve two encounters
of our Lord's, one outside of Jericho with the blind man Bartimaeus, who begged for the Son of David's healing mercy (Mk
10:46–52), and one inside the city with the short tax collector
named Zacchaeus, a wealthy man who mounted a sycamore tree

because he was "seeking to see who Jesus was" (Lk 19:1–10). Whether or not this latter encounter happened at the tree that today "marks the spot" is indeed beside the point, as the current memorial tree well secures a moment for reflection on these, respectively, merciful and gracious encounters, both of which reveal to us just how much Jesus wants to be with us, no matter our misery or our sins.

SCRIPTURE ON SITE:
Mark 10:46
Luke 19:1-10

The fourth episode is perhaps a little less well-known, but still quite relevant to what pilgrims see today while visiting Jericho. Consisting of two moments, it involves the prophet Elisha. We read in 2 Kings 2:4–6 first about Elisha's persistent fidelity to Elijah, who was about to be taken up into heaven, despite Elijah's insistence that Elisha not follow him past Jericho and beyond the Jordan, and also in spite of the taunting of the sons of the prophets of Jericho. Second, we read later in the chapter about a curious occasion in which Elisha purifies the foul . . . a spring in Jericho:

Water from the spring which has fed Jericho since the time of Elijah and Elisha (2 Kings 2:19-22).

The inhabitants of Jericho complained to Elisha: "The site of the city is fine indeed, as my lord can see, but the water is bad and the land sterile." Elisha said: "Bring me a new bowl and put salt into it." When they had brought it to him, he went out to the spring and threw salt into it, saying: "Thus says the Lord: I have purified this water. Never again shall death or sterility come from it." And the water has stayed pure even to this day, according to the word Elisha had spoken. (2 Kings 2:19–22)

The biblical "to this day" applies, literally, to *this* day, as the spring of water continues to flow, as can be seen in modern Jericho at the parking lot for the archaeological site Tell es-Sultan.

Archaeological History

At 258 meters below sea level, Jericho is the lowest—and, as it turns out, oldest—city on earth. Sitting strategically between desert and lush green landscapes, Jericho's climate attracted prehistoric nomads to the area. They settled at the hill Tell es-Sultan near a powerful perennial spring, whose waters flow at 1,000 gallons/minute and are still distributed throughout the oasis, now by a complex system of gravity-flow irrigation. This water source has allowed, and still allows, Jericho to produce abundant fruit, flowers, and spices.[1]

A view of the site of ancient Jericho, with its desert oasis of fruit and gum trees in the background.

---

[1] Jerome Murphy-O'Connor, *The Holy Land: An Oxford Archaeological Guide from Earliest Times to 1700*, 5th ed. (Oxford: Oxford University Press, 2008), 327.

Jericho has had a long history of defensive walls built around it. The first massive wall was built around the settlement sometime around 8000 BC, when the inhabitants shifted from being wandering food-gatherers to settled food-producers. Waves of desert invaders repeatedly took the town, and then Joshua and the Israelites captured the city around 1200 BC. Occupation of the tel—the technical word for an archaeological mound—ended at the Babylonian Exile, in 587/586 BC.[2]

Ruins of ancient Jericho's defensive walls and towers.

In the late sixth century BC, Jericho became a Persian administrative center with rich plantations. From the time of Alexander the Great (336–323 BC), the oasis around Jericho was considered the private estate of the sovereign in power; this dynamic, however, impeded any true urban development of Jericho.[3] Herod the Great at first leased the oasis from Cleopatra, who had been given it by her lover, Mark Antony. After Cleopatra and Mark Antony's joint suicide in 30 BC, Octavian rewarded Herod's shrewd diplomacy by entrusting Jericho to him. Herod set up new aqueducts to irrigate the area below the cliffs and to supply a luxurious winter palace of his.[4] He also built a hippodrome with a theater here for entertainment.[5] Jericho, however, suffered from the negligence of the Roman army as Vespasian waited for Jewish factions in Jerusalem to weaken each other, as well as for his engineers of the Tenth Legion to complete the road they needed in order to bring their massive siege equipment up to Jerusalem[6] for the battle that would eventually ruin the city.

---

[2]   Ibid.

[3]   Ibid.

[4]   Ibid., 327.

[5]   A huge oblong track for horses and chariot races—much like the Circus Maximus in Rome, as immortalized by the movie *Ben Hur*.

[6]   Ibid., 330.

For most of its history, Jericho has been a center of agricultural production, namely of fruits and sweets. The Greek philosopher, geographer, and historian Strabo describes just how verdant this desert oasis was, which contained a Phoenicon (palm grove) mixed with other kinds of cultivated and fruitful trees, as well as shrubs of spicy-flavored balsam, the juice of which is a costly, glutinous, white substance that serves as a cure for headaches and beginning cataracts.[7] Not surprisingly, Jericho was known, among Hebrews, as the City of Palms (Deut 34:3).

Jesus would most certainly have traveled through Jericho, and this many times over on pilgrimage for feasts (Jn 2:13; 5:1), because following the valley of the Jordan River south until reaching this city was the safest and best way to reach Jerusalem from Galilee in his time. Once at Jericho, Jesus would have turned westward, beginning the ascent to Jerusalem.[8]

Issues Raised

Issue 1

The story of Joshua and the Battle of Jericho (Josh 6:1–27) raises the issue of the historicity of the Bible—and provides us a chance to do a little archaeology, which science is most helpful in understanding the Bible.

Excavations from 1952–1958 on Jericho by the renowned archaeologist Kathleen Kenyon demonstrate that Jericho was destroyed, with its walls having collapsed, around 1550 BC during a well-known Egyptian campaign of that period, and that Jericho was subsequently deserted until 1400 BC,[9] and then again later

---

[7]   From Strabo's *Geography* 16.2.41, cited in Murphy-O'Connor, *The Holy Land*, 328.

[8]   John J. Kilgallen, *A New Testament Guide to the Holy Land* (Chicago: Loyola, 1998), 116–17.

[9]   Kathleen M. Kenyon, *Archaeology of the Holy Land* (London: Ernest Benn Limited, 1965), 197–98. Evidence for the destruction of Jericho, Kenyon writes, is dramatic: "All the Middle Bronze Age buildings were violently destroyed by fire. The stumps of the walls are buried in the debris collapsed from the upper stories, and the faces of these stumps and the floors of the rooms are strongly scorched by fire. This destruction covers the whole area." Moreover, she says, the "gap of occupation" in Jericho is "confirmed by a gap in the use of tombs" there, such that "when the material is analyzed in the light of our present knowledge, it becomes clear that there is a complete gap"

from 1325 BC until at least 1200 BC.[10] For some, this could render problematic the biblical account of Joshua and the Hebrews's destroying Jericho because, based on the best timing that we can surmise from an attempt to corroborate history and archaeology with the biblical account of the exodus from Egypt and the conquest of Canaan, Joshua hypothetically should have passed over the Jordan, and so conquered Jericho, during the time in which Kenyon showed that the city was already abandoned and in ruins.[11]

What do we do with this seeming disparity between the Bible and archaeology? Do we despair of the Bible's authenticity—or, worse yet, doubt its inerrancy? No! This difficulty should neither shake our faith nor disturb our peace. In order to address and resolve it, we should simply adopt a reasonable understanding of what kind of history we should consider especially the Book of Joshua to be.

In short, I understand the conquest accounts of the "historical book," as we Catholics are wont to call it, of Joshua to be a combination of folkloric[12] history and theologically motivated history. The articulation of the former, teased out well by Kenyon,[13] is the result of being practically realistic about the nature of the Old Testament books that cover ancient Israel's post-Egyp-

---

of occupation "both on the tel and in the tombs between ca. 1580 BC and ca. 1400 BC."

[10] And possibly even later, as a strong kingdom was not established there until 1000 BC (ibid., 211).

[11] The details of how to arrive at this apparently problematic dating of the Battle of Jericho are beyond the scope of this book. However, 195–212 provide a good, thorough, and concise breakdown of the archaeology of this important site. Some of the facts and figures might not be exactly familiar to someone who has not taken classes in archaeology, but Kenyon does a wonderful job of taking a step back and explaining what her findings mean in the grand scheme of things.

[12] I could foresee a seminarian, well-versed in traditional readings of the Old Testament, taking a bit of alarm at this term, as if it were somehow to suggest that these books are entirely ahistorical. Such is certainly not at all what I am claiming here, as the succeeding paragraphs demonstrate.

[13] Who has quite convinced me on these points here. I make her arguments and musings my own, of course hereby acknowledging that, though their presentation in this book originates in me, the content of these positions do not!

tian history, while the articulation of the latter is the result of an equilibrated diachronic analysis of Old Testament books whose stories often appear to exhibit the same literary genre. In other, simpler words, once we interpret biblical Jericho from the points of view of folkloric memory and theologically motivated (rhetorically and narratively) history, we shall see that biblical history and archaeology do not, indeed, disagree with or invalidate each other with regard to Joshua and the Battle of Jericho.

Firstly, following Kenyon, I sustain that the accounts contained, in the form in which they have come down to us, in Exodus and Joshua should be understood as the result more of folkloric memory than historiographical motivations. Let us work up to this notion in steps, beginning with Exodus and then arriving at Joshua.

To begin, we can point out, as many scholars do, that no Egyptian archaeological source "give[s] any hint of the events recorded in Exodus."[14] However, to adopt Kenyon's words, the event of the exodus "was of such primary importance in Hebrew history, and the divine assistance of which it was held to be evidence was such a basic concept in the development of Yahwism, that its historical basis must be accepted, particularly in view of recent evidence as to the possibility of written records at a date earlier than used to be supposed."[15]

The striking of such a balance is hard to find in scholarship at large. Yet Kenyon has found, I think, a good way to reconcile it. With regard to Exodus and its historicity, we can sustain with her that the book itself gives us indications that it should not be read as a work of historiography, which seeks an exact chronology of events. For example, in Exodus, the "even time spans of 40 or 30 years mentioned in the Bible" stand out as being "largely conventional expressions for the passage of an appreciable period of time." They also show that "the length of folk memory,

---

[14] Kenyon, *Archaeology in the Holy Land*, 207. We should not, of course, take this archaeological silence too far, since arguments from absence of evidence are quite pernicious. A propos, Kenneth Kitchen well insists that we should not overvalue such archaeological silence regarding the Hebrews's stay in and departure from Egypt; after all, he points out, Nile floods have, for centuries, washed away most ancient things buried or left in its vicinity (Kenneth A. Kitchen, *On the Reliability of the Old Testament* [Grand Rapids, MI: Eerdmans, 2003], 246).

[15] Kenyon, *Archaeology in the Holy Land*, 207–8.

though it may be reasonably accurate as to the occurrence of important events, is short as regards chronological exactitude."[16]

In a similar way that the apparently historical claims of Exodus should be considered more folkloric than historically pinpoint precise, the account of Joshua's conquering of Jericho should also be read within the folkloric, and not historiographic, lens according to which it was likely written. The archaeological data, or lack thereof, with regard to Jericho's biblically purported destruction at the hands of the Hebrews should prompt us to read Joshua's conquering of Jericho as a certain kind of storytelling that is *rooted in history* but does not always accurately relate the exact succession of past events. Kenyon, on this note, is right on: given that "of all the captures of towns by the Israelites, that of Jericho is the most dramatic . . . it is difficult to avoid the impression that [Jericho in Joshua] is the record, committed to writing perhaps after very many years, of a folk memory of an important event."[17]

By claiming that Joshua is heavily folkloric, I am not ahistoricizing this book. Rather, I am attempting humbly to admit that, "for the present, the part played by the Hebrews" in the historical course of events as revealed by archaeology at Jericho "must remain uncertain."[18] Jericho was likely, per archaeology, uninhabited and in ruins at the time of Joshua's passing into the land of Canaan. Moreover, the vivid drama of Joshua's account of the Battle of Jericho leads one to think that some of its details are incredibly emphasized, which pronouncement undermines its credibility as a source of historically accurate information. However, the Bible says that Joshua captured Jericho! Something there must have happened! What exactly? We do not know; perhaps the Hebrews, witnessing the burned and toppled walls of the city, slightly inflated the account of their victorious campaign over Jericho by incorporating the strong, destroyed walls into

---

[16] Ibid., 208. She has a good point at the end of this page: "In the absence of a fixed calendar (and there is no evidence that the Israelites made use of the Egyptian calendar), a man would remember that an event took place in the lifetime of his father, or even his grandfather, but it is very unlikely that he would be sure that it took place in that of his great-grandfather or alternatively of his great-great-grandfather." To be sure, this is where history proper becomes folklore.

[17] Ibid., 209.

[18] Ibid., 212.

the story of their success. Or maybe, simply, the historically accurate memory of that event diminished over time, and so allowed for certain embellishments to the story, indeed even along theological-political lines.[19]

So, to recapitulate, the biblical account of Joshua at Jericho is quite likely more folkloric history[20] than strictly historiographical history. Loose, well-rounded, disparate, and dramatic details combine to elicit the impression of folklore in the biblical accounts of the Exodus and of Joshua's defeating of Jericho. Not only do I find this approach realistic; I also find it quite helpful in confronting the claim of contradiction, with regard to Jericho in particular, between the Bible and archaeology. These two, in light of the above considerations, should not be thought to contradict, since the two were never more capable of coinciding than an apple does to an orange—both of which are fruit, but which are, on many levels, incomparable because they are so different individually.

Secondly, in order not to pit the Bible and history/archaeology against each other, we should view the books of Exodus and Joshua through the important optic of *genre*:

> Since God speaks in Sacred Scripture through men in human fashion, the interpreter of Sacred Scripture, in order to see clearly what God wanted to communicate to us, should carefully investigate what meaning the sacred writers really intended, and what God wanted to manifest by means of their words. . . . To search out the intention of the sacred writers, attention should be given, among other things, to "literary forms." For truth is set forth and expressed differently in texts which are variously historical, prophetic, poetic, or of other forms of discourse. The interpreter must investigate what meaning the sacred writer intended to express and actually expressed in particular circumstances by using contemporary literary forms in accordance with the situation of his own time

---

[19] See the next part of this argument, following the paragraph, further on, which begins with "Secondly."

[20] Which, again, does not mean *made up*, *artificial*, or *fake*. To claim that folklore has no connection to actual history is to create a false dichotomy.

and culture. For the correct understanding of what the
sacred author wanted to assert, due attention must be
paid to the customary and characteristic styles of feel-
ing, speaking and narrating which prevailed at the time
of the sacred writer, and to the patterns men normally
employed at that period in their everyday dealings with
one another.[21]

In light of these principles in *Dei Verbum* §12, we must ask:
was the writer of the Book of Joshua intending, by this story in
particular, to compose a piece of historiography? Perhaps not. In
fact, our Jewish brethren do not even refer to Joshua, or other
books near it in our canons, as a "historical book," but rather as
a "former prophet," coming, as it does, before the major prophets of Isaiah, Jeremiah, and so on. Most scholars, too, think that
Joshua was written primarily so as to convey a theological schema in which Israel and its leaders are judged by their fidelity to
the Deuteronomic covenant; in fact, scholars speak of this book
comprising one of the principal works of the Deuteronomistic
historian or redactor, who would have sprinkled Joshua, Judges,
1–2 Samuel, and 1–2 Kings with certain theological refrains and
motifs that hearken back to the theological messages of Deuteronomy.

With those opinions I am in a *qualified* agreement.[22] I think
it wise to look at the Book of Joshua not so much as a work of
modern history, but rather, thanks to a consideration of literary
forms, to see its primary intention in theological terms. Or, in the
least, perhaps we could say that the author of Joshua was less interested than we are in historiography and more interested than
we are in conveying and advancing an ethic of singular fidelity

---

[21] Second Vatican Council, Dogmatic Constitution on Divine Revelation, *Dei Verbum* (1965), §12, accessed June 4, 2017, http://www.
vatican.va/archive/hist_councils/ii_vatican_council/documents/vat-
ii_const_19651118_dei-verbum_en.html.

[22] I stop short of asserting, as many scholars do not, that the entire
conquest of Canaan—so, the Book of Joshua—and even a large part
of the Book of Deuteronomy, itself, were simply, more or less, expressions of the cult-centralizing polemic of the reformer-King Josiah,
composed and/or compiled after the Babylonian Exile ended in 538
BC. Such claims are hardly proven, and hardly provable, insofar as
they constitute deductive assertions made by an inductive methodol-
ogy and are therefore made improperly.

to Almighty God. Such a perspective helps us to avoid pitting so fiercely, as some do, the Battle of Jericho against archaeology and history.[23]

Issue 2

The Battle of Jericho also raises the issue of how to interpret the violent parts of the Old Testament, which sections cause problems for many of the faithful who read them. At the end of the victory over Jericho, we read about the Hebrews: "They observed the ban by putting to the sword all living creatures in the city: men and women, young and old, as well as oxen, sheep and donkeys" (Josh 6:21). Such actions seem quite ruthless; why did innocent citizens, especially children, need to be killed underneath this seemingly divinely instituted law of extermination known as the "ban?"[24] We can approach an answer to this question—and, by extension, to the larger problem of the other violent parts of the Old Testament—through a few contextualizations.

Firstly, considering the theological nature of this and many other Old Testament writings, we can understand the message that this story, especially when read in light of the rest of the Conquest, would convey to its Hebrew readers—that is, the importance of being, like Joshua, "strong and steadfast, careful to observe the entire law which Moses [the Lord's] servant enjoined on [Joshua]." "Do not," the Lord said to Joshua at the outset of his mission, "swerve from it either to the right or to the left, that you may succeed wherever you go. Do not let this book of the law depart from your lips. Recite it by day and by night, that you may carefully observe all that is written in it; then you will attain your goal, then you will succeed" (Josh 1:7–8). The entire conquest was preceded by an order toward fidelity—and, hence, was meant to be taken in reference—to the commands of Deuteronomy, wherein we read, in chapter 7:

---

[23] We should, however, insist that Joshua *is* in some way history—that is, not all of the conquest narrative in Joshua is fabrication, in whole or in part. The archaeological evidence of some of the destroyed cities that the Book of Joshua mentions does, indeed, match the biblical account—namely, at Hazor, where a burn level dating to the Late Bronze Age has been found in the walls of that settlement, which city *alone*, of all the cities he conquered, Joshua burned (11:11).

[24] "Whoever sacrifices to any god, except to the Lord alone, shall be put under the ban" (Ex 22:19).

When the Lord, your God, brings you into the land which you are about to enter to possess, and removes many nations before you . . . when the Lord, your God gives them over to you and you defeat them, you shall put them under the ban. Make no covenant with them, and do not be gracious to them. You shall not intermarry with them, neither giving your daughters to their sons nor taking their daughters for your sons. For they would turn your sons from following me to serving other gods, and then the anger of the Lord would flare up against you and he would quickly destroy you. (Deut 7:1–4).

In other words, Joshua and the Hebrews committed very violent, even terrible acts as an exercise in fidelity to the demands of Deuteronomy, according to which the Hebrews were commanded to stay utterly faithful to God, and to secure this exclusive loyalty by eradicating any possible temptation toward infidelity against Almighty God.

But, does this redirection from Joshua to Deuteronomy, wherein are found the awful laws of *ḥerem* warfare known as the "ban," help to solve the problem of the violent parts of the Old Testament? In fact, it does, as it puts into the context of covenant these laws that God commanded Moses to speak (Deut 1:3).

The Deuteronomic Covenant was given after the Israelites's sinning against the Lord at Peor, where they worshipped Baal (Num 25), much like the Exodus Covenant (Ex 34:10–26) was made after Israel sinned against God by crafting and adoring the Golden Calf (Ex 32). In other words, these two "laws" were given, like Paul says, "on account of transgressions" (Gal 3:19)—that is, as a divine concession to sinful humanity's fallen state. "In the beginning," though—to appropriate Jesus's words on divorce, which Moses allowed "for the hardness of hearts"—"it was not so" (Mt 19:8). Without man's sin, God would have never given these laws, some of which he himself admits were "not good laws" (Ezek 20:25–26) but were given out of necessity to the people so as to safeguard even a modicum of fidelity to him, on their part. That, I think, is why there exist such violent texts in our history of revelation—not because God wanted them, for he himself revealed his eternal desire for mankind as abundant life ("I came that they might have life, and have it abundantly" [Jn 10:10]), but because God "begrudgingly" knew that we needed them.

Thus we can see, through theological lenses, that the horribly violent parts in the Old Testament stem back not to an eternal command or the particular intention of God our Father, as if it were a reflection of the supposedly violent nature, but rather as a divine *concession* to mankind, who would, by these laws, at least preserve a shred of fidelity toward him and his eternal covenant with mankind.[25]

Of course, another conciliatory reading of such "problematic" texts is the allegorical reading adopted by St. Augustine. Recalling how he at first balked at such violent texts, the doctor of the Church writes in his *Confessions*: "I delighted to hear Ambrose often asserting in his sermons to the people, as a principle on which he must insist emphatically, *The letter is death-dealing, but the spirit gives life.* This he would tell them as he drew aside the veil of mystery and opened to them the spiritual meaning of passages which, taken literally, would seem to mislead."[26] Such a spiritual expounding of the *herem* texts could, for example, emphasize the need to remove evil from the "land" of one's heart, or could prompt one to "declare war" on sin within his heart. In this way, one could allegorically read texts that appear problematic on a literal level of interpretation well.

Of course, this kind of spiritualized reading would not satisfy a reader keenly intent on the importance of a literal reading of the biblical text. However, Augustine points out, in his *On Christian Doctrine*, an important hermeneutical key for proper biblical interpretation:

> Whatever there is in the word of God that cannot, when taken literally, be referred either to purity of life or soundness of doctrine, you may set down as figurative. Purity of life has reference to the love of God and one's neighbor, soundness of doctrine to the knowledge of God and one's neighbor.[27]

---

[25] For a full treatment, see John S. Bergsma and Scott W. Hahn, "What Laws were 'Not Good'? A Canonical Approach to the Theological Problem of Ezekiel 20:25–26, " *Journal of Biblical Literature* 123, no. 2 (2004): 201–18.

[26] Augustine of Hippo, *The Confessions*, trans. Maria Boulding (New York: Vintage, 1997), 140.

[27] Augustine of Hippo, *De Doctrina Christiana* 3.10.14, trans. Edmund Hill (New York: New City Press, 1996).

Those things, again, whether only sayings or whether actual deeds, which appear to the inexperienced to be sinful, and which are ascribed to God, or to men whose holiness is put before us as an example, are wholly figurative, and the hidden kernel of meaning they contain is to be picked out as food for the nourishment of charity.[28]

Correct biblical interpretation, Augustine says, should always lead to charity—that is, to love of God and love of neighbor. Hence, if a literal reading of something found in Scripture does not lead one to these ends, then the literal reading, per Augustine, should be abandoned in preference for a spiritual reading that elicits charity within the soul, and the works, of the reader. In light of these considerations of the "Doctor of Grace," we could then seek to interpret the *herem* passages of the Old Testament not in a literal way—that is, God commanding his people to do horrible things because he wants them to do such things or because he is so horrible himself—but rather in a spiritual way, such as this: bash your sins against the rock of Christ in the Sacrament of Penance, and watch your sins dissipate like water striking coastal rock.

POINTS FOR REFLECTION

• The words of Bartimaeus ("Jesus, son of David, have pity on me!" [Mk 10:48]) constitute one of the options for a penitent's Act of Contrition during the Rite of Penance. It is in fact the shortest of those listed in the ritual. Have you ever used it? If not, I recommend you try it, perhaps even here during your pilgrimage, so that the pilgrimage can already begin to shape and realize your relationship with the Lord, before whom you, in the Sacrament of Confession, cry out like Bartimaeus for mercy. Moreover, if you are trying to shrug off some habitual sin or temptation, you would do well to entrust yourself to the fortifying power of God's mercy with Bartimaeus's words. If we read the Greek of Mark carefully, we should translate it as "Master, that I may see again" (*ana-blepsō*), as if to say: "Lord, I have struggled with this sin before, and

---

[28] Ibid., 3.12.18.

when I last confessed it, I saw the light of your love which remembers not our sins, and I had confidence in 'the help of your grace' to help me to so 'sin no more' . . . but, here now, I have fallen again. O Lord, may I see again—that I may see your forgiving and patient eyes, and feel again your confidence in my good will and the protective power of your grace. Lord, that I may see again."

• Bartimaeus's action of following Jesus on the way after his being forgiven and healed (Mk 10:52) is for all of us a fitting image of the necessity of professing, in the Sacrament of Confession, a firm resolve to make amends for our sins. Each of the longer acts of contrition conveys this resolution in some way: "I firmly resolve, with the help of your grace, to sin no more, and to avoid the near occasions of sin"; "I firmly intend, with your help, to do penance and to amend my life as I should"; and so on. This firm resolution should not be a generic or general intention to be better; it should be practical and measurable, just as one's penance assigned by the priest should be.

Furthermore, the execution of this firm resolve to make amends should also take a cue from the witness of Zacchaeus who, having come down quickly from the tree and having received the Lord with joy, promised Jesus that he would make reparation for the wicked things he had done: "Behold, half of my possessions, Lord, I shall give to the poor, and if I have extorted anything from anyone, I shall repay it four times over" (Lk 19:8). Just as Jesus's forgiving love is adequate for, and pertains to, the specific sins that each penitent commits, so too should that penitent seek to correspond his or her contrition towards a concrete, commensurate reparation for the sins that he or she commits.

Especially for Seminarians

• As a priest, you will need to listen carefully for the penitent's pledge to attempt to live a sin-free life. In fact, if he or she is unwilling even to attempt to avoid committing again in the future a certain sin (meaning, if the penitent refuses to change his or her life), you will need to work, sometimes hard (of course aware that the Lord is "slow to anger and merciful" [Ex 34:6]), to elicit even the faintest amount or expression of amendment, without which the integrity of the penitent's contrition[29] can legitimately be doubted, and so absolution justly withheld. Of course, this circumstance quite rarely occurs. However, a priest-to-be should be aware of the necessity of a penitent's making a firm resolution to sin no more, as such is prime evidence of the penitent's contrition for sins committed.

For this reason, it is good for a priest to offer a penance corresponding to the sins that he has just heard, so that, by the penance, the penitent might already begin re-forming that part of his or her life in which he or she has fallen short of the perfect love toward which we are all called (Mt 5:48). If one struggles with taking the Lord's name in vain, for example, offer as a penance a repetition of Jesus's name with great tenderness, love, and devotion, or to say the Hail Mary and, when the penitent comes to the end of the first half of the prayer, have him or her bow the head at the name of Jesus. If one confesses pride and arrogance, suggest that he or she pray slowly and deliberately the Litany of Humility. If one shares difficulties with the Sixth Commandment, commend to him or her some kind of corporeal self-denial,[30] so as to learn how to say no, in small things, to what the body craves, in the hope that "the person who is trustworthy in very small matters [will be] also trustworthy in great ones" (Lk 16:10).

---

[29] Which is part of the sacrament's matter—a *sine qua non* for the sacrament's validity.

[30] Abstain from meat, sweets, condiments, alcohol, listening to music in the car, etc.

QUMRAN

*This is the heritage of the tribe of Judahites by their clans
. . . in the wilderness: Beth-arabah, Middin, Secacah,
Nibshan, the City of Salt, and Engedi; six cities and their
villages.*

(Joshua 15:20, 61–62).

The village of Qumran, once known as the City of Salt because it
was near to the Dead Sea, is taken by many to be the community
center of the Essenes who produced the famous Dead Sea Scrolls.
The Essenes of Qumran lived in natural caves in the adjoining
cliffs, in tents, and in underground chambers cut in the soft rock,
gathering here for their sect's religious activity.[1]

From the plethora of documents that have been discovered
here,[2] and principally from the witness of Josephus,[3] we can
describe the Essenes in these ways. Theirs was a pious and as-
cetical community, bound to a rule of life. The members of the
Essenes had a more severe discipline, as well as a greater mutual
affection,[4] than the communities of the Pharisees and Sadducees,

---

[1] Murphy-O'Connor, *The Holy Land*, 436.

[2] The history of which is recounted in the informational section of the
   Qumran office, and so will be skipped here.

[3] Josephus dedicates a large space in his writings to describing the Es-
   senes, as in *Wars of the Jews* 2.119–60, in *The Works of Josephus:
   Complete and Unabridged*, trans. William Whitson (Peabody, MA:
   Hendrickson, 1987), 605–7.

[4] Essenes observed a more strict application of the Sabbath rest than

which were the two other principle sects of Judaism at the time. They rejected pleasures as evil and esteemed continence as a virtue.[5] The Essenes despised riches, holding property in common among the brethren.[6] They had extraordinary piety, praying often,[7] and practiced thorough and frequent ritual cleansing in baths known as *miqvots* for the forgiveness of sins. Dressed in white robes, they would take these ritual baths before sitting at table in their refectory, where the priest would bless the food before they ate it.[8] The silence of their community environment always appeared to foreigners "like some tremendous mystery," while, for them, it was a "perpetual exercise in sobriety."[9]

The Essene communities could certainly seem like a kind of early form of monasticism! However, we should note, with Josephus, that "there is another order of the Essenes, who agree with the rest as to their way of living, and customs, and laws, but differ from them in the point of marriage, as thinking that by not marrying they cut off the principal part of the human life, which is the process of succession."[10] The Qumran community, in other words, was not the only community of the Essenes; some communities were spread covertly among the common people in various cities.[11] Each community of Essenes seemed to have had its own spin on a rule of life. As noted earlier, the Qumran community had the men live celibately, though they could adopt children,[12] but other communities were allowed to marry and have a family. For this reason, it is better to speak about the *Qumran* Essenes, rather than simply the Essenes.

---

any other sect (*Wars* 2.147–50) and a harsh process of excommunication for grave sinners, who were thrown out to eat only grass and, so, die of famine, save perhaps a last-gasp reconciliation and reintegration into the community out of "mercy" (*Wars* 2.143–144 Whitson, *Works*, 606; here and earlier).

[5] *Wars* 2.119–20 (Whitson, *Works*, 605).

[6] *Wars* 2.122 (Whitson, *Works*, 605).

[7] Essenes were forbidden from saying a profane word before sunrise, allowing only the prayers of their forefathers (*Wars* 2.128 [Whitson, *Works*, 605]).

[8] *Wars* 2.128–29 (Whitson, *Works*, 605).

[9] *Wars* 2.133 (Whitson, *Works*, 605).

[10] *Wars* 2.160 (Whitson, *Works*, 607).

[11] "They have no certain city but many of them dwell in every city" (*Wars* 2.124 [Whitson, *Works*, 605]).

[12] *Wars* 2.120–21 (Whitson, *Works*, 605).

The Qumran Essenes likely chose this location for their community because it helped them to await, in the best way possible, the coming of the Messiah. From these ruins, you can look over to nearby Jericho, where Elijah was taken up to heaven in a fiery chariot and whirlwind (2 Kings 2:4.11), for which reason he was thought to be coming again at the end of time (Mal 4:5–6). You can also look across the Dead Sea and see Mount Nebo, where Moses died (Deut 34:1–5), and ponder the Lord's promise that he would raise up another prophet like Moses (Deut 18:18). Such figures, tied to these locations, inspired the apocalyptic attitude of the desert-dwelling Essenes of Qumran.

The members of this sect gathered at what is now the collection of ruins for all their religious and economic activities. This site, to be sure, was not first occupied by the Essenes. In the eighth century BC, the Israelites established a small fort here, likely as a farming settlement.[13] This fort, though, was already long-abandoned when the early Essene leader known as the "Teacher of Righteousness," along with some fifty Essenes, settled here in 150 BC. A large influx of new members arrived at the end of the reign of John Hyrcanus (134–103 BC), requiring the community to rebuild their settlement. The Essenes were then forced to leave the site during the military conflicts fought and

The ruins of the Essene settlement at Qumran.

---

[13] Murphy-O'Connor, *The Holy Land*, 436.

won by Herod the Great (40–37 BC), and an earthquake damaged the buildings further in 31 BC. The Essenes returned here after some time, remaining until Rome expelled them in AD 68, when the expanding empire set up here a garrison to moderate Dead Sea trade.[14]

However, the details of this standard theory regarding the settlements are not universally accepted. It is uncertain why the Essenes came here. Some suggest that they fled Jerusalem after a falling-out with the Temple leaders, whom the Essenes believed corrupted the priestly line and the Temple calendar by changing them. Also, it is not certain whether or not these Essenes brought scrolls along with them to their desert monastery; identical inkpots in the caves and settlement suggest that they arrived empty-handed, then composed all of their writings on site.

The Essenes have some very interesting parallels with, and possibly also points of influence on, the early Christian religion:[15]

1. The Essenes shared property in common—as did the early Church, see Acts 2:44—though it was not to the exclusion of private property, since their rule of life prescribes that, if you offend a brother, you should make up for your offense by giving to him of your own supplies and livelihood.[16]

2. Many think that John the Baptist was an Essene and then broke off from them to begin his own ministry. He lived a solitary life in the desert, used water for purification (of sins[17]), lived intensely awaiting the coming of the kingdom, preached such things as: "Whoever has two tunics should share with the person who has none. And whoever has food should do likewise" (Lk 3:11). John also warned of the wrath to come (Lk 3:17). Moreover, Josephus says that John's baptism was a sign, not an effecting of, forgiveness of sins and conversion—much like

---

[14] Ibid., 438.

[15] For further reading, see James C. Vanderkam and Peter Flint, *The Meaning of the Dead Sea Scrolls: Their Significance for Understanding the Bible, Judaism, Jesus, and Christianity* (San Francisco: HarperCollins, 2002).

[16] Josephus, *Wars* 2.127 (Whitson, *Works*, 605).

[17] Josephus, *The Antiquities of the Jews* 18.117 (Whitson, *Works*, 484).

the Essenes's insistence that baptism with water means nothing without conversion.[18]

Also, Josephus describes, separately, the Baptist and the Essenes with the same words: "They practiced piety toward God and charity towards neighbor."[19] All of these Josephan resonances could very well be more than merely coincidental, insofar as they suggest an identification of the early Baptist and the Essenes. The Qumran community was a fixed, stationary community, and John likely broke off from the community when he felt called to take his preaching on the road. Also, the Essenes interacted only with the "sons of the light" and not with the "sons of darkness,"[20] but John reached out to the crowd, which included tax collectors, sinners, and others forbidden to the Essenes.

A unique icon of St. John the Baptist, from a hermitage in the wilderness beyond Ein Kerem. The Baptist is holding a scroll containing a Hebrew version of his famous words in John 1:29 and 34: "Behold, the Lamb of God, who takes away the sins of the world" (or, literally from this Hebrew, "…who takes away sins forever."). "Now I have seen and testified that he is the Son of God." See Issue 1 of the chapter Ein Kerem.

3. Early Christian baptismal baths had two separate sets of stairs, one on each end of the pool. The movement of

[18] Ibid.

[19] Ibid. (the Baptist). See also *Wars* 2.139 (Essenes) (Whitson, *Works*, 606).

[20] Terminology that recurs throughout almost the entirety of the collection of Dead Sea Scrolls.

descending into the water impure, bathing and cleansing, and then ascending by a different set of stairs from the water purified, might have its roots in the *miqveh* structure of the Essenes, whose purification baths had two different access points separated by a wall.[21] The Essene baptism was completed when the newly purified put on a white robe after leaving the pool—much like the early Christians later did—before their common meal.[22]

4. Though this will be mentioned later as part of a larger picture and issue, the Essene Gate in Jerusalem was discovered by Pixner to be immediately next to the Upper Room. This potentially suggests an Essene presence there on Mount Zion that might have secured immediate exchange and possible overlap of ideas and praxis between the first Christians and Jerusalem Essenes, who, by physical proximity, would have been among the first of peoples to whom the Gospel was preached. Some have thought that the Essenes's calendar might have influenced the timing of Jesus's celebrating the Last Supper[23] (however, this Gospel–Essene approximation has been challenged, especially with regards to the issue of the dating of the Last Supper[24]).

Despite all this, we should note that, though some Essenes surely converted to the faith and became Christian, the early Christians were not Essenes. How could the early Christians be Essenes when their master, Jesus, often took stances with regard to ritual purity[25] that could not contrast more strongly with

---

[21] Bargil Pixner, *Paths of the Messiah: Sites of the Early Church from Galilee to Jerusalem—Jesus and Jewish Christianity in Light of Archaeological Discoveries*, ed. Rainer Riesner, trans. Keith Myrick and Sam and Miriam Randall (San Francisco: Ignatius, 2010), 211.

[22] Josephus, *Wars* 2.129 (Whitson, *Works*, 605).

[23] That is, according not to the Temple calendar, but rather according to the calendar of the surrounding Essenes, which redirection ostensibly harmonizes an otherwise apparent, uncomfortable difference between Gospel accounts on the timing of the Last Supper (Murphy-O'Connor, *The Holy Land*, 118–19; Pixner, *Paths of the Messiah*, 198–215).

[24] See *Issues Raised* in the Holy Thursday chapter, further on.

[25] See Matthew 15:1–20, in which Jesus says that it is not what goes into, but rather what comes out of, one's mouth that defiles him.

those of the meticulous, even scrupulous, Essenes? It's interesting to compare these two communities, but we should not take the parallels between the Essenes and early Christians too far.[26]

Issues Raised

Qumran is a good place to discuss biblical manuscripts and textual traditions. Firstly, if we had to describe the importance of the Dead Sea Scrolls, we could provide the following:

- They constitute the oldest—by about 1,000 years!—manuscripts of the Hebrew Old Testament in our possession.

- They prove that the content of the Hebrew Scriptures was faithfully transmitted throughout the centuries.

- They show that, at the time, there existed as yet no standard canon of Old Testament texts, much less the order of the books.

- They reveal much about the culture, and its messianic expectations, immediately preceding the Incarnation.

- They reflect the linguistic development, and in some cases the simplification and/or degradation, of the Hebrew language in terms of orthography and syntax.

- They demonstrate that the quest for the "original version" of Old Testament texts is extremely complicated, insofar as the Qumran texts differ so greatly at times from the versions of the texts found in the Masoretic (Hebrew) and Septuagint (Greek) traditions that the Qumran texts comprise their own "textual tradition."[27]

---

[26] Pixner, I believe, takes Essene enthusiasm a little too far, suggesting very tenuous points of overlap and influence, such as: the Baptism of Jesus site being determinable based on an elusive treasure hoard from the Essene Copper Scroll; the Holy Family's upbringing, especially the supposed Essene reference in/underneath Joseph's description as a "just" man (Mt 1:19), which term was very dear to the Essenes; etc.

[27] Which could be defined as a version of a text unique in its form, though similar in its content to that which is found in other traditions.

- They reveal that the Essenes were a community that tend-ed to read the Scriptures in such a way as to actualize the texts, making them refer to *them* in their life and life-style—a procedure that would later be imitated among Christian communities.

POINTS FOR REFLECTION

- The liturgical and legalistic scruples of the Essenes not-withstanding, there is something to be said for the care that they took to be *separate* from the presence and activ-ity of sin in the world, to live *differently* than did those "sons of darkness" who forsook God's law. In fact, such care accords with the Old Testament understanding of holiness, as is seen in God's commands to the Israelites: "You shall be holy to me; for I the Lord am holy, and have separated you from the peoples, that you should be mine" (Lev 20:26). We Catholics hear this very sentiment echoed in the First Preface of Ordinary Time, in which the priest, explaining why it is right and just to give God praise, proclaims: "For through his Pascal Mystery, he accomplished the marvelous deed, by which he has freed us from the yoke of sin and death, summoning us to the glory of being now called a chosen race, a royal priest-hood, a holy nation, a people for your own possession, to proclaim everywhere your mighty works, for you have called us out of darkness into your own wonderful light."

- What is your understanding of holiness? How would you describe it? How would you practice it, and seek to incul-cate it? Do you strive to separate yourself from the sinful desires and activity that we often call "the world"?

Especially for Seminarians

- If all of God's people are called to holiness, how much more so are his priests called to be holy! As a priest, you will be often approached by the faithful and asked for help in growing in holiness. If you are not actively striv-ing to be a student and agent of holiness, then you will not be able to assist those who turn to you looking for advice in this area. Do you pray for holiness? Do you consciously attempt to do, think, and love holy things and to distance yourself from anything that is evil? Just as God separated light from darkness, etc., and an iconostasis or rail sets apart the sanctuary of a church, separate yourself from the ways of the world, and be holy, as God your father is holy (Lev 19:3, 11:44–45).

JORDAN RIVER BAPTISM SITE

It happened in those days that Jesus came from Nazareth of Galilee and was baptized in the Jordan by John. On coming up out of the water, he saw the heavens being torn open and the Spirit, like a dove, descending upon him. And a voice came from the heavens: "You are my beloved Son; with you I am well pleased."

(Mark 1:9–11)

Jesus's Baptism in the Jordan is found throughout the Gospels (Mk 1:9–11; Mt 3:11–17; Lk 3:21–22), but John's Gospel does not explicitly contain it. Moreover, the Synoptic Gospels seem to place our Lord's Baptism by John here in the south of Israel, but John seems to locate the Baptist's ministry in the north, in the region of Gaulanitis.[1] I will treat this potential discrepancy further on.

In this area, John the Baptist is portrayed as a very dynamic speaker who was able to tailor his message of repentance to the specific life circumstances of his addressees (Lk 3:10–14). Three groups of people interrupted John, asking him what they

---

[1] The southern region of ancient Israel was that of Judah. Galilee was a northern region, and Gaulanitis was an area of Galilee that is now known as the Golan Heights.

SCRIPTURE ON SITE:
Mark 1:9-11

should do to repent. To the ordinary person of the crowd, he simply answered: "Whoever has two tunics (and food) should share with the person who has none" (Lk 3:11). From the tax collectors, John demanded that they stop collecting more than what is owed (Lk 3:13). Then, to the soldiers from the Temple area, John commands that they not extort from, falsely accuse, or intimidate anyone (Luke 3:14). All in all, John asks two things of those who seek repentance: charity and fairness.[2] These, according to the preaching of the Baptist, are what straighten out and prepare our heart to meet our God.

Issues Raised

Locating the exact place where Jesus was baptized by John has proven to be a difficult task over the years. The traditional site is here in the south not far from Jericho, per the Synoptic Gospels.[3] Moreover, the Pilgrim of Bordeaux (AD 333) identified, as *the* place, this spot on the eastern bank of the Jordan, north of Jericho and near the hill from which it was believed that Elijah was taken up into heaven.[4] Many Protestants, however, claim a site in the north, near the city of Tiberias and just below the Sea of Galilee where the Jordan begins its southern course. Lastly, some would sustain that the baptism happened on the eastern side of the Sea of Galilee: Pixner has made a very suggestive pitch for the region called *Batanea*, with which he identifies the biblical *Bethany*, "beyond the Jordan" (Jn 1:28).[5]

So, which one is it? A great question! And one that we should answer, as some take this baptismal disparity as yet another instance in which the Bible contradicts itself. I, of course, quite disagree; it is fairly clear to me that, here, we are decisively *not* dealing with evangelical contradiction. I think that we can and should read the Synoptics and John together as witnessing to the same southern location for Jesus's Baptism.

2   Kilgallen, *New Testament Guide*, 111.
3   Matthew 3:1 says that John the Baptist was baptizing "in the desert of Judea," in which this southern baptism site is found.
4   Pixner, *Paths of the Messiah*, 177.
5   See ibid., 177–91.

Let us begin with Pixner's argument for a northern location, since his is the best I have read. Were it correct, his reasoning could cause problems for reconciling some indications of John with indications in the Synoptic accounts of the Lord's Baptism, but even aside from this, at the end of the day, I deem Pixner's theory inconclusive. Why? Well, while temporal and spatial indications from the first two chapters of John seem to locate Jesus's Baptism in the north,[6] we should firstly point out that these indications are not very clear; unlike the Synoptics, John does not give evident context clues as to where he places this "Bethany beyond the Jordan" (1:28). Secondly, we should insist that we can, though, find some evidence in John's Gospel itself for a southern location. We see this in the early progression of his Gospel. At one point, we read that Jesus was in Judea baptizing (3:22), as was John the Baptist (3:23). Then we read that Jesus left Judea and returned to Galilee and, importantly, that "he had to pass through Samaria" (4:2–4) to get there. This means that he was departing from the south (Judea) and going to the north

One of several Jordan River candidates for a northern location of the Baptism of Jesus, just below the Sea of Galilee. Tradition, though, has located the Baptism of Jesus further south in a muddy section of the Jordan River near Jerusalem.

---

6 Ibid., 181–84.

(Galilee), since Samaria is between Judea and Galilee, and this cannot mean that he was departing from the east side of the Sea of Galilee, for it would not be necessary to pass through Samaria were he simply on the other side of the sea. Hence, even as John's Gospel relates, Jesus must have been baptizing in the south, in Judea—which is precisely what the Synoptics claim, as we have seen above.

In summary, then, this convergence of Synoptic and Johannine witnesses is strong evidence in favor of a southern location for Jesus's Baptism by John the Baptist.

POINTS FOR REFLECTION

- Do you know the date of your baptism? We commit to memory various dates on the calendar that recall or celebrate events (and people) that are important to us, but yet sometimes we fail to esteem the day of our baptism as much as we ought to. It was at that moment that the supernatural life of faith began to live in our souls! It was in the waters of Baptism that the life of the Trinity came to dwell within us, cleansing us from the stain of original sin, making our bodies temples of the Holy Spirit, and opening up for us the way of salvation, for which Baptism is necessary (CCC 1257). Spiritually speaking, Baptism is a big deal! Or at least it should be seen as such. How much importance do you place on the day in which you were baptized? Should you not know and hold dear this special date?

Especially for Seminarians

- The Sacrament of Baptism should be one that priests hold dearly in their hearts, because in this liturgical action our spiritual paternity shines through. Early Church Fathers used to refer to the baptismal font as the womb of Holy Mother Church, where she gives birth to her new children. Indeed, since it is by the Trinitarian formula and the triple infusion on the part of the priest that the spiritual life of faith is born in a soul, we can see here the priest exercising his spiritual fatherhood, in which he sacramentally begets the life of faith in the newly baptized. Have you already begun to think about the Sacrament of Baptism from the perspective of the priest? Let your prayer over your future role in the sacrament be a moment for you to appreciate ever more deeply how Baptism is yet another instance justifying priests' title of "Father."

JERUSALEM

The ascent from the Mount of Olives across the Kidron Valley to the walls of the Old City of Jerusalem.

JERUSALEM

*Behold, I cast out demons and I perform healings today
and tomorrow, and on the third day I accomplish my purpose. Yet I must continue on my way today, tomorrow, and
the following day, for it is impossible that a prophet should
die outside of Jerusalem.*

(Luke 13:32–33)

Jerusalem is one of the oldest continually inhabited cities in the
world. Featuring the central part of world's three great mono-
theisms, the city has for millennia captured the fascination and
religiosity of countless people. At the outset of our journey to
and through Jerusalem, it would be good to examine just what
this city means and has meant to our "elder"—to use the word
of St. John Paul II—brothers and sisters, those of Jewish faith.
As the Pope rightly pointed out, Judaism "is not 'extrinsic' to the
Church," but rather, "in a certain way is 'intrinsic' to our own
religion."[1] Such a consideration will help us take more owner-
ship of this city so important to our own history, to *our* story, as
a people of God.

In his book *Quale rapporto tra i due Testamenti?* ("What

---

[1]   Pope John Paul II, "The Roots of Anti-Judaism in the Christian Envi-
      ronment," Discourse at the Synagogue of Rome, April 13, 1986, ac-
      cessed June 4, 2017, http://www.vatican.va/jubilee_2000/magazine/
      documents/ju_mag_01111997_p-42x_en.html.

kind of relationship is there between the two Testaments?"),[2] Massimo Grilli paints a picture of Jerusalem that I believe can help us in this regard. An astute writer, he is also my thesis director! I relay below a little over one page of his work:

> In the twenty-four books of the Hebrew Bible, *Yerushalayim* recurs about 750 times. The quantity of such references testifies to the qualitative strength of this city as a symbol. . . .
>
> The name is due probably to the fact that, originally, the city was constructed as a foundation for the God *shalem*, and hence its name meant "possession of *shalem*,"[3] which perhaps allows us to identify Jerusalem with the city of *shalem* mentioned in Genesis 14:18, the city of which Melchizedek was king. Later, a popular etymology—which hence has little philological or historical basis—identified the name of the god *shalem* with the Hebrew word *shalom*, which prepared the way for the interpretation of Jerusalem as *city of peace*, which is found many times over in the Bible: "Wish for peace on Jerusalem" (Ps 122:7, etc.).
>
> The Septuagint translates the name with *Ierousalem*, but from the 2nd century BC, we find also the form *Hierosolyma*, which alludes to the sacred character of the city,[4] which derives from the Temple. The Old Testament, in fact, speaks of Jerusalem as *'ir haqqodesh*, which means "the Holy City" (Is 48:2; 52:1; Neh 11:1).
>
> In terms of the meaning of Jerusalem within the Bible and in history, we must say that the city is indissolubly bound to the presence of God in his temple, and to the Davidic promise. Jerusalem is the compendium, the epitome, of the hopes of Israel: it represents the Law, the Temple, and the fulfillment of the promise of the Land, and constitutes a city intimately united to the history of

---

[2]   Massimo Grilli, *Quale rapporto tra i due Testamenti? Riflessione critica sui modelli ermeneutici classici concernenti l'unità delle Scritture* (Bologna: EDB, 2007)."

[3]   The Hebrew word *yarash*, from which come the first three consonants of *Jerusalem*, means "to possess" or "to inherit." So, *yarash* + *salem* gives us "possession of shalem."

[4]   The Greek word *hieros* means "holy."

Israel, as Psalm 132 witnesses: "The Lord swore an oath
to David in truth, he will never turn back from it: 'Your
own offspring I will set upon your throne.' Yes, the Lord
has chosen Zion, desired it for a dwelling: 'This is my
resting place forever; here I will dwell, for I desire it'"
(vv. 11.13–14). The prophets then gave to Jerusalem a
universal and cosmic dimension, with the pilgrimage of
peoples to Zion (Is 2:2–4; 60; Zech 8:22). In the course
of history, the promise of God about Jerusalem was put
into crisis: the city has endured more than thirty sieges
and terrible massacres, including that of Hebrews and
Muslims on the part of the Crusades. On the other hand,
though, Hebraism has looked upon the city of Jerusalem
as a symbol of the perennial promise of God, and hence
the dream of restoration (see Jeremiah 32). Linked to this
aspect is another [one]; . . . Hebraism has looked at times
to the future, to a restoration of the city beyond its purely terrestrial dimension (Is 2:2; Mic 4:1; Ezra 17:22). In
some Hebraic groups, one encounters in this way also
the hope of a Jerusalem preserved in heaven, which will
be rendered visible only at the end of times. The Fourth
Book of Ezra speaks of an apparition of the city which
now is invisible (4 Esdras 7:26; 13:36), and the Testament
of the Twelve Patriarchs affirms that "the saints will rest
in Eden and the just will rejoice in the new Jerusalem"
(Test. Dan 5:12). Also at Qumran, the Temple Scroll contains a schema of the eschatological sanctuary, which will
be situated in the earthly Jerusalem. The heavenly Jerusalem, in opposition to the actual one, appears also in many
rabbinic writings.

Hence, we can understand that the categories "Jerusalem above" and "Jerusalem below" were not created by Christianity; in reality, these have a rich Jewish
background. Judeo-Christianity took up this category of
thought and developed it, above all else in Hebrews and
Revelation, applying it to the full realization of the kingdom of God instituted by Christ with the Resurrection.[5]

[5]   Grilli, *Quale rapporto tra i due Testamenti?* 121–22.

Those things that Jerusalem, then, represents within a Judeo-Christian imagination are: holiness; peace; prayer; divine promise, presence, and defense; and future glory. For the Jews, it is a place of tragedy and triumph, and it is so, too, for Christians, who saw our Lord there not only lament over her (Lk 13:34–35), suffer within her walls, and die just outside them (Jn 19:17; Heb 13:12), but also *rise* at Jerusalem victorious over sin and death. That is what this city should mean to us: the wonder of God made man who, by dying, destroyed our death and, by rising, restored our life. Truly, Jerusalem is *our* happy home, too. Made new, it ever shall be so long as we remain faithful: "On the victor I will inscribe the name of my God and the name of the city of my God, the new Jerusalem, which comes down out of heaven from my God, as well as my new name" (Rev 3:12).

I have chosen to balance a site-based approach and a Passion-chronology-based approach to Jerusalem. This combination, I pray, will reduce the amount of potentially confusing page turning should a group visit these locations in an order different from that in which I lay everything out. We will start from the outside of the Old City, examining its walls and gates. Then, we will cover the holy places of and near the Mount of Olives (so, some of Holy Thursday), the sites of Mount Zion (more of Holy Thursday), and finally the locales constitutive of Good Friday and Easter Sunday. An additional section on St. Anne/Bethesda will follow. Bethlehem and Ein Kerem will then be treated separately afterwards, as they are outside of the city but indeed not far away.

WALLS AND GATES

I rejoiced when they said to me,
"Let us go to the house of the Lord."

And now our feet are standing
within your gates, Jerusalem.

Jerusalem, built as a city,
walled round about.

There the tribes go up,
the tribes of the Lord. . . .

For the peace of Jerusalem pray.

Psalms 122:1–4b, 6a (NABRE)

Jerusalem is built on two high hills with two valleys around it and one running through it.[1] The city is located in the Judean hills and hence reaches a high altitude of about 2,400 feet. Such would explain the language of the pilgrimage Psalms of Ascent, such as Psalm 122:4a, which reads: "There the tribes go up." Such would also explain John's note that Jesus, travelling south from lower-el-

---

[1] For a tremendous view of the Old City, go to the roof of the Austrian Hospice (in the Muslim Quarter, near the Fourth Station of the Cross), from which you can see not only how Calvary is on a high point of the city, but also how the entire city really was built on valley-tops, in particular above the Tyropoeon Valley, which cuts across the city. Also, stop and enjoy there an Italian cappuccino!

evation Galilee,[2] went *up* (*anebē*) to Jerusalem as the Passover of the Jews came to hand (Jn 2:13). Moreover, not only do the Judean highlands, upon which Jerusalem sits, have a quite elevated altitude; they also exhibit a very *precipitous* altitude change. In

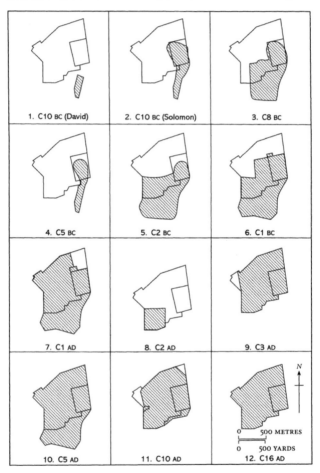

Jerusalem: Historical expansion and contraction (p. 10, fig. 1, in Jerome Murphy-O'Connor, *The Holy Land*; used by permission of Oxford University Press).

---

2   The lake of which sits at about 700 feet below sea level.

the less than twenty miles from Jerusalem east to the Dead Sea, the elevation drops from around 2,600 feet above sea level at the Mount of Olives to 1,400 feet *below* sea level at the surface of the Dead Sea! All of this is to say that if a Hebrew wanted to go to Jerusalem to celebrate the sacred feasts in the Temple, he or she would have ahead of him or her a steep, arduous trek across desert and up rocky hills—fitting adversity, of course, for a pilgrimage!

The "Old City" today comprises an area of 0.35 square miles, or 224 acres. The present-day walls surrounding Jerusalem run 2.7 miles long, and within these walls live around 3,500 people, mostly Muslims, Christians, and Jews. Jerusalem proper, however, was not always of this size, nor were her walls always the walls that are seen to surround the Old City today. An excellent display of this pattern of shifting growing and shrinking is found in the figure above, which traces the size of the city of Jerusalem along various centuries from the time of David (tenth century BC) to the time of the Ottomans (sixteenth century AD).

The first thing that you might note about the city is the massive fortification system that it has. Its walls are strong and impressive, indeed! It makes me think of Psalm 48:13–15: "Go about Zion, walk all around it, note the number of its towers. Consider the ramparts, examine its citadels, that you may tell future generations that this is God, our God for ever and ever. He will lead us until death." The sheer might of the walls serve as a fitting image for the protective strength that Almighty God exercises on behalf of his people.

I now relay selections of Jerome Murphy-O'Connor's excellent, concise treatment of the walls and size of the city:

> The city of David was a small settlement on the eastern hill, close to the only spring and defended on two sides by deep valleys. By bringing the Ark of the Covenant within its walls, David made it the symbol of a religious ideal which transcended the petty jealousies of the twelve tribes of Israel. To underline this dimension, his son Solomon (965–928 BC) built the first temple to enshrine the Ark. He had to extend the city, and the valleys gave him no choice but to move northwards along the ridge.
>
> In subsequent centuries, suffering caused the city first to expand and then to contract. The Assyrian invasion of the north in the latter part of the 8th century BC sent ref-

ugees flooding towards Jerusalem. Failing to find space, many built outside the city to the west. They had to be protected when Sennacherib menaced the city in 701 BC, and a new wall was built to enclose the western hill, quadrupling the size of the city. This was the city devastated by the Babylonians in 586 BC. After its inhabitants returned from exile some 50 years later, they were refused authority to rebuild the walls; it was [finally] accorded to Nehemiah (445–443 BC), but a greatly reduced population forced him to revert to a line which encompassed less than the city of Solomon.

Only after the Maccabean revolt in the first part of the 2nd century BC had restored Jewish independence did the city grow again. . . . It was destined to grow further to the north, but the lines of the eastern and western walls have remained constant ever since.

Herod [the Great] (37–4 BC), surprisingly, does not appear to have touched the walls; he concentrated his attention to buildings within the city. . . . After [Titus's] victory in AD 70, Titus ordered the walls of Jerusalem to be razed, leaving only the loftiest of the towers, Phasael, Hippicus, and Mariamme, and the portion of the wall enclosing the city on the west. . . . The destruction begun by Titus was completed by Hadrian in AD 135. In his new city, Aelia Capitolina, only the camp of the Tenth Legion was walled. A wall became necessary only when the Legion left at the end of the 3rd century. The area it enclosed was very close to that of the present Old City, whose street plan (such as it is) is conditioned by the layout of Aelia; the main arteries are still the same.

The Ottoman sultan Suliman the Magnificent (1520–1566) erected the present rampart.[3]

So, from its origins as a small, Jebusite town on the eastern hill that David conquered for Israel (2 Sam 2:5–6), Jerusalem expanded, contracted, and finally stabilized to the size that it is today. You can see traces of this history in the outermost wall

---

[3] Jerome Murphy-O'Connor, *The Holy Land: An Oxford Archaeological Guide from Earliest Times to 1700*, 5th ed. (Oxford: Oxford University Press, 2008), 11–12.

itself: going just uphill from the Jaffa Gate, you can observe within the wall three different layers of stone—the top being Suliman's (1500's), the lowest being possibly Herodian, as the stones of Herod the Great and Herod Agrippa I (here) are characteristically large.

We will now go around the city clockwise, highlighting a few of the city's gates (and skipping others). The map below is very helpful in this regard, as it not only demonstrates how the city is broken up into four quarters, but also where each gate is located—that is, along which part of the wall and within which quarter. We will start at the Jaffa Gate, as the area immediately outside of it provides a good place at which to begin the trek around the city.

Jerusalem: Gates and quarters of the old city (p. 13, fig. 2 in Jerome Murphy-O'Connor, *The Holy Land*; used by permission of Oxford University Press).

Jaffa Gate

Arabs call the Jaffa Gate by its official name, "Bab el-Khalil," which means: "The Gate of the Friend." It refers, and points, to Hebron, which takes its Arabic name from Abraham, the "friend of God" (Is 41:8), who pitched his tent near the Oaks of Mamre in Hebron (Gen 13:8), buried his wife, Sarah, there

The Jaffa Gate.

where she died (Gen 23:2.19), and is thought to be buried there himself. This Arabic term derives from the Qur'an calling Abraham "*Khalil* al-**Rahm**an," which literally means "Beloved/ Friend of the Merciful (God)." Going through the gate, we see on the right two mounted figures on the saluting platform outside the Citadel; they represent very accurately the equipment of Crusader and Muslim cavalry during the period of the Latin Kingdom (1099–1187).[4] Flavius Josephus tells us that it was at this area that the Romans, after a month of frantic effort, finally broke through into the Upper City (*Wars of the Jews* 6.374–99) in late September of AD 70, the year in which Titus destroyed the city of Jerusalem.[5]

---

4   Ibid., 17.

5   Ibid., 18.

When Titus leveled the city, he left standing a few towers, one of which was named Mariamme (see below), who was the second wife of Herod the Great. It is still visible above what is called "The Citadel," or the "Tower of King David." It is likely not actually a tower of the king, who ruled a Jerusalem that did not encompass this part of the current city. Byzantine Christians believed this site to be the palace of David,[6] perhaps borrowing the name "Tower of David" from the Song of Songs, attributed to Solomon: "Like a tower of David [is] your neck, built in courses, a thousand shields hanging upon it, all the armor of warriors" (4:4). Herod stayed there, building three towers on the spot.

Josephus witnesses that this place was transformed later into a praetorium where judgments and condemnations took place (see below). Many believe that it is likely that Pontius Pilate condemned Jesus to die here.[7] I, though, think that our Lord's being

The fortress of Herod, also known as "The Citadel," with its famous, ancient towers.

---

[6]   Ibid., 23.

[7]   Ibid.

consigned to die happened in a different spot (see the chapter on Good Friday and Easter, further on).

While Herod's tower and palace do not explicitly appear in the New Testament, they nevertheless provide us with a chance to enlighten our prayer with the Gospels. As Bargil Pixner, O.S.B., writes:

> Herod the Great became Emperor Augustus's crafty and devoted vassal. The people, though, hated this Judaized Idumean, who had become a Jew only by way of his father. In 37 BC, he defeated Antigonus, the last king of the Hasmonean priestly dynasty (War 1.238f), becoming a much feared tyrant and cruel,[8] . . . intensely jealous and plagued by distrust. In 23 BC, Herod built a royal palace in the northwestern corner of the city of that time for himself and his numerous wives and children. Here he received an endless stream of guests from all corners of the world (Ant 15.317f; War 5.156–83); here he was visited by the magi from the east who, guided by the star, had set out to find the newborn King of the Jews (Mt 2:1–9). . . . Joseph and Mary, on their way to Bethlehem through Jerusalem, must have passed this place. Did Mary, riding on her mule, look up at the imposing edifice already sensing the danger posed to her child by the powerful man hidden behind these forbidding walls?[9]

Indeed, as our Benedictine friend points out, in this Citadel the Magi were received by Herod the Great, who died in 4 BC, and the Holy Family must have passed it on their way to Bethlehem for our Lord's Nativity. And here we are, looking at the same tower! History—biblical history—happened right here!

Damascus Gate

The most elaborate of the city gates, the Damascus Gate, is the finest example of Ottoman architecture in the entire region.[10] The

---

[8]   Bargil Pixner, *Paths of the Messiah: Sites of the Early Church from Galilee to Jerusalem—Jesus and Jewish Christianity in Light of Archaeological Discoveries*, ed. Rainer Riesner, trans. Keith Myrick and Sam and Miriam Randall (San Francisco: Ignatius, 2010), 4.

[9]   Ibid., 7.

[10] Murphy-O'Connor, *The Holy Land*, 14.

first gate on this site was built by Herod Agrippa I (AD 41–44) and was rebuilt by Hadrian in AD 135 as the freestanding, monumental entrance to the Roman-crafted capitol Aelia Capitolina.

The Damascus Gate.

This gate gave way to a semicircular plaza from which ran the two principal roads of the ancient Roman city that correspond to the present-day roads Tariq el-Wad and Suq Khan ez-Zeit.[11]

You can see that this particular gate is usually quite abuzz with activity: markets, meetings, and many other things. Such should not surprise us, if we consider the importance of the city gate in Old Testament times. Besides being a protection against invaders, city gates encompassed a variety of functions in biblical times: sacrifices, monument installation, processions (military or liturgical), appearance of a king, public assemblies, jurid-

---

[11] Ibid., 15. *Suq* is the Arabic word for "market," many of which engulf the inner streets of the Muslim quarter, to which part of the city this gate gives entrance.

ical activities, public executions, and markets.[12] The following are some biblical examples of these activities:

1. In Ezekiel 46:2, the prince is to enter by the way of the porch of the gate from outside and shall stand by the post of the gate, and the priests shall prepare his burnt offering and his peace offerings, and he shall worship at the threshold of the gate.[13]

2. In 1 Samuel 18:6–7, the women come out of the cities to meet Saul and David returning from the victorious war with the Philistines, and there form a triumphal procession.[14]

3. In Nehemiah 8:2–3, the people of Jerusalem assembled at the city gate to hear the Torah read aloud.[15]

4. In Deuteronomy 17:2–9, the gate becomes the court of justice, to which witnesses are called to testify and at which judgment is to be passed.[16]

5. In Ruth 4:9–11, Boaz, at the city gate, buys the field of Naomi and announces that Ruth is to be his wife, taking the city elders and the people at the gate as his witnesses.[17]

6. In Deuteronomy 17:5 and 21:18–22, respectively, idolaters and rebellious sons are to be stoned to death at the gate.[18] Our Lord, of course, was himself "led out" (Jn 19:17) of the city and crucified along a road near a gate

---

[12] Natalie N. May, "City Gates and Their Functions in Mesopotamia and Ancient Israel," in *The Fabric of Cities: Aspects of Urbanism, Urban Topography and Society in Mesopotamia, Greece and Rome*, ed. Natalie N. May and Ulrike Steinert (Leiden: Brill, 2014), 77–121, at 78.

[13] Ibid., 82.

[14] May, "City Gates," 89.

[15] Ibid., 93–94.

[16] Ibid., 98.

[17] Ibid., 99.

[18] Ibid., 104.

so that his very public agony would obtain maximum shock value on those passing by.

St. Stephen's Gate

This gate received its name once Christian pilgrims were not permitted, after the fall of the Latin Kingdom (1187), to go near Jerusalem's northern wall, where Byzantine Christians had located this gate and church of St. Stephen. Instead, they had to leave the city by this eastern gate when they wanted to visit the Mount of Olives and Jericho, and so they named *this* gate St. Stephen's Gate. Such does "illustrate the tendency," at times, "of places in Jerusalem to move to suit the convenience of the visitors."[19]

Regardless, the gate is named after St. Stephen because the Protomartyr was taken outside the city near the Temple and there stoned (Acts 7:58–60). This gate has also been called the Sheep's Gate, as it was the place where sheep were brought and sold. Lastly, the gate is currently also called, in Hebrew, "Lions's Gate," even though this is technically a mistake. The two animals that line the doorway are in fact panthers, the heraldic emblem of the Mamluk sultan Baybars (1260–1277), which Suliman the Magnificent set on either side of the gate to celebrate the Ottoman defeat of the Mamluks in 1517. As has been noted, it seems that, here, pride trumped the religious prohibition of images. Not long thereafter, then, a more acceptable rationale was developed. Here, Selim I, the first Ottoman sultan (1512–1520), was supposed to have met two lions who were about to consume him as he was leaving the city. Selim was able to escape, so the story goes, because he promised that he would protect Jerusalem by building a wall to surround it.[20]

Golden Gate

From the Mount of Olives, or from the Kidron Valley down below, you can look toward the Dome of the Rock and former Temple Mount and see a double gate that has been sealed shut. This gate has been called many things: the Golden Gate, the "Beautiful Gate," the Gate of Mercy, and the Gate of Penance

---

[19] Murphy-O'Connor, *The Holy Land*, 21.
[20] Ibid. The lion continues, to this day, to be the symbol of the Jerusalem municipality. Of course, we could also read in this symbol the theme of the "Lion of the Tribe of Judah" (Gen 49:9; Rev 5:5).

The Golden Gate, as seen from the Kidron Valley

through which the just will enter with their final Judge.

The Golden Gate is the focus of many traditions, though there is little certitude regarding its origins.[21] Some thought that, before the Messiah comes, Elijah, or at least the "Prince" (Ezek 44:1–3), would return and enter through this door into the Temple—

---

[21] Ibid., 100.

which, of course, the Ottomans wanted to prevent and, so, placed tombs in the valley below the gate, since Jews could not come into contact or proximity with a corpse without becoming ritually unclean (Lev 21:11). Others, relying on the Mishnah, identified this gate with the Shushan Gate of the Temple, where recurred the purification ceremony of the red heifer (Num 19:1–10).

Murphy-O'Connor, not surprisingly, is not too fond of the identification of this gate with Peter's healing, and as evidence against it, he cites the lack of any such description on the part of the Pilgrim of Piacenza (AD 570) and the fact that it had been suggested that Empress Eudokia built the present edifice in the mid-fifth century AD to commemorate the miracle.[22] Our Dominican archaeologist thinks that the present structure was built by the Ummayad caliph Abd al-Malik (685–705) as part of his rehabilitation of what had been the Jewish Temple. It was probably blocked in the eighth century AD, he thinks, when access to the Haram al-Sharif (Temple Mount) was denied to all unbelievers.[23]

Crusaders unblocked the gate twice a year: on Palm Sunday and on the feast of the Exaltation of the Cross. The present Western name also took firm root at this period, though it was attested already in the seventh century AD. The Greek *hōraia* (beautiful) was confused with the Latin *aurea* (golden) because of the similarity in sound.[24] Hence, the gate can properly be called both the Golden Gate and the Beautiful Gate!

Here, at the Beautiful Gate, Peter healed the beggar who was crippled from birth.

POINTS FOR REFLECTION

- In order to celebrate the Feast of Passover, Jesus's family went up to Jerusalem every year. The road from Nazareth was an arduous trek—about seventy miles long, and rising over 2,000 feet in elevation. Concerning pilgrimage to the Holy City, we have it so easy compared to them! Still, despite the creature comforts rightly built into your trip, surely there have been aspects of it that have been physi-

[22] Ibid., 101.
[23] Ibid., 102.
[24] Ibid.

cally and mentally demanding. What are those difficulties or challenges that have made your journey a pilgrimage, rather than a vacation? Have you offered those up to the Lord, thereby consecrating your time and the self-denials that it surely entails? Throughout your life, you will have many chances to sanctify trips—family vacations, work trips, even running errands—by offering up any inconveniences or trying moments and effectively turning them into pilgrimages that will both benefit you spiritually and please God.

• In a very small space of land there live, side by side, people from the three great monotheistic faiths—to each of which this city, and even at times the same points of the city, is so dear. That such differing, deep traditions of religious zeal can cohabitate in such close quarters, and typically peacefully, is a testament to the universal call to love one's neighbor (Mt 22:39–40), and it challenges us to examine the ways in which we live together, especially with people of, at times, vastly differing temperaments and *modi operandi*, within the close quarters of our own communities. The hustle and bustle of this city, in which personal space comes at a premium while walking down the streets, challenges us to exercise patience towards people of other races and religions, who, in this moment, are, in fact, our neighbor. In *Amoris Laetitia*, Pope Francis comments on this first attribute that Paul lists in his famous "Ode to Love" (1 Cor 13:1–13):

> Patience takes root when I recognize that other people also have a right to live in this world, just as they are. It does not matter if they hold me back, if they unsettle my plans, or annoy me by the way they act or think, or if they are not everything I want them to be. Love always has an aspect of deep compassion that leads to accepting the other person as part of this world, even when he or she acts differently than I would like.[25]

---

[25] Pope Francis, Post-Synodal Apostolic Exhortation *Amoris Laetitia* (March 19, 2016), §92, accessed June 4, 2017, http://w2.vatican.va/

Let your time in the Old City be a time in which you grow in patience.

- You have a unique opportunity to enhance your contemplative prayer with the experiences you are having right now. The next time you read about the Magi, or about the Holy Family travelling to Bethlehem, remember this Herodian tower. Insert it into your mental prayer and use it to help you recreate the scenes, to experience the emotions of wonder, alarm, and scheming on the part of Herod, and also whatever must have gone on within the hearts of the Holy Family passing by this imposing edifice. In this way, you will let the Holy Land change—or better yet, inform—the way you pray, which I hope the Land thereby enhances.

- We should pay attention to how Luke portrays Peter responding to the crippled, poor man asking for alms: "But Peter *looked intently at him*, as did John, and said: 'Look at us.' He paid attention to them, expecting to receive something from them. Peter said: 'I have neither silver nor gold, but *what I do have I give you*: in the name of Jesus Christ the Nazorean, rise and walk.' Then Peter *took him by the right hand and raised him up*" (Acts

content/francesco/en/apost_exhortations/documents/papa-francesco_esortazione-ap_20160319_amoris-laetitia.html.

3:5–7, emphasis mine). Would that we could be like Peter when we, ourselves, encounter on the street a poor person asking for money! By making eye contact with the crippled man, Peter affirmed the man's dignity as a human being. Then, despite the poor man's disinterest in Peter—or, rather, perhaps his interest solely in getting money out of the Apostle (the statement that he "paid attention to them" really means he turned his attention to them when he thought they might be giving him money)—Peter shared with him what really mattered: the power of Christ—the uplifting joy of the love of God enfleshed in fraternal charity and concern.

When you encounter poor people asking for money, what goes through your head, and what do you do? Do you make eye contact with them and, smiling, offer them a greeting—thereby affirming their dignity as human persons? Do you tell them the truth, or do you lie to get out of a potentially uncomfortable moment? Do you wish them a blessing and assure them of your prayers for them? And, lastly, do you give them, when appropriate, a handshake—some kind of physical, human contact for which, in many cases, they hunger just as much as food? Follow the example of the Apostles and share God's love with those most in need.

Especially for Seminarians

- You will have many a chance as a young priest to sanctify your various trips (March for Life, Steubenville Conferences, SEEK, etc.) by offering up, with a positive attitude, the taxing moments that can transform any adventure into a pilgrimage that is not only graciously beneficial for you and those you bring with you (even spiritually) but also sacrificially pleasing to Almighty God.

- Many priests will say that their pilgrimages to the Holy Land changed the way they pray with the Scriptures and the way that they preach. One way in which this has been true for me is how what I have seen here helps me in (to borrow an Ignatian term) the *"composition of place"*[26] by means of which I try to *plug in* to a biblical account while I'm reading it and praying with it. Take the opportunity to start praying this way, using the sense memory of the places you are visiting to enhance your contemplation.

- As priests, you will represent to our brothers and sisters who are poor not only the Church, but also our Lord. Do not pass up the chances you are given to share the love of Christ with the least of these (Mt 25:40).

---

[26] "When the contemplation or meditation is on something visible . . . the representation will consist in seeing in imagination the material place where the object is that we wish to contemplate. I said the material place, for example, the temple, or the mountain where Jesus or His Mother is, according to the subject matter of the contemplation" (Louis J. Puhl, *The Spiritual Exercises of St. Ignatius: Based on Studies in the Language of the Autograph* [Chicago: Loyola Press, 1951)], 25).

MOUNT OF OLIVES

*As Jesus was sitting on the Mount of Olives opposite
the Temple area, Peter, James, John, and Andrew asked
him privately, "Tell us, when will [the destruction of the
Temple] happen, and what sign will there be when all these
things are about to come to an end?" Jesus began to say
to them, "See that no one deceives you. Many will come
in my name saying, 'I am he,' and they will deceive many.
When you hear of wars and reports of wars, do not be
alarmed; such things must happen, but it will not yet be
the end."*

(Mark 13:3–7)

The Mount of Olives has a fascinating history. In the time of David (1004–965 BC), there was a Jewish sanctuary on the summit
(2 Sam 15:30–32), and David escaped this way when faced with
the treachery of his son Absalom. In the generation after David,
more sanctuaries appeared: Solomon built on the hill temples for
the gods of his foreign wives (2 Kings 23:13). Much later we see
that Jesus himself frequented the Mount of Olives. While he was
near Jerusalem, he stayed with his friends in nearby Bethany (Lk
10:38; Mk. 11:11). Since those who were poor could not afford
to stay inside the city when its population tripled for the feast

days, Jesus would walk each day over the hill to Jerusalem, and then over again back to Bethany at nightfall (Lk 21:37). On one such evening, Jesus sat with his disciples opposite the Temple, and spoke of the future of the city, whose faithlessness reduced him to tears (Lk 19:37, 41–44; see *Dominus Flevit*, further on). Moreover, at the bottom of the mount's slope is the garden of Gethsemane where he was arrested a few days later (Mk 14:26–52). Finally, at the top of this hill, Luke locates the Ascension (Acts 1:6–12).[1]

Separating the city of Jerusalem from the Mount of Olives is the Kidron Valley, which flows down into the Valley of Hinnom.[2] Jesus had to process through this valley when he made his triumphal entry into Jerusalem, which we commemorate every Palm Sunday (Mt 21:1–11). The Kidron Valley is mentioned by name only in John's Gospel, when Jesus and the disciples left Jerusalem and passed through it over to the garden on the other side, where Judas betrayed him (Jn 18:1). You will note in this valley and at the foot of the Mount of Olives a large concentration of ceme-

View from the Mount of Olives of the Kidron Valley and Old City.

[1]   Murphy-O'Connor, *The Holy Land*, 139.
[2]   Also known as "Gehenna." See the discussion about the church of St. Peter in Gallicantu in the next chapter.

teries—Christian, Jewish, and Muslim. This could be due to the belief that Kidron is the Valley of Jehoshaphat where humanity will assemble to be judged by God.[3]

The Mount of Olives is frequently depicted with apocalyptic imagery. John J. Kilgallen writes:

> Imaginatively, the Jewish Scriptures portray God, the great Lord, as the One who would come from the east, like the sun reaching out over the Jewish world each dawn.[4] When this God comes to judge Israel and to purify Jerusalem, the many hills on his way would be leveled and the many valleys would be filled up, all to make his royal passage fittingly a smooth and easy one.[5] The Mount of Olives, in particular, would be divided in half from east to west, so that between the newly created northern and southern parts God could approach his city with stately ease. That Jesus would "return as you have seen him go up," in the words of the angels to the disciples, suggests that it is Jesus who will perform this role of judge of Israel at the end of time.[6]

For the Mount of Olives discussion, I deem that it will be easiest to proceed, as we did in Galilee around the Sea, place by place and church by church. Still, at each pilgrimage point, the material that follows will provide scriptural and archaeological data for each site, pausing at each for some Scripture reading and then concluding the entire chapter with *Issues Raised* and *Points for reflection*. As you might by now expect, I draw heavily from Murphy-O'Connor for the background material, and then from Pixner and Kilgallen for considerations of the meaning for us of these places and the happenings therein.

---

[3] Ibid., 141.

[4] As in Ezekiel 43:1–2: "Then he led me to the gate facing east, and there was the glory of the God of Israel coming from the east! His voice was like the roar of many waters, and the earth shone with his glory."

[5] See Isaiah 40:4, on the lips of John the Baptist in Luke 3:5.

[6] John J. Kilgallen, *A New Testament Guide to the Holy Land* (Chicago: Loyola, 1998), 148–49.

Mosque of the Ascension

The place from where Luke has Jesus ascending into heaven is dominated by an edifice that is now a mosque. We will get to the history of this building in a moment, but first, let us examine the biblical sources for this spot.

The mosque built over the spot from which many believe that Jesus ascended into heaven.

Luke 24:50–52 has: "Then Jesus led them out as far as Bethany, raised his hands, and blessed them. As he blessed them he parted from them and was taken up to heaven. They did him homage and then returned to Jerusalem with great joy, and they were continually in the temple praising God." The exact place at which this happens is not precisely given, though we get the impression that it happened on Easter Sunday itself.[7] In Luke's second work, the Acts of the Apostles (1:12), the Ascension occurs forty days after the Resurrection (1:3) somewhere on the Mount of Olives, which is a Sabbath's day journey (2,000 steps) from the city.[8]

SCRIPTURE ON SITE:
Acts 1:6-12

So, from these indications, we can be fairly certain that, per Luke, the Ascension

---

[7]   Murphy-O'Connor, *The Holy Land*, 141.
[8]   Ibid., 142.

The spot from which some believe that Jesus was lifted up toward heaven.

of our Lord happened somewhere in this vicinity, which is sufficiently close to Jerusalem, and on the way to Bethany, to match Luke's account.[9]

Why, then, is there a mosque here? It is a long story. The first Christian church here was built sometime before AD 392. It was octagonal, and its center was not enclosed—that is, it was open to the sky, which is appropriate to the event it commemorated! The Crusaders made it round and surrounded it with fortified masonry, which we still see today. In the Middle Ages, a small footprint, supposed to be that of our Lord's when he "touched off" to the heavens, became quite venerated in the middle of the shrine. However, when the Muslims won the city from the Crusaders, Saladin gave the site to two of his followers, and the building complex has remained in Muslim hands since. They added a roof and a *mihrab*, which is the gothic-looking niche inside mosques that points to Mecca, toward which Muslims orient themselves for prayer. This place has become holy to Muslims, who believe—though it is not mentioned in the Qur'an—that Jesus ascended into heaven.[10]

Pater Noster/Eleona Church

This church bears two names: that of "Our Father," and that of "Eleona." Why the double name? Let us begin with explaining the latter.

As the Church historian Eusebius has it, the Roman emperor Constantine undertook a massive church-building program in Palestine, focusing especially on three caves linked to the key

---

[9] For an explanation of the differences between these two accounts from the same author, Luke, see Kilgallen, *New Testament Guide*, 150–51.

[10] Murphy-O'Connor, *The Holy Land*, 143.

mysteries of the Christian faith: the cave of Jesus's birth in Beth-lehem, the rock-cut tomb near Golgotha, and the cave on the Mount of Olives with which the Ascension was connected. Con-stantine's mother, Helena, oversaw the building of the church here. Egeria beheld it and described it as the starting point of the Holy Thursday procession from the Mount of Olives into

The central section of the church here which bears two names: Eleona, and Our Father.

the Old City. She also, it turns out, was the first to record what became for the church a common name: Eleona, which comes from the Greek word *elaion* (meaning: olive) and a final "a" that represents the Aramaic definite article ("the")—making, of the name, the phrase "the olive (grove)."[11] This name is appropriate, given the church's setting on the Mount of Olives!

Over time, the site commemorating the Ascension was moved further up the hill, and so the cave became associated exclusive-ly with the teaching of Jesus on the final battle between good and evil (Mt 24:1–26:2), which Gospel Egeria heard read aloud on Holy Thursday. The church was destroyed by the Persians in 614, but the memory of Jesus's teaching remained.[12]

Then there occurred a major shift in the content of what Jesus taught here: this place became the spot where Jesus, in

---

[11] Ibid.
[12] Ibid.

fact, taught the disciples the Our Father. How did this happen? Through a "sophisticated harmonization," it seems,[13] of Luke 10:38–11:4[14] and Mark 11:12–25.[15] Apparently, an 1102 Crusader pilgrim heard a story about there being found on the top of this hill a marble plaque with the Lord's prayer inscribed in Hebrew, and then another pilgrim in 1170 saw one such plaque in Greek underneath the altar at the church that was here. When the destroyed church was recently excavated, an inscribed Latin version was indeed found amidst the rubble.[16] All of this justified the decoration of one of the current walls of the complex with large ceramic tile plaques on which is written, in over sixty languages, the Our Father.

However, it is rather doubtful to me that our Lord taught the Our Father here, as such a description does not easily sync with this Bethany's location. In Luke, it is clear that this prayer was taught by Jesus long before he reached Jerusalem. Two chapters after Luke relates the giving of the Our Father, Luke says that Jesus was going through towns and villages teaching, making his way to Jerusalem (Lk 13:22). Likely, Matthew is more accurate when he places the teaching of the Our Father in Galilee.[17] Or, perhaps we could wonder if Jesus did not simply give this prayer twice—once in Galilee,

One of the many Our Father plaques that line the walls of this church's complex. This plaque contains a Hebrew and Aramaic version of the Lord's Prayer (which was, of course, first written down in Greek).

[13] Ibid.

[14] Jesus with anxious Martha and meditative Mary in Bethany, followed immediately by the Our Father.

[15] Which has Jesus's apocalyptic teaching on the "secrets of the end of the world," per Eusebius (Pixner, *Paths of the Messiah*, 234), taking place near this Bethany close to Jerusalem.

[16] Murphy-O'Connor, *The Holy Land*, 143.

[17] Kilgallen, *New Testament Guide*, 153.

and once here. That seems to be a better explanation.

Nonetheless, we should keep the Our Father in mind when passing to the far side of the complex where there can be seen, in an excavation pit some feet below the ground, an old baptistery that was attached to this church. Consider here the significance of the Our Father in the Rite of Baptism, according to ancient—and, though less obviously so, current—sacramental praxis. In the first centuries of the Byzantine period, when the newly baptized—having received the gift of faith in the sacramental immersion under the Trinitarian formula (Mt 28:19)—emerged from the water, they immediately recited the Our Father, a prayer that they had to memorize as catechumens, but which they could pray only once they were baptized. Why the wait? Well, Baptism is the precise moment in which one becomes a son or daughter of God the Father, who, at that instant, says to the one being baptized just what he said to his own Son at Jesus's Baptism: "You are my beloved Son, with you I am well pleased" (Mk 1:11). Hence, it was fitting that only once one was sacramentally con-

The ruins of the ancient baptistery discovered here at the Eleona/Our Father Church.

stituted God's beloved child could that person call God "Father," just as Jesus did, and instructed the disciples to do, when he taught them the Our Father (Mt 6:9). Even to this day, the recitation of the Our Father happens after the immersion in, or infusion of, water.

At baptisms, though, we can sometimes easily tend to blow through this prayer, or at least recite it on sheer autopilot. We should, rather, say it deliberately, knowing that this is the first time in which we are fully able to address God as "our Father" with our newly made brother or sister in Christ who, having just received the gift of faith and spiritual adoption (see Rom

8:14–17), finally gets to call God his or her Father, too—surely, a very special moment![18]

Dominus Flevit Church

This church, whose name means "The Lord Wept," was designed by Antonio Barluzzi in the fitting form of a teardrop. The building commemorates our Lord's lament over the Holy City and his prophecy of the destruction of its Temple, both of which sayings he made during his approach to Jerusalem from the Mount of Olives:

These grim words foretold Jerusalem's future destruction at the besieging hands of Rome's Tenth Legion in AD 70. Matthew's version of our Lord's lament differs slightly and is more emotive:

The church Dominus Flevit.

Jerusalem, Jerusalem, you who kill the prophets and stone those who are sent to you, how many times I yearned to gather your children together, as a hen gathers her young under her wings, but you were unwilling! Behold, your house will be abandoned, desolate. I tell you, you will not see me again until you say: "Blessed is he who comes in the name of the Lord" (23:37–39).

SCRIPTURE ON SITE:
Luke 19:41-44

Inside the chapel, a look through the glass window over the altar offers an amazing view of the Old City—specifically

---

[18] For a series of great Scriptural reflections on the Our Father, see Scott W. Hahn, *Understanding "Our Father": Biblical Reflections on the Lord's Prayer* (Steubenville, OH: Emmaus Road, 2002).

the area where the Jewish Temple once stood. On the floor of Barluzzi's church, you will also see traces of the earlier monastery (fifth century AD) that had been built here. Outside of the chapel, you will notice various tombs; these come from cemeteries which date from 1600–1300 BC, 100 BC–AD 135, and AD 200–400. Egeria's Holy Thursday procession stopped here, but it is not certain what exactly it commemorated here.

Church of All Nations

Going down to the bottom of the hill, we reach the area of Gethsemane,[19] in which is found the large basilica called the Church of All Nations. This church, which was built in 1924, is located on the traditional site of the garden in which Jesus collapsed in prayer, sweating blood in his anguish before his Passion.

The church into which we will go houses a very precious relic: the rock that is held to be the rock on which Jesus prayed in the Garden of Gethsemane. This building is the latest in a series of three churches, all of which were built in order to commemorate the prayer of Jesus before his arrest. As Murphy-O'Connor writes:

The basilica of the Church of All Nations, at the foot of the Mount of Olives.

---

[19] The name *Gethsemane* comes from the Hebrew words *gat* ("press") and *shemen* ("oil," often "olive oil"), which together make this word signify "oil press."

It covers the "elegant Church" (Egeria) built between 379 and 384 on the site where the pre-Constantinian Jerusalem community commemorated the prayer of Christ. Willibald, in 724–725, is the last

pilgrim to mention this church; it was destroyed by an earthquake some 20 years later. The Crusaders first built an oratory in the ruins which they later replaced by a church; they gave it a slightly different orientation in order to have a piece of rock in each apse—a rather material interpretation of the triple prayer of Christ.[20]

The designs of this present-day church help us to contemplate the importance and power of praying in time of suffering. Jesus gives himself completely, in trustful, filial submission, over to the will of the Father, despite an anguish so deep as to cause hematidrosis.[21] So, too, should we pray when we find ourselves in any kind of spiritual agony, especially when it is intense. For a consideration of Jesus's agony in the Garden, see *Issues Raised*, further on.

The mosaic above the entrance to the Church of All Nations.

Before going inside, note the mosaic above the front door. In this triangular piece, Jesus is shown in glory, offering his sufferings

and those of the world to the Father.[22] With this mosaic, the

---

[20] Murphy-O'Connor, *The Holy Land*, 147.

[21] The condition in which subcutaneous capillaries dilate so intensely as to burst into the sweat glands, resulting in blood being carried to the surface of the skin by the sweat coming from those glands.

[22] Kilgallen, *New Testament Guide*, 167.

church invites all pilgrims to unite their personal sufferings to the agony of Christ, for the sake of whose sorrowful passion we beg that God have mercy on us and the whole world.

Inside the basilica you will note on the ceiling representations symbolizing various nations. These are the countries who have donated money for this building's construction, maintenance, and operation—hence the name "Church of All Nations." Look down, then, to the mosaic floor, as it helps us to get in touch, literally, not only with the history of this place but also with our faith's own history of devotion expressed here. The mosaics are an exact representation of the mosaic floor of the church built when Theodosius was Emperor of Constantinople (AD 379–393), and which are called "elegant" in Egeria's pilgrimage journal.

Beneath the covers of the floor is the mosaic flooring of the original Theodosian basilica. "We are," in this way, "by virtue of this original flooring, in touch with a long tradition of veneration on this spot."[23] Such a prayerful connection with our faith's past is one of the special things that pilgrimage to the Holy Land seeks to instill in the hearts of the faithful traveler.

After going up to the rock that is preserved under the altar, and upon

SCRIPTURE ON SITE:
Mark 14:43-52
John 18:1-13

The main altar of the Church of All Nations. The mosaic above the altar depicts that which occurred—the agony of Jesus, who sweat blood—on the very stone in front of the altar.

---

23 Ibid., 168.

which it is remembered that Jesus sweated blood in prayer-filled agony, do not miss the mosaics that crown the back walls of the three apses. These images of Jesus's betrayal, agony, and power are very evocative of the trusting, yet intense, prayer of Our Lord, as well as his might contained in the expression of his divine name.

You will also notice outside of the church a grove of olive trees that, with their gnarled bark and branches, seem quite old. Indeed, it was recently discovered that these trees have the same DNA as those of Jesus's time, such that, while what we see of them above ground is not from the first century AD, what is beneath them underground could very well be! The Roman Emperor Hadrian burned the grove when he destroyed Jerusalem in the mid-second century AD. Similar trees can be seen in the grove across the street, where many suppose Jesus left his soon-to-be-sleepy disciples (that is, Gethsemani) in order to pray alone to his heavenly Father. This is also, then, the place where Jesus was arrested and taken to the house of Caiaphas.

One of the very old olive trees in the Garden of Gethsemane near the Church of All Nations.

Issues Raised

Issue 1

When we notice the *mihrab* in the Mosque of the Ascension, we recognize how important proper orientation in prayer is to our Muslim brothers and sisters. Here it would be good to recognize how important orientation in prayer is to our Christian faith, as well.[24]

In his book *Spirit of the Liturgy*, Cardinal Ratzinger treats at length the purpose and boon of prayer *ad orientem*—that is, the facing east, towards the "rising sun" (*oriens*), of both priest and people at the celebration of Holy Mass.[25] Pope Emeritus Benedict XVI recently reiterated his view on this matter in a reflection piece in homage of Patriarch Bartholomew, published in the Vatican newspaper *L'Osservatore Romano*:

> A shepherd of the flock of Jesus Christ is never oriented merely to the circle of his own faithful. The community of the Church is universal also in the sense that it includes all of reality. That becomes evident, for example, in the liturgy, which signifies not only the commemoration and realization of the saving deeds of Jesus Christ. It is [also] on the way toward the redemption of all creation. In the liturgy's orientation to the East, we see that Christians, together with the Lord, want to progress toward the salvation of creation in its entirety. Christ, the crucified and

---

[24] Even though our faith traditions share an emphasis on physical orientation in prayer, the Christian and Muslim religions share significantly different understandings of what prayer is, based on each faith's understanding of who God is, especially in relation to mankind. For a clear and compelling presentation of these differences, see Scott W. Hahn, *Abba or Allah: Important Differences between Catholicism and Islam* (audio book on CD) (Sycamore, IL: Lighthouse Catholic Media, 2012). Every seminarian should read what I consider to be the most important speech of the last half-century: Benedict XVI, "Faith, Reason, and the University: Memories and Reflections" ("The Regensburg Address"), September 12, 2006, accessed June 4, 2017, https://w2.vatican.va/content/benedict-xvi/en/speeches/2006/september/documents/hf_ben-xvi_spe_20060912_university-regensburg.html. See the sixth paragraph from the top. For official, German citation, see the bibliography.

[25] Joseph Ratzinger, *The Spirit of the Liturgy* (San Francisco: Ignatius Press, 2000), 151.

risen Lord, is at the same time also the "sun" that illumines the world.[26] Faith is always directed toward the totality of creation.[27]

Reading these words, we see that there is real, spiritual merit to celebrating the Mass facing east with the people—which position, of course, is never (at least, never should be) an instance of the priest "turning his back to the people."[28] How and when to implement such a practice—say, in a parish— is of course a decision that should be formed and regulated by prudence. However, it has been done well by some American bishops, such as Bishop James Conley of Lincoln, Nebraska, where he established the practice that, during Advent—the great season of expectation!—and for the Christmas Vigil, Masses in his cathedral would be celebrated facing the east; he also gave priests in his diocese permission to do likewise.[29]

Finally, and by way of recapitulation, Bishop Arthur Serratelli begins his piece on "Praying Ad Orientem" precisely with the image of the Muslim *mihrab*. The entire column is fascinating, instructive, and non-polemical. One paragraph deserves mention here:

St. John of Damascus gives three explanations for the eastward stance of Christians at prayer. First, Christ is "the Sun of Righteousness" (Mal 4:2) and "the Dayspring from on high" (Luke 1:78). Facing the light dawning from the east, Christians affirm their faith in Christ as the Light of the world. Second, God planted the Garden

---

[26] Much like, we could add, the sun of Ezekiel 43, cited earlier, which shines with the glory of God from the east, from where our hope tells us Christ will come again to visit his people like the "dawn from on high" (Lk 1:78).

[27] Pope Benedict XVI, "Travel Companions: A Reflection of Benedict XVI," *L'Osservatore Romano*, October 12, 2016, accessed June 4, 2017, http://www.osservatoreromano.va/en/news/travel-companions. Creation was marred—"cursed" (Gen 3:17)—by sin, but one day, it will again be made new (Rev 21:5), to which renewal we look forward in the liturgy.

[28] Ratzinger, *Spirit of the Liturgy*, 151.

[29] James Conley, "Looking to the east," Nov 21, 2014, accessed June 4, 2017, http://www.lincolndiocese.org/op-ed/bishop-s-column/3004-looking-to-the-east.

of Eden in the east (Gen 2:8). But, when our first parents sinned, they were exiled from the garden and moved westward. Facing east, therefore, reminds Christians of their need to long and strive for the paradise that God intended for them. And, third, when speaking of his Second Coming at the end of history, Jesus said, "For just as lightning comes from the east and is seen as far as the west, so will the coming of the Son of Man be" (Mt 24:27). Thus, facing the east at prayer visibly expresses the hope for the coming of Jesus.[30]

Issue 2

The agony of Jesus in the Garden of Gethsemane contains a paradox: how could Jesus, who in his humanity enjoyed the beatific vision, have undergone such painful anguish there at the foot of the Mount of Olives? In other words, since he knew who he was (God, powerful over sin and death) and what the future held in store both for him (Resurrection and glory) and for all who would believe in him (eternal life, won by his triumphal Passion), why is Jesus depicted suffering? A good explanation is traced by St. John Paul II in his Apostolic Letter *Novo Millennio Ineunte*. The Holy Father, putting this paradox in the context of the inexhaustible mystery of the hypostatic union, explains that Jesus's human nature was revolting from the idea of his own suffering and from seeing how profound his own suffering would be. His vision indeed allowed him to see the face of the Father, but it also allowed him to know, without distraction and in complete purity of thought, our sin, every sin, and the gravity of every sin. His consideration of all these things—tied to the awareness that he was going to enter into the suffering that these sins caused—was what caused Jesus to suffer. In the Holy Father's very instructive words:

> However valid it may be to maintain that, because of the human condition which made him grow "in wisdom and in stature, and in favor with God and man" (Lk. 2:52), [Jesus's] human awareness of his own mystery would also

---

[30] Arthur J. Serratelli, "Praying ad Orientem," *Catholic News Agency*, February 28, 2017, accessed June 4, 2017, http://www.catholic-newsagency.com/column/praying-ad-orientem-3713/.

have progressed to its fullest expression in his glorified humanity, there is no doubt that already in his historical existence Jesus was aware of his identity as the Son of God. John emphasizes this to the point of affirming that it was ultimately because of this awareness that Jesus was rejected and condemned: they sought to kill him "because he not only broke the Sabbath, but also called God his Father, making himself equal with God" (Jn 5:18). In Gethsemane and on Golgotha, Jesus's human awareness will be put to the supreme test. But not even the drama of his Passion and death will be able to shake his serene certainty of being the Son of the heavenly Father.[31]

. . . The intensity of the episode of the agony in the Garden passes before our eyes. Oppressed by foreknowledge of the trials that await him, and alone before the Father, Jesus cries out to him in his habitual and affectionate expression of trust: "Abba, Father." He asks him to take away, if possible, the cup of suffering. But the Father seems not to want to heed the Son's cry. In order to bring man back to the Father's face, Jesus not only had to take on the face of man, but had to burden himself with the "face" of sin. "For our sake he made him to be sin who knew no sin, so that in him we might become the righteousness of God" (2 Cor 5:21).[32]

. . . At the very moment when he identifies with our sin, "abandoned" by the Father, he "abandons" himself into the hands of the Father. His eyes remain fixed on the Father. Precisely because of the knowledge and experience of the Father which he alone has, even at this moment of darkness he sees clearly the gravity of sin and suffers because of it. He alone, who sees the Father and rejoices fully in him, can understand completely what it means to resist the Father's love by sin. More than an experience

---

[31] Pope John Paul II, *Novo Millennio Ineunte* (January 6, 2001), §24, accessed June 4, 2016, https://w2.vatican.va/content/john-paul-ii/en/apost_letters/2001/documents/hf_jp-ii_apl_20010106_novo-millennio-ineunte.html.

[32] Ibid., §25.

of physical pain, his Passion is an agonizing suffering of the soul. Theological tradition has not failed to ask how Jesus could possibly experience at one and the same time his profound unity with the Father, by its very nature a source of joy and happiness, and an agony that goes all the way to his final cry of abandonment. The simultaneous presence of these two seemingly irreconcilable aspects is rooted in the fathomless depths of the hypostatic union.[33]

Clearly, then, it would be improper to say that, at his agony and at the moment of his crying out in the words of Psalm 22 on the Cross, Jesus was wavering in his salvific resolve, wrestling with the "decision"[34] to carry out his mission, or even worse, doubting or denying the presence of God in his life. Jesus, in his divinity and humanity, knew God better than that. But here, at these dark moments, he also knew in a preeminent way the gravity of sin, and this knowledge caused him to suffer bitterly in his humanity.

POINTS FOR REFLECTION

• At the outset of his brilliant commentary on the Our Father, Kilgallen offers this powerful observation, with which I completely agree:

> It is a constant source of wonderment that the Being we know as the one and true God is revealed to us by Jesus as Father, and that God wants to be known this way. For thousands of years, human beings more easily have understood God as Power, Authority, Lord, awesome Master, and Judge, than they have accepted him as Father in the living out of their lives with their God. Yet this is the title that Jesus knew is best with which to address God, . . . [and] he asks the Christian to apply to God all the positive meaning [that] human beings attach to this figure. The Christian thus imitates

---

[33] Ibid., §26.
[34] Murphy-O'Connor, *The Holy Land*, 146.

Jesus who rarely spoke of God as anyone but Father, and never addressed God directly by any other name.[35]

Wow! The Lord of heaven and earth is first and foremost "Father" (Mt 11:25), which is the only way that Jesus ever addressed God! As he has done, so should we! And not only that, we should also pray for those who have a hard time relating to God as Father, because either they have no father of their own or they have a very broken one. The Eleona Church would be a good place to pray an Our Father or two for them.

- Luke conveys our Lord's weeping as a reaction to the lack of repentance from sins committed on the part of the Jewish people of Jerusalem: "You did not recognize the day of your visitation" (19:44). We cannot fail to hear in these words of Jesus the many pleas for return from sinful ways directed at Jerusalem by Isaiah, Jeremiah, and other prophets. "Sobering," indeed, "are the words of John's first chapter: 'He came to his own, and his own received him not' (Jn 1:11)."[36] In this light, you might benefit from asking yourself: is there some sin for which I am not adequately repentant—some sin perhaps that I know I should not commit, and even tell myself that I do not want to commit, but cannot find it within myself fully to shake that shred of desire to commit again? Let us pray for the grace of true contrition.

Especially For Seminarians

- Frequent prayers on the part of a priest for the fatherless, such as saying the Our Father, are an eminent way in which we can exercise our spiritual paternity—that is, praying for the begetting of new life, freedom, and hope within a soul, especially those entrusted to our care and for whom our fatherly hearts should be "moved to compassion" (Mt 9:36).

---

[35] Kilgallen, *New Testament Guide*, 154–55.
[36] Ibid., 161.

MOUNT ZION

*When they entered the city, they went to the upper room
where they were staying, Peter and John and James and
Andrew, Philip and Thomas, Bartholomew and Matthew,
James son of Alphaeus, Simon the Zealot, and Judas son
of James. All these devoted themselves with one accord to
prayer, together with some women, and Mary the mother
of Jesus, and his brothers.*

(Acts 1:13–15)

Nowadays, the term "Mount Zion" refers to the part of the western hill that extends beyond the south wall of the Old City and is bordered by the Hinnom Valley to the west and south and by the Tyropoeon Valley to the east. In Old Testament times, Zion was the eastern hill,[1] which was the location of the Jebusite stronghold that David captured and which became known as the City of David (2 Sam 5:7). The name changed in the fourth century AD, presumably on the basis of such passages as Micah 3:12 (NABRE):

> Zion shall be plowed like a field,
> and Jerusalem reduced to rubble,
> And the mount of the temple
> to a forest ridge

---

[1] As has been mentioned in the previous chapter, which can be seen well from St. Peter in Gallicantu, sits on the slope of the western hill, and is separated from the eastern hill by the Tyropoeon Valley.

(though the prophet probably was speaking about the selfsame area under three different names[2]). Christians like the Bordeaux pilgrim (AD 333) understood the prophecy as a description of the two hills on which Jerusalem is built, such that (working backwards through the citation), if the eastern hill were the Temple Mount, then Zion had to be the western hill.[3]

A model, located in the Israeli Museum, of the narrow, eastern hill of Jerusalem in the time of King Solomon. Above the small, eastern hill stands Solomon's Temple. Below Solomon's Temple stood David's palace, which he built on the narrow, eastern hill after he seized the Jebusite stronghold there (2 Sam 5:7).

It is possible that the transfer of the name "Zion" to the western hill—and, hence, the Christian appropriation of that name—occurred in the early second century AD. Coins from the Bar Kokhba rebellion (AD 132–125), though they take their form and inscription from the coins of the Hasmonean period and the first revolt against Rome (AD 70), make a curious replacement in their inscription: rather than having written on them "Salvation of Zion" or "Freedom of Zion" (as coins read beforehand), these later coins replaced "Zion" with "Jerusalem." Why the change? Well, it could be that the rebels saw that a new heretical group (in their eyes) of Jewish Christians (who

---

[2]   Such parallelism is common in Hebrew poetry and prophecies. Here, this would mean to say that Micah meant "Zion," "Jerusalem," and "the mount of the temple" to refer to the same place.

[3]   Murphy-O'Connor, *The Holy Land*, 115.

did not participate in the revolt) had come to usurp the name "Zion," and the rebels, spiteful of those Christians, sought to distance themselves from them.[4]

Why, you might ask, is this area of Zion outside of the (current) city walls? This is a fair question, given that this part of the city was, indeed, first brought within Jerusalem's walls in the second century BC.[5] As it turns out, the walls surrounding this area were torn down and rebuilt over the millennia for bellicose reasons, until Suliman the Magnificent, in the sixteenth century, decided to include this territory within Jerusalem's walls, finally and forever. However, there happened a hiccup in his plans. His architects wanted to make the Franciscans pay for the extension that would encompass their property there, which included the Cenacle/Upper Room. The friars, of course, had no money, and so the Cenacle and its environs were left outside of the walls. Suliman was furious; he wanted his wall to honor and protect all the places of popular devotion. So he executed his architects. However, as Murphy-O'Connor

A view of both the western and eastern hills of old Jerusalem from the Mount of Olives. The start of the cluster of houses in the bottom left, just above the steep descent of the valley, is the eastern hill, which is also known as the City of David, who established this place as the center of his kingdom. Above the cluster of houses and across the street stands a round church with a bell tower. This church—the Dormition Abbey—stands on the western hill, which is also known as Mount Zion.

---

[4]   Pixner, *Paths of the Messiah*, 338.
[5]   Murphy-O'Connor, *The Holy Land*, 15.

adroitly remarks: "The depredations of modern urban development reveal more clearly every day that no one ever gave Jerusalem a finer gift" than Zion's exclusion from the Old City of Jerusalem.[6] *O felix culpa!*[7]

It was on this hill that the first Christian community gathered together after the Ascension. It is likely that this area became an epicenter for early Christianity, as is suggested by the name of the major church built here: first the Upper Church of the Apostles, which was a fourth-century AD reconstruction of an earlier "Little Church of God," per Epiphanius (AD 315–403), and then "Zion, Mother of all the Churches."[8]

St. Peter in Gallicantu

This church's name comes from the Latin words *gallus* and *cantare* and means, quite literally, the cockcrow. Here, the infamous rooster sang twice upon the third denial of Jesus on the part of Peter,[9] who was waiting outside the house of Caiaphas within earshot of Jesus's trial before the Sanhedrin (Mk 14:53–72). The low-

The church of St. Peter in Gallicantu.

6   Ibid., 12.

7   This term is taken from the Easter Exultet, which at one point reads: "O *happy fault* . . . O truly necessary sin of Adam, which won for us so great a redeemer!" The phrase conveys the wonder that believers in Jesus experience when they realize that it was only on account of something so bad as our sin that we have been able to be redeemed and know Jesus as our Redeemer. In this way, the "fault" of sin becomes a "happy" or "fortunate" one, because it in a way made this Easter joy of ours even possible!

8   Ibid., 117.

9   Predicted by our Lord in Mark 14:27–30 and occurring in Mark 14:66–72.

A statue commemorating Peter's triple denial of Jesus.

SCRIPTURE ON SITE:
Acts 3:1-10

est level of this church houses what is likely the pit in which Jesus spent the night, imprisoned (see Mk 15:1).

Some doubt the historical veracity of the assertions just made. I, however, consider it tenable. Murphy-O'Connor, perhaps unsurprisingly one of the doubters, admits that this property "enshrines most interesting rock-cut structures, cellars, cisterns, and stables, dating to the Herodian period (37 BC–AD 70)," and that, moreover, "beside the church runs an ancient stepped way from the top of the hill down the valley to Siloam." He even proffers that "enough traces have been found to demonstrate the existence of a monastic church of the 6th century AD, which a very late document (AD 675) identifies as the place where Peter went after his betrayal; 'he went out and wept bitterly.'" Lastly, he notes that the same text "places Jesus's confrontation with Caiaphas, and Peter's denial, in the immediate vicinity of the church of Zion." However, Murphy-O'Connor thinks that "it is much more likely that the house of the high priest was at the top of the hill," where "luxurious houses of the Herodian period" have been found in the Armenian property (another purported house of Caiaphas is exhibited here).[10]

---

[10] Murphy-O'Connor, *The Holy Land*, 119. The ancient steps he describes beside the church that go down to the valley of Siloam are visible, and at time walkable, to this day. They are the steps up which Jesus ascended on Holy Thursday evening after his arrest.

Pixner, though, offers good arguments for why this *other* candidate for the house of Caiaphas should not be believed and why the current, Gallicantu church should be preferred. To begin, we note that the Israeli archaeologists discovered, in the debris of those magnificent, Herodian buildings, a series of very fine frescoes that contained an unusual characteristic: representations of birds, which depiction was an offense against the

Mosaic prohibition of animal illustrations (Ex 20:4). It would be "astonishing," indeed, to find such a violation of the Torah in the house of a high priest of Jerusalem at the time of Jesus; even Herod the Great, who was not scrupulous in his religious observance, avoided such representations in his buildings and palaces, such as Masada.[11]

Furthermore, a few archaeological features of the Gallicantu church suggest that it is more likely the location for the events of Mark 14 in the house of Caiaphas. A fragment of a door lintel there was discovered to have inscribed on it the Aramaic word *qorban*—"offering", as in Mark 7:11—which would befit a place that once was the high

Upward view from the pit underneath the House of Caiaphas, in which Jesus spent the night after his arrest.

priest's house.[12] Moreover, the ancient staircase just outside of the church leading down to the Siloam Pool proves that the site of the Gallicantu church corresponds to a certain church[13] that is seen on the Madaba Mosaic to be the House of Caiaphas.[14]

---

[11] Pixner, *Paths of the Messiah*, 255–57.

[12] Ibid., 259.

[13] See the Byzantine Way of the Cross according to the Madaba Mosaic Map on the following page from p. 301 of Pixner's work. No. 5 stands for the staircase to Siloam, and number 7 stands for St. Peter in Gallicantu/Caiaphas's house.

[14] Ibid., 260.

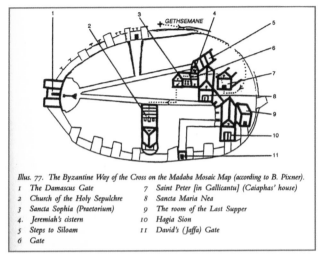

Illus. 77. The Byzantine Way of the Cross on the Madaba Mosaic Map (according to B. Pixner).

1	*The Damascus Gate*	*7*	*Saint Peter [in Gallicantu] (Caiaphas' house)*
2	*Church of the Holy Sepulchre*	*8*	*Sancta Maria Nea*
3	*Sancta Sophia (Praetorium)*	*9*	*The room of the Last Supper*
4	*Jeremiah's cistern*	*10*	*Hagia Sion*
5	*Steps to Siloam*	*11*	*David's (Jaffa) Gate*
6	*Gate*		

The Byzantine Way of the Cross on the Madaba Mosaic Map (p. 301, illustration 77, in Bargil Pixner, *Weges des Messias*, Brunnen Verlag, 1991, www.brunnen-verlag.com).

For these reasons, I think it is safe to say that St. Peter in Gallicantu stands on what used to be the House of Caiaphas, where Jesus was brought under arrest late Holy Thursday evening, was beaten and ridiculed, and was betrayed by Peter to the crow of a rooster.

You should make sure not to miss the fantastic panoramic view just uphill from the church, at which vista you can see not only the City of David—that is, the eastern hill of Jerusalem and the original Zion, where David established his kingdom—but also the three valleys that shaped Jerusalem: the Kidron, the Tyropoeon, and the Hinnom.

The last of these valleys has a notorious history within the Bible. Mentioned in Joshua 15:8 as one of the boundaries of Judah's portion of the Promised Land, it is called either the Valley of the Son of Hinnom (literally in Hebrew: *ge-ben-Hinnom*) or simply the Valley of Hinnom (*ge-Hinnom*), the latter of which was transliterated into the Greek of the Septuagint as *Gehennah*. From the first century AD on, both Christians[15] and

---

[15] "Gehennah of fire" (Mt 5:22).

Jews[16] use it as the name of the place of eternal punishment. How did such a beautiful, sunlit valley give its name to hell? Murphy-O'Connor explains:

> Symbolic values were most important. The bottom of the Hinnom valley is the lowest point of the city, the antithesis of the Temple Mount. If the latter evoked the Mountain of the Lord (Is 2:3), the former symbolized Sheol, the underworld (Amos 9:2), the kingdom of Death (Hab 2:5), the universal grave to which all individual tombs gave entrance. The end of the valley was also the beginning of the desert, which was both the continuation of the primeval chaos and the home of the demons, in particular Azazel (Lev 16:10). . . .
>
> The heinous crimes committed in the Hinnom valley were also a factor. It was the place of the Topheth ("the Burner"), where children were burnt alive in sacrifice to the god Moloch (2 Kings 23:10). Isaiah prophesized that Moloch—and by implication his adherents—would be burnt there (30:33; 33:14), a theme repeated by Jeremiah (7:31–33). "The furnace of Gehenna shall be made manifest, and over against it the Paradise of delight" (4 Ezra 7:36).[17]

Tomb of David

Nestled adjacent to the Dormition Abbey church, we find the so-called Tomb of David, where pious Jews keep constant, prayerful vigil. It is most certain, however, that this is not the actual tomb of the king; after all, David was buried in his city on the eastern hill (1 Kings 2:10), not the western hill. With that text in mind, and understanding the transfer of the term "Zion" from the eastern to the western hill, we can hence approach the so-called Tomb of David with warranted suspicion. The cenotaph, or tomb, of David that we see comes from the Crusader period. It got here on the western hill because, in the Byzantine period, David and James—the Jewish and Christian, respectively, *founders* of Jerusalem (see Acts 12:17; 15:13; and 21:18)—were the

---

[16] "Gehenna, the pit of destruction," (Mishnah, Aboth 5:19 [cited in Murphy-O'Connor, *The Holy Land*, 137]).

[17] Murphy-O'Connor, *The Holy Land*, 137.

focus of a liturgical celebration in the Church of Mount Zion. Eventually, this devotion gave rise to the popular belief that the two were both buried here on Mount Zion.[18]

More interesting than the cenotaph are the walls behind it and the floors beneath it. Crusader, Byzantine, and Roman floors lie underneath the present ground level of the Tomb of David. It is very possible that the ground level of this room is that of the Little Church of God mentioned by Epiphanius as having been in existence on Mount Zion in AD 130 and then built over so as to construct the church known as Hagia Sion. Moreover, when we consider the fact that this revered site was, in the second century AD, dangerous and difficult to access, we can assume that, if Christans "continued to frequent the site, it must have been of great importance in the previous century,"[19] and so it is quite likely the place of that Little Church of God.

It is quite possible, if not very likely, that this room was ini-

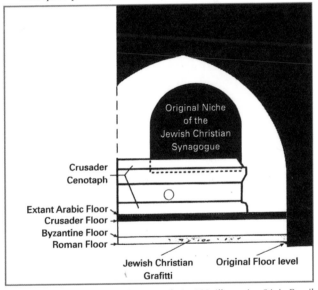

Floor levels beneath David's cenotaph (p. 330, illustration 84, in Bargil Pixner, *Weges des Messias*, Brunnen Verlag, 1991, www.brunnen-verlag.com).

---

[18] Ibid., 116–17.
[19] Ibid., 117.

tially a Jewish-Christian synagogue, where the first believers and their fellow Jewish converts met and prayed. In the early Church, there co-existed two distinct groups, or kinds, of faithful: Jewish Christians, who came to the faith from Judaism, and Gentile Christians, who came to the faith from outside of Judaism.[20] The very first Christians, of course, were "exclusively" Jews who "did not think of themselves as having left Orthodox Judaism."[21] Hence, initially, the place for Jewish-Christian services was called a synagogue, which is a Hellenization of the Hebrew term for meeting-hall (*knesset*), at which the Jews would gather to pray.[22] This early church on Zion, therefore, was probably a Jewish-Christian synagogue.

How can we know this? Firstly, note the alignment of this room. The niche in the wall behind the cenotaph is not oriented northeast in the direction of the former Temple, as many Jewish synagogues throughout ancient Israel were, but rather to the north—that is, precisely toward the Church of the Holy Sepulcher, which was the place of Jesus's crucifixion on Golgatha and of Jesus's tomb. This choice of orientation was quite likely intentional: "It seems logical that Jewish Christians selected an orientation to replace the traditional Jewish orientation towards the Temple, particularly after its destruction, with a new focus, i.e., the place of Jesus's burial and Resurrection."[23] That such a re-orientation occurred is also seen in the construction of the Martyrion church, built by Constantine in AD 326, which was itself oriented not toward the east but rather towards Christ's tomb.[24]

Secondly, we note a series of graffiti written on the plaster of the original wall of the synagogue-church from the Roman period. One *graffito* has the initials of Greek words that might be translated as: "Conquer, Savior, mercy." Another *graffito* has

---

[20] That there actually were two such groups is attested by the fact that the first Christian council, held in Jerusalem (Acts 15:1–29), was convened in order to ask if Gentile converts needed to become Jewish first before receiving the Christian faith.

[21] Pixner, *Paths of the Messiah*, 327.

[22] In order to differentiate themselves from Jewish Christians, Gentile Christians called their gatherings *ekklesia*. Only later were Christian assembly places called *churches*, from the Greek *kyriake* (ibid., 328).

[23] Ibid., 329–30.

[24] Ibid., 330.

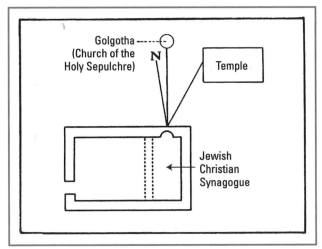

Orientation of the Jewish-Christian synagogue (p. 327, illustration 82, in Bargil Pixner, *Weges des Messias*, Brunnen Verlag, 1991, www.brunnen-verlag.com).

letters that can be rendered: "O Jesus, that I may live, O Lord of the autocrat." "Autocrat" could refer to David,[25] which would make the *graffito* claim that Jesus is the Lord of David,[26] which figure, of course, the *Jewish*-Christians held very dear, even and especially in their sacred worship space.

Thirdly, the works of a number of later ecclesiastical figures imply that this building was a Jewish-Christian place of worship—and exclusively *Jewish*-Christian, at that. The most telling is the witness of Cyril, who would later become bishop of Jerusalem. In 348, just a few years after Constantine made Christianity a legal religion in Rome, Cyril held a series of famous catecheses in the newly built Church of the Holy Sepulcher. During his sixteenth catechesis, which was about the Holy Spirit, he remarked that it would be more suitable to discuss this topic at the place where the Spirit descended onto the first Christians—that is, "in the Upper Church of the Apostles." This statement has been tak-

---

[25] See Matthew 22:43–44 and Psalm 110:1 (NABRE):
   The Lord says to my lord:
   "Sit at my right hand."
[26] Ibid., 331.

en by many to mean that Cyril, who was a presbyter of the Gentile Christian Church, was lamenting the fact that he could not go to Zion to preach in the church there, known as the Church of the Apostles, which was probably a Jewish-Christian synagogue in the exclusive control of that community.[27]

Cenacle

Within the same building complex as the so-called Tomb of David, you will find the Cenacle, which is thought by many to be the famous "Upper Room" where occurred both the Last Supper (Mk 14:15) and the event of Pentecost (Acts 1:13; 2:1). However, not a few scholars doubt that the Last Supper happened here. They point to the fact that this tradition is first attested only in the early fifth century and "appears to be a derivation from the better supported tradition which located on Mount Zion the

The famous Upper Room in which likely both Jesus celebrated the Last Supper with his disciples and the Holy Spirit descended on them at Pentecost.

---

[27] Ibid., 348. As mentioned earlier, the Jewish and Gentile Christians were not recognized until close to the year 400. See also the archeological history section of the chapter on Capernaum in part I (Galilee) above.

descent of the Spirit on the apostles at Pentecost," a location identified by Cyril of Jerusalem before 348.[28] Moreover, they point out the fact that, in Luke, different words are used for the place where the disciples gathered for the Last Supper (*anagaion*; Lk 22:12) and for the place where they found themselves at the moment of the Descent of the Holy Spirit (*uperōon*, Acts 1:13). We might expect, based on Luke's precision in recounting and ordering the events of the early Church's life (Lk 1:1–4), to see him use the same words here, had those events happened in the same room. For these reasons, many scholars, hesitating to identify the upper room of Pentecost with the upper room of the Last Supper, assert that it is likely that Pentecost happened in the current space, but not the Last Supper.[29]

However, another consideration leads me to give more credence to the possibility of it being the same place—even though, to be sure, in the end, I do not believe that we can be 100 percent certain based on the evidence we have. We find that Epiphanius, again in the fourth century AD, at one point writes: "For the fulfillment of the Passover, Jesus went on the mountain (*eis to opos*), where he ate the Passover, after he had been in such demand, as he said [Luke 22:15]. There he ate the Passover meal together with his disciples. He carried it out not any differently than them [the Jews?], in order also in this 'not to dissolve the law, but to fulfill it' [Matt. 5:17]."[30] The phrase "on the mountain" is key one. From all four Gospels, it is clear that Jesus took the Last Supper within Jerusalem: in the Synoptic Gospels (Mt 26:18; Mk 14:13; Lk 22:10), he sends two disciples *into* the city to find a suitable place, and in John (18:1), he departs with his disciples *from* their farewell meal to the other side of the Kidron Valley to the Mount of Olives, which means that they were somewhere in the city beforehand. So, if Epiphanius writes that Jesus went "on *the* mountain" for the Last Supper, then that can refer only to Mount Zion, which was, at the time, the top of Jerusalem's western hill. Moreover, lastly, Epiphanius also reported that, in AD 130–131, Emperor Hadrian visited

---

[28] Murphy-O'Connor, *The Holy Land*, 118.

[29] Murphy-O'Connor says that it was simply "natural to assume" that this upper room was "the same one in which Jesus ate his last meal with his disciples" (ibid).

[30] Pixner, *Paths of the Messiah*, 251.

Zion and discovered a church built there at the site of the Upper Room of the Pentecost event in Acts 1:13.[31]

So, at the end of the day, I think we can say the following: this is likely the place where the Holy Spirit descended upon the apostles and Mary—per the witness of Epihanius of Salamis and Cyril of Jerusalem, regarding Hadrian—and there is a tradition attested as early as the time of Epiphanius (fourth century AD) which suggests that the Last Supper happened here, too, or at least nearby on Mount Zion.

Much more interesting than such a historical debate, however, is the meaning of the Pentecost event and the Last Supper. First, let us pause and read these accounts.

SCRIPTURE ON SITE:

Luke 22:14-23
Acts 1:13-14
Acts 2:1-13

To begin, we can note that many early Christian writers saw, in the apostolic aftermath of the Pentecost event, a fulfilling of the prophecy of Isaiah 2:2–3 (NABRE):

In days to come,
The mountain of the Lord's house
shall be established as the highest mountain
and raised above the hills.
All nations shall stream toward it.

Many peoples shall come and say:
"Come, let us go up to the Lord's mountain,
to the house of the God of Jacob,
That he may instruct us in his ways,
and we may walk in his paths."
For from Zion shall go forth instruction,
and the word of the Lord from Jerusalem.

The Christian reading of this text saw in the apostles's post-Pentecost preaching (Acts 2:5–13) the fulfillment of this passage. Here are the points of contact: Pentecost was the "day to come"; the "mountain . . . raised above the hills" was Mount Zion; and "from Zion shall go forth instruction [*torah*, in Hebrew]" refers to the disciples who, upon exiting the Upper

---

[31] Ibid.

Room, began to carry out the Lord's final instructions to them: "Go, make disciples of all nations, baptizing them . . . *teaching* them to observe all that I have commanded you" (Mt 28:19–20, emphasis mine). The fact is that, on and from Mount Zion, the teaching and *new Law* of the Gospel and its way of life went "out to all the earth" (Ps 19:5) in the persons whom Jesus sent (*apostellein*) for just such a purpose.[32]

Continuing on, with regard to the meaning of the Last Supper, we note how this account, in the Synoptic Gospels, presents Jesus for us to "behold"—as the priest says at Holy Mass before distributing Holy Communion—"the Lamb of God . . . who takes away the sins of the world." How do the Synoptic Gospels do this? By recording that the Last Supper coincided with the slaughter, in the Temple, of the Passover lambs on Preparation Day for the Jewish Passover (Mk 14:12). Hence, when Jesus offered the cup to his disciples, saying, "Drink from it, all of you, for this is my blood of the covenant, which will be shed on behalf of many for the forgiveness of sins" (Mt 26:27–28), he was showing himself to be *the* sacrificial Lamb who will be slain (Rev 5:12) and who alone would take away all of our sins in a way that the slaughter of the Passover lambs in the Temple could never do (Heb 10:1–10).

How do we know that the Synoptic Gospels made the Last Supper and the Temple slaughter of Passover lambs coincide temporally? It has to do with what Exodus 12 intended to happen on Preparation Day and on Passover Day. At the time of Jesus, "mainstream" (i.e., not Qumranite) Judaism applied the Passover rules of Exodus 12 in this way: the Passover lambs were slain in the Jerusalem Temple on the fourteenth day of the month of Nisan, which was Preparation Day.[33] Moreover, Exodus 12:8

---

[32] For an excellent explanation why Christian Pentecost occurred on the Jewish feast of Pentecost, see Kilgallen, *New Testament Guide*, 238–39. Recalling that the Jewish Pentecost was a feast of thanksgiving for the spring harvest, which crops had been planted fifty days beforehand, he writes: "Just as the death and Resurrection opened up the harvesting of souls, so the gift of the Spirit now makes that harvesting power complete." Also, for a wonderful exposition of Peter's Scripture-packed post-Pentecost preaching, especially in light of Joel 3:1–5, see ibid., 240–41.

[33] Per Josephus, Jews at the time applied the directive in Exodus 12:6 to slaughter them "during the evening twilight" (literally "between the two evenings") by sacrificing the spotless lambs between 3 p.m.

directs that the Passover lambs be eaten "on that night," which in context must mean *after* the sun went down over the lambs being sacrificed. Since sundown, according to the Jewish way of calculating liturgical days at the time of Jesus, would mark the beginning of a new day—which, in this case would hence be the 15th of Nissan—we see that the Passover lambs were eaten on Passover Day,[34] even perhaps as early as 5:01 p.m., immediately after the slaughtering of the lambs occurred.

Therefore, when we read that the disciples prepared the upper room for the Passover meal on the day in which Passover lambs were sacrificed in the Temple (Mk 14:12) and then that Jesus came to that upper room with the Twelve *when it was evening* (Mk 14:17), we can safely say that, according to the Synoptics, Jesus consumed with the disciples a Passover meal, which taken probably right around 5 p.m. on the cusp of both the end of Preparation Day and the beginning of Passover Day, showed him to be the true Lamb of God who takes away the sins of the world by his precious body and blood.

Issues Raised

Issue 1

Who exactly were these Jewish-Christians? What about their faith was distinct from Gentile Christians—that is to say, what were the Jewish elements thereof? These Christians kept the Sabbath and were, probably since the end of the first century, what we might call *Quartodecimans*, which means that they celebrated Christian Easter on the *fourteenth* of Nissan, following the Jewish calendar. They ate no pork, as well, and referred to each other not as Christians, but as Israelites, Nazarenes, or Ebionites. Some of them also were called *chiliastics*, as they expected a "thousand-year realm" (see Revelation 20:1–3). Based on such "outdated" beliefs and practices, St. Jerome accused them of damaging the unity of the Church.[35]

---

and 5 p.m. See *Wars of the Jews* 6.423, in *The Works of Josephus: Complete and Unabridged*, trans. William Whitson (Peabody, MA: Hendrickson, 1987), 749.

[34] John P. Meier, *A Marginal Jew: Rethinking the Historical Jesus*, vol. 1, Anchor Bible Reference Library (New York: Doubleday, 1991), 388.

[35] Pixner, *Paths of the Messiah*, 348.

It should be noted that Jewish and Gentile Christians began to be reconciled fully in Jerusalem by John II. This bishop of Jerusalem blessed the Jewish Christians's expiation altar (*kapporet*) located in the Byzantine church built, by Emperor Theodosius I (379–395), on top of this Jewish-Christian synagogue here on Mount Zion, which the larger church incorporated into the overall design. This blessing appropriately occurred on the great reconciliation day of the Jewish calendar (Yom Kippur) in 394. In this way, Bishop John II is remembered for absorbing Jewish Christians into the Gentile Christian Church.[36]

Issue 2

I have found that, in the Holy Land, some tour guides highlight uncertainty of historical identification. When they do this, pilgrims tend to lose heart and interest and, consequently, do not fully enter into the consideration of a real event in the life of Jesus and the early Church. For example, once a pilgrim realizes that the "Ecce Homo Arch" (see below) does not predate Hadrian (so, AD 120), and thus cannot be the place where Pilate declared "Behold the man" and then handed Jesus over to be crucified (Jn 19:5, 16), and that, hence, the current "Way of the Cross" is in fact only a twelfth-century Crusader tradition, that pilgrim might not engage the spirit of prayer that can happen there. For this reason, I think that it is always best first to affirm the traditional identification, and then to mention its disputability. For example, in the case of the Cenacle, we could say: "Here, based on a suggestive, fourth-century tradition, we believe the Last Supper happened. However . . ." Too many guides swiftly dismiss any historical association they deem tenuous—to the sure detriment of their pilgrims's religious experience. My pilgrims will hear me say the above, and then follow with, "And, if the Cenacle is not the place of the Last Supper, then that sacred meal took place in a similar upper room within a stone's throw," for the aforementioned reasons. Such a delivery, I believe, better fosters within the hearts of pilgrims the prayerful spirit of contact with Christ and the events on which is founded our faith, which we see here in the Holy Land is not only rooted in mystery, but is also *real*—that is, connected to *things*.

---

[36] Ibid., 349.

Issue 3

The discussion of the timing of the Last Supper can generate a certain perplexity when we read the Passion narratives of the Synoptic Gospels and then the Passion account of John's Gospel. Following their respective chronologies, we notice that the Synoptic Gospels place Jesus's Last Supper on the day "when they sacrificed the Passover lamb" (Mk 14:12), meaning Preparation Day for Passover (14 Nissan). John, on the other hand, appears to put not the Last Supper but rather the Crucifixion of the Lord on "Preparation Day" (Jn 19:14, 30–31). This scenario could create confusion, as it ostensibly makes the Synoptic Gospels and the Fourth Gospel stand in contradiction with regard to the dating of the Last Supper and of the Crucifixion of Jesus. Such also, by consequence, calls into question the exact nature of the meal that Jesus shared with his disciples immediately before his arrest: if, as the temporal indications in John seem, to many, to imply, the meal happened before Preparation Day, then it could not have been, in John, a Passover meal—as it clearly is in the Synoptics—but must rather have been some other kind of meal, like a "solemn farewell meal."[37]

However, I have found[38] that the two accounts are not, in fact, contradictory, either in terms of the (Passover) nature of the meal of the Last Supper or in the larger terms of evangelical chronology. In short, I argue that it is improper to read John in contradiction to the Synoptic (though many scholars do). Even though his account lacks the words of institution, John indeed

---

[37] Meier, *A Marginal Jew*, 388–89.

[38] I use "I" loosely and "have found" strictly. Until recently, my opinion on this matter followed in the long line of scholars who have concluded, or at least implied, that the Gospels's texts as we have them stand in contradiction to each other regarding the timing of the Last Supper. These scholars conjure up various means of explaining away this apparent disparity. Meier thinks they can be reconciled by recourse to redaction criticism, which would assert that John's account contains two levels of traditions, the earliest of which stands in continuity with the Synoptic Gospels's chronology. Ratzinger rightly critiques this theory as "artificial," but still accepts it "with a certain caution" (Joseph Ratzinger, *Jesus of Nazareth. Holy Week: From the Entrance into Jerusalem to the Resurrection* [New York: Image, 2011], 113), only then to build on it and advance his own theological explanation for the Last Supper scenario. I was then pointed to the work of Brant Pitre (cited further on), whose theory on the matter I found to be utterly convincing. I relay his argument in this section.

depicts *as a Passover dinner* the meal taken by Jesus and his disciples "before the feast of Passover" (Jn 13:1)—just as the Synoptics do. Furthermore, even though John seems to put the Crucifixion of the Lord on Preparation Day for the Passover (Jn 19:14, 30–31), he in fact does not do so. John's references to Preparation Day need not be read exclusively in reference to the day before the Passover—and, hence, need not be read in contradiction of the clear, temporal indicators of Passover Preparation Day provided in the Synoptics at the Last Supper (Mk 14:12).

Let us begin with the nature of the meal in John and proceed to the larger issue of the Gospels's chronology. For one, consider the disciples's reclined position in John 13:23–25. This position ritually conveyed the Hebrews's status as freemen—that is, no longer slaves in Egypt. This historical liberation fed into a potentially explosive expectation for Passover on the part of Jews at the time. By the time of Jesus, Jews had for many years harbored the hope for a certain political deliverance from their Roman overlords. At Passover, the Romans brought extra soldiers—and even the region's prefect, Pontius Pilate—from their usual station at Caesarea Maritime. All of this is to say that the reclined position, in John, of the disciples at table with Jesus quite adequately conveys the imagery and dynamic (historical, religious, and political) of the celebration of Passover. For two, consider other Jewish Passover dinner elements found in John's account: the dipping of the morsel by Jesus (Jn 13:26–27); the custom of giving something to the poor during a festal meal (Jn 13:29); and the last-minute purchase of something for the feast (Jn 13:29–30).[39] In light of these quite likely intentional elements in John's Gospel, we can say with considerable confidence that not only the Synoptic Gospels but *also* John intends to depict Jesus's final meal with his chosen band as a Passover meal.

Let us move on, then, to a consideration of chronology. We need to realize that we are dealing here, in the various Passion accounts (but especially in John), with an "inherent ambiguity" and "multiple meanings" of the term "Passover" in Jewish Scripture, Second Temple literature, and rabbinic tradition.

---

[39] Brant Pitre, *Jesus and the Last Supper* (Grand Rapids, MI: Eerdmans, 2015), 346.

Once we realize this, we will see that this semantic range can actually help to harmonize what would otherwise be a problematic discord between the chronologies of the Synoptic Gospels and John. In fact, "interpreters who see a contradiction between John and the Synoptic Gospels assume that on the three occasions when John uses the word 'Passover' (*pascha*) he is referring to the Passover lamb sacrificed on 14 Nisan."[40] It seems, though, that in these three instances in John 19, the evangelist is *not* referring to the Passover lamb, but rather to other things. When seen in this way, the "problem" of the seemingly contradictory chronologies of the Last Supper in the Synoptic Gospels and John effectively disappears.

In short, "Passover" could refer to:

1. the Passover lamb (sacrificed on 14 Nisan);
2. the Passover meal (during which the initial lamb was eaten, 15 Nisan);
3. the Passover peace offering (which could also be a lamb, and which was sacrificed and eaten during the seven-day Feast of Unleavened Bread, 15–21 Nisan);
4. or the Passover week (the entire seven days of the celebration, and sacrifice, of Passover, 15–21 Nisan).[41]

When applied to John's Gospel, these distinctions line up as follows: (i) by "Before the feast of Passover" (Jn 13:1—in reference to Jesus at table with his disciples) is intended the moments just before the Passover *meal* on 15 Nisan (so, definition 2, above); (ii) by "To eat the Passover" (Jn 18:28—in reference to the Jewish leaders not entering the praetorium so as not to become ritually unclean for the upcoming meal) is intended the Passover *peace offering* eaten on 15 Nisan (definition 3); and (iii) by "The preparation of Passover" (Jn 19:14—in reference to the hour in which Jesus was crucified) is intended the Friday of Passover *week* (definition 4).[42]

When these citations in John, which are usually taken to argue that John, in contradiction to the Synoptic Gospels, bumps up Jesus's last meal with his disciples to 13 Nisan (which makes

[40] Ibid., 331.
[41] Ibid.
[42] Ibid.

it not a Passover meal) and Jesus's crucifixion to 14 Nisan (which thus takes place during the Preparation Day lamb-slaughtering in the Temple, which is when the Synoptics say that Jesus ate the Passover meal at the Last Supper), are read in the manner outlined earlier, then "the contradiction between John and the Synoptic Gospels on the date of the Last Supper [becomes] more apparent than real, and [can be seen as] the result of a misconstrual of the linguistic and historical realities of the Passover festival in the Second Temple period."[43] The terminological-linguistic arguments, hence, of the Johannine contradictorians need not and, indeed, cannot stand, because other meanings that put John in harmony with the temporal indications of the Synoptic Gospels can also make perfect sense. Thus, the latter should be preferred as they respect the integrity of the Gospel text and its semantics and also prevent us from making claims about the Gospels that no Catholic scholar should claim.

Brant Pitre puts it bluntly: the "popular theory that John altered the chronology of Jesus's death in order to have Jesus's condemnation in 19:14 coincide with the noon sacrifice of the Passover lambs founders" on two facts. The first is the fact that John's Gospel "does not actually say anything about Jesus's dying at the same time that the Passover lambs were being sacrificed in the Temple," as is often presumed or asserted without evidence by scholars. While John tells us that Jesus was on the Cross at noon, the sixth hour (Jn 19:14), "*there does not appear to have ever been a noon sacrifice of Passover lambs,*" which were sacrificed, rather, between 3 p.m. and 5 p.m., per Josephus. Scholars, especially Johannine contradictorians, chronologically identify Jesus's death on "Preparation Day" in chapter 19 with the timing of the sacrifice of the Passover lambs in the Temple. They, perhaps unknowingly, harmonize John with the Synoptic account on this note, which is in fact the account that tells us that Jesus died at 3pm (Mt 27:46, Mk 15:34, Lk 23:44–46).[44]

The second fact on which this common conjecture founders is the fact that the phrase "preparation of Passover" (Jn

[43] Ibid., 332.

[44] Ibid., 330. The position advanced concerning such a shifting of the chronology by John is that it would manifestly depict, in an appealing way, the crucified Jesus as *the* Lamb of God who takes away the sins of the world.

19:14) does not refer, as the Johannine contradictorians would have it, to "the Preparation Day for the Passover" (that is, 14 Nisan), but rather to the "Friday of Passover week,"[45] which hence means preparation for the Sabbath, not preparation for the Passover meal. This usage is attested in Mark 15:42–43 ("since it was *Preparation*, that is, the day before the Sabbath, Joseph of Arimathea . . . "), and most tellingly in John 19:31 ("Since it was *Preparation*, in order to prevent the bodies from remaining on the cross *on the Sabbath* . . . the Jews asked Pilate that their legs might be broken, and that they might be taken away") and John 10:40 and 42 ("They took the body of Jesus and bound it in linen cloths with the spices. . . . So because of *the Preparation of the Jews*, as the tomb was close at hand, they laid Jesus there").

In these Johannine texts, the word "Preparation" (*paraskeue*), especially "the Preparation of the Jews," is simply a reference to the Jewish Friday[46] and, so, does not place John's Passion chronology at odds with that of the Synoptic Gospels with regard to what was happening on 14 Nisan (Preparation Day for the Passover meal). For this reason, John 19:14 should be translated not as "Preparation Day [for the Passover meal]" but rather "Friday of Passover week."[47] The former translation would put John at odds with the Synoptic Gospels, whereas the latter would line them up perfectly.

In summary, I conclude with Pitre's own recapitulation:

> When the chronological evidence in the Gospel of John is interpreted in its linguistic, literary, and historical contexts, there are good reasons for concluding that the date of the Last Supper in the Gospel of John and the synoptic gospels is basically the same: the account of Jesus's final meal begins on the afternoon of 14 Nisan, continues through the night of 15 Nisan, on which Jesus and his disciples celebrate a Passover meal together, and then concludes with the crucifixion of Jesus on 15 Nisan, the first day of the weeklong feast of Passover celebrated by the Jews in the city of Jerusalem, and the day before a

---

[45] Ibid., 337. This is definition 4, above.
[46] Ibid., 359.
[47] Ibid.

Sabbath which, in that year, coincided with the feast of the sheaf offering in the Temple (Nisan 16).[48]

Pitre's Passover hypothesis is especially laudable in that it respects both the Gospel text and the extra-biblical witnesses, Jewish and Christian.

POINTS FOR REFLECTION

- Considering the "coming" (Acts 2:2) of the Holy Spirit at Pentecost, you might ask yourself: have you ever found yourself praying for just that—that the Holy Spirit come? How wonderfully fructifying for personal prayer is the simple invocation: "Come Holy Spirit!" If you are stuck in prayer, if you seek a special outpouring of one of his Gifts, if you need the presence in your life of him who is our Paraclete, our comforter—invite him to come!

- We go to Mass so often that we perhaps—especially if the liturgy is celebrated in a banal way—lose an appreciation of just what is the Holy Sacrifice of the Mass: a re-presentation of Calvary, the act of obedience that won for us our salvation, reversing the curse of sin into which humanity fell with the sin of Adam. How much we have for which to be thankful after Mass—that we have been temporarily caught up into the heavenly liturgy, to the angelic voices with which we join our own in acclaiming Jesus as the thrice-holy God! Are you gratefully aware of this awesome mystery, or has the Mass become so habituated and routine that this fervor gets easily lost on you? If so, make it a point to offer after each Eucharist what has traditionally been called a "thanksgiving after Mass." Look up some old forms of it, if you wish (St. Thomas

---

[48] Ibid., 367. My only question regarding this "Passover Hypothesis" is this: Why did John not, if he intends (as I now see that he does) the final meal of Jesus with his disciples to be a true Passover meal, utilize, in the context of the meal initiated in chapter 13, any explicit either terminology of "preparation" or reference to the slaughtering of the lambs, as do the Synoptic Gospels (see Mk. 14:12)? Perhaps he does not have to do so, as the Passover imagery is conveyed in his account in other ways (see above).

Aquinas has a very lovely one!), and use them yourself. Allow this habit to reintroduce you to the glory and power of the Mass.

Especially For Seminarians

- When you, as a priest, are called upon to offer a spontaneous prayer with a group or an individual, call down the Holy Spirit, and what to say will be given to you (Lk 12:11–12).

- Developing a habit of offering a prayer of thanksgiving after Mass will serve your priesthood enormously, so that celebrating Mass does not become just another thing that you do every day. It is far too grand, too mysterious, too heavenly, to be only that—thanks be to God!

GOOD FRIDAY AND EASTER SUNDAY

So they took Jesus, and carrying the cross himself, he went out to what is called the Place of the Skull, in Hebrew, Golgotha. There they crucified him, and with him two others, one on either side, with Jesus in the middle. Pilate also had an inscription written and put on the cross. It read, "Jesus the Nazorean, the King of the Jews."

(John 19:16–19).

Now in the place where he had been crucified there was a garden, and in the garden a new tomb, in which no one had yet been buried. So they laid Jesus there because of the Jewish preparation day; for the tomb was close by.

(John 19:41–42)

Praetorium of Pilate

Three principal places have been offered, throughout history, as potential locations for the Praetorium of Pilate, which is where Jesus was handed over by the Roman prefect to be crucified (Jn 19:16):

1. the Temple fortress, which Herod the Great named "Antonia" after his Roman friend Marc Antony, and which sat just north of the Temple Mount;[1]
2. the old, Hasmonean kings's palace, at the southwest corner of the Temple complex; and
3. the upper palace, built by Herod in the middle of his reign in 23 BC in the area of today's Citadel by the Jaffa Gate.

A late Crusader tradition puts it in Antonia, from where the *Via Dolorosa* has been starting since around the twelfth century. The discovery of a nearby impressive limestone pavement, thought to be the "Stone Pavement" (*lithostrōtos*) of John 19:13 and resting under what was known as the "Ecce Homo" arch,[2] proved, however, to be a false discovery, as the pavement and arch there are dated to the time of Hadrian, around AD 135, which is obviously much later than the time of Jesus's death. It is certain that, at least by the eighth century, the Byzantine Christians located the Praetorium at the Church of St. Sophia somewhere near the Temple.[3] However, most scholars argue that "it is more probable that Pilate condemned Jesus to death on the other side of the city at the Citadel, the 'high point,' *Gabbatha* according to John 19:13," as Murphy-O'Connor writes:

> This was the palace of Herod where Pilate normally resided when he came up from Caesarea to ensure control during the great Jewish feasts (Philo, *Delegation to Gaius*, 38). According to the gospels, the trial took place on a platform (Mt 27:19) in the open (Lk 23:4; Jn 18:28). Such a structure existed at the palace in AD 66, as we know from what Josephus says of one of Pilate's successors: "Florus lodged at the palace, and on the following day had a platform placed in front of the building and took his seat; the chief priests, the nobles, and the most eminent citizens then presented themselves before the tri-

---

[1]   *Wars* 1.401 (Whitson, *Works*, 575).
[2]   The Latin of Pilate's words in John 19:5: "Behold the man!"
[3]   Murphy-O'Connor, *The Holy Land*, 37.

bunal" (War 2:301); as in the case of Jesus, the affair ended in crucifixion.[4]

However, on the other hand, a very suggestive case for the second scenario listed above—that is, the ancient, royal palace of the Hasmoneans—can be made. Pixner best makes this pitch, and his arguments consist in a very probable interpretation of the same historical (Roman) and biblical texts, as well as a convicting presentation and defense of Byzantine Christian sources paired with archaeological findings. The latter is most striking: "If the [pre-Byzantine and Byzantine] Christian community of Jerusalem retained a genuine memory about the place of Jesus's trial, then only the ancient Hasmonean palace is a possibility, and warrants further investigation."[5] It is most fitting that this location be considered, because those Byzantine Christian sources locate at this supposed place of the Praetorium the Church of St. Sophia, which was purportedly built over Pilate's tribunal so as to remind people how—as Sophronius of Jerusalem, in 635, dramatically captured the irony of the scene—when Jesus, about to be condemned, stood before Pontius Pilate, Godly Wisdom stood on trial before a terrestrial judge.[6] That so many scholars forthwith dismiss the Byzantine Christian witness as historically unreliable is the cold result of arrogant, reductive, Hegelian historicism; as J. R. R. Tolkien once wrote in a poem: "All that is gold does not glitter, not all those who wander are lost; *the old that is strong does not wither, deep roots are not reached by the frost.*"

SCRIPTURE ON SITE:
John 18:28–19:16

Let us read John's dramatic account of Jesus's trial before Pilate.

Firstly, what was the Hasmonean palace? There existed near the Temple a palace that served for over one hundred years as the royal residence of the Hasmoneans. In 40 BC, Herod the Great took this palace from the Hasmonean Hyrcanus II (63–40 BC), and after being recognized in 37 BC by the Romans as Jewish

---

[4] Ibid., 38.
[5] Pixner, *Paths of the Messiah*, 268.
[6] Ibid., 279.

king, he took up his residence in the royal palace, where Josephus tells us he lived until 23 BC.[7] Josephus also writes[8] that, here, Herod exercised judicial office, as when he uncovered a conspiracy against him by his mother-in-law Alexandra, who was probably angry that her son-in-law had killed his wife who was her daughter.[9] What we can note from this brief history is that, at this Hasmonean palace, Herod both resided *and* judged—that is, the palace had a juridical precedent before Rome took it over.

In 23 BC, Herod decided to build his own palace, complete with three towers, in the area of today's Jaffa Gate, so as to control the whole city. Here, Herod lived with his women and his large retinue.[10] However, it is likely that the lower, Hasmonean palace was not deserted upon this transfer of regal residence, but rather continued to be utilized for administrative purposes, similar to Herod's palace at Masada, where: "The so-called west palace built by the Hasmoneans served as an administrative building once Herod renovated it and built, on the opposite corner, a three-story palace for his residence. A similar division between living and administration seems also to have taken place in the Herodian palaces of Jericho and Caesarea Maritime (Acts 23:35, 24:2, 23)."[11] Those palaces resembled the Jerusalem one in adopting a particularly Pompeian style of architecture (peristyle, frescoed walls, etc.),[12] which suggests that they served similar purposes and were envisaged for the same use.

If this division between Herod's—and then Pilate's—living quarters (up in the Citadel by the Jaffa Gate) and administrative/juridical quarters (downhill near the southwest corner of the Temple) is accepted, even cautiously, then the details within certain biblical passages of the Passion can make sense, which would, in turn, bolster the argument that the Praetorium was actually in the old Herodian palace southwest of the Temple. If the trial of Jesus took place in this lower palace, then we can understand the remark made by Luke that Pilate "sent up [*anepempsen*] Jesus" (23:7) as an accused to Herod, who would have

---

[7]   Josephus, *Antiquities* 15.292 (Whitson, *Works*, 416).

[8]   Ibid., 15.286 (Whitson, *Works*, 416).

[9]   Pixner, *Paths of the Messiah*, 269.

[10]   Ibid.

[11]   Ibid., 270.

[12]   Ibid., 274.

been residing up at the Citadel. On the other hand, if the trial took place in a praetorium already up on the Citadel hilltop in the same complex as the royal residence, then this passage from Luke might make little sense—or, better, could make sense only if that verb in Luke 23:7 could be taken to mean simply *sent him upstairs*, which meaning seems unlikely, seeing as how the private and public doings of Herod had two different epicenters.

To be sure, this Scripture passage just cited could be taken either way in support of one or the other possible location of the Praetorium. So, too, can the historical event of Florus, mentioned earlier, which most take in support of the upper Herodian palace. I think, though, that this latter episode actually proves Pixner's case for the Hasmonean palace! The fact that the judgment throne had to be *brought* to the upper palace and set up there implies that it was not there beforehand—meaning, that that Citadel residence was not regularly used as a praetorium. In light of this consideration, it is reasonable to suspect that the Praetorium was at the lower palace, which had been used in the past (by Herod the Great) as a place of judgment.[13] Such a possibility is supported by the fact that most praetoria were located in the middle of the city, rather than—say—at a distance, as up on a hill away from the center of action.[14]

Despite the slightly ambiguous historical and biblical arguments, the case for this praetorial preference is buttressed by the extensive Byzantine witness, which surely seems to speak in Pixner's favor. The Good Friday procession along the Way of the Cross changed over time—see below—and did not include stops at the ruins of the Praetorium of Pilate or the House of Caiaphas at the time of Cyril and Egeria (AD 383). We can note, however, that, between 417 and 439, both of these places were in fact included in the procession. How do we know this? From an unlikely source—ancient lectionaries! Armenian lectionaries show that the Byzantine procession stopped at the "House of the High Priest" and then the "Palace of Pilate."[15] Further, the Georgian lectionary, which describes liturgical life in Jerusalem in the mid-fifth century, gives the names of churches at these two stations: Saint Peter (House of Caiaphas) and Saint Sophia (Prae-

---

[13] Ibid., 272.

[14] Ibid., 291.

[15] Ibid., 278.

torium of Pilate), which churches were likely built around 450 by Empress Eudocia. Older still is the report of Peter the Iberian, who *descended* from the Church of the Holy Sepulcher down the Tyropoeon Valley to the church called Pilate, which was soon thereafter (per an AD 510 breviary) renamed *Hagia Sophia*.[16]

Where was this Byzantine, Praetorium Church located? It had to be near the house of Caiaphas, because the Book of Theodosius from AD 530 says: "From the house of Caiaphas up to the Praetorium of Pilate, there are nearly 100 (double) steps. Here is the Church of Holy Wisdom."[17] The lower Hasmonean palace is, of course, just such a distance from the house of Caiaphas! Moreover, and more exactly, the location of the great Sancta Maria Nea Church, built by Emperor Justinian, secures this location of the Praetorium/Holy Wisdom Church. After the grand, Marian church was dedicated in 543, it always gets mentioned together with the Holy Wisdom Church,[18] which of course suggests the close proximity of the two—a proximity that can be noted in the Madaba mosaic map.[19] The witness of the Pilgrim of Piacenza seals the deal: "We came [from Zion] to the basilica of Sancta Maria [Nea] . . . and we prayed in the Praetorium, where the Lord was condemned, and where the basilica of the Sancta Sophia is; opposite the ruins of the temple of Solomon, under the road, water flows down to the source of Siloam."[20] Based on this description and the other Byzantine witnesses, it seems "likely"[21] that the Praetorium of Pilate, where Jesus was condemned to die and where he took up the Cross for the salvation of the world, was to be found in the complex of the lower Hasmonean palace near the southwestern corner of the Jewish Temple complex.

Certainly, more archaeological work on this Hasmonean palace needs to be done before we can posit a certain conclusion about the Praetorium's location, but in the absence of more definitive historical indications, I am partial to the preferential option that Pixner affords the tradition, and especially to the integrity of the Byzantine Christian witness. The memory of the

---

[16] Ibid., 279.
[17] Ibid.
[18] Ibid., 281.
[19] Ibid., 282.
[20] Ibid., 284.
[21] Ibid., 287.

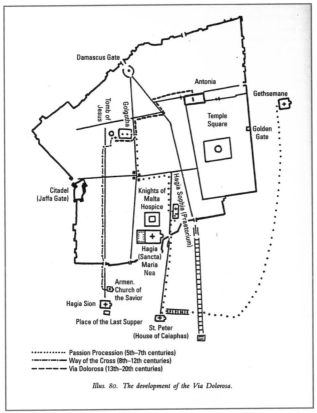

Illus. 80. The development of the Via Dolorosa.

The development of the *Via Dolorosa* (p. 312, illustration 80, in Bargil Pixner, *Weges des Messias*, Brunnen Verlag, 1991, www.brunnen-verlag.com).

early Church and its preservation in the Byzantine period should not be so quickly dismissed as dubiously rooted in real history or merely fanciful. In some cases, we need to be both "cunning as serpents" and, even more so, "meek as doves" (Mt. 10:16), trusting in the good and competent faith of those (Byzantine Christians) who precede us.

Way of the Cross

In the (above) illustration, one can see historical development of the *Via Crucis* (Way of the Cross) into the path that it currently takes, following its fixation in the eighteenth century.[22] On Holy Thursday night, early Byzantine pilgrims used to process from the Eleona Church atop the Mount of Olives to Calvary. From Gethsemane, the way went around the city to the south, to the house of Caiaphas on Mount Zion, then on to the Praetorium of Pilate at St. Sophia,[23] and finally on to the Holy Sepulcher. After the Christian community had lost the real Praetorium of Pilate with the Sophia Church to the invading Persians in 614 and then to the Umayyad Muslims in 638, the Praetorium relocated to Mount Zion at the location of the Armenian Church of the Savior, just north of the present-day Dormition Abbey. Though this arrangement of places was originally considered "provisional"— since Muslim areas of the city were, in that time, off-limits to Christians—it was regarded by later Crusaders as final.[24]

Still, not all Christian Crusaders were happy with the improbable location for the Praetorium of Pilate on Mount Zion. So, in 1172, the knight Theodoric "suggested another possibility: the ruins of the Antonia Fortress, near the Jerusalem headquarters of the Knights Templar at the north end of the Temple Mount." This "discovery, convinced an increasing number

The pilgrimage Way of the Cross route that the Crusaders developed in the late eleventh century.

---

[22] A number of stations (1, 4, 5, and 8) trace their present location only to the nineteenth century.

[23] Murphy-O'Connor, *The Holy Land*, 37. Murphy-O'Connor only indirectly admits that this church was believed to be situated above the Praetorium of Pilate, "somewhere near the Temple." He rarely gives credit to any of Pixner's contributions. Murphy-O'Connor's book is certainly one of the best for information, but often comes across as arrogant, and otherwise quite skeptical and critical.

[24] Pixner, *Paths of the Messiah*, 311.

of Christians,"[25] and the tradition that they established has held until this day, in which the weekly devotional Way of the Cross begins just outside of the Church of the Flagellation, where the old Antonia Fortress once stood.

So, it is very unlikely that the current *Via Crucis* follows the actual path of Jesus to Calvary. We can comfortably assert this on the basis of archaeology[26] and history—that is, the historical fact that the current trek goes back only to the days of the Crusaders, who crafted the Way of the Cross according to historical exigencies and perhaps contemporary fancies. Should we, then, even bother doing it as a devotional? Absolutely! For one, the closer that you get to Calvary, the more closely your path will merge with what is most likely to be Christ's actual path. For two, this devotional, which weaves through and stops in spots of great commotion on the streets of the Old City, will give you a sense of the chaos that Jesus surely encountered on his way bearing the Cross to Calvary. For three, doing such a public prayer is a great group witness to our faith in Jesus and our love for the wood of the Cross, "on which hung the Savior of the world"—as we chant aloud during the beginning of Good Friday's liturgy.

Church of the Holy Sepulcher

The importance of the Church of the Holy Sepulcher for the Christian cannot be understated. In it are contained the actual locations of two of the key events of the life of Jesus—and hence, of our salvation history and identity as believers: Calvary, where our Savior died on Good Friday, and the tomb, where our Savior was first buried and then rose victorious over sin and death on Easter Sunday. Here, we are able, in a preeminent way, to literally get *in touch* with our faith and the principle mysteries thereof. Thank you, Father, for the Incarnation, death, and Resurrection of your Son!

For all the sure excitement of being able to see, touch, and pray at these holy places, one's experience of this church in its

SCRIPTURE ON SITE:
John 19:16-37
John 19:38-20:18
Luke 23:50-24:12

---

[25] Ibid., 311.
[26] That is, the "Ecce Homo" arch dating only to the time of Hadrian, AD 135.

The dome mosaic above the old, Crusader nave of the Church of
the Holy Sepulcher.

actual state might likely be a mixture of joy beyond words and,
frankly, disappointment. Murphy-O'Connor well describes this
melancholic medley:

> One expects the central shrine of Christendom to stand
> out in majestic isolation, but anonymous buildings cling
> to it like barnacles. One looks for numinous light, but it
> is dark and cramped. One hopes for peace, but the ear is
> assailed by a cacophony of warring chants. One desires
> holiness, only to encounter a jealous possessiveness: the
> six groups of occupants—Latin Catholics, Greek Ortho-
> dox, Armenian Orthodox, Syrians, Copts, Ethiopians—
> watch one another suspiciously for any infringement of
> rights. The frailty of humanity is nowhere more apparent
> than here; it epitomizes the human condition. The empty
> who come to be filled will leave desolate; [however,] those
> who permit the church to question them may begin to
> understand why hundreds of thousands thought it worth-
> while to risk death or slavery in order to pray here.[27]

---

[27] Murphy-O'Connor, *The Holy Land*, 49.

Indeed, much of the basilica could seriously taint a pilgrim's naïve expectation of beholding therein a glorious church. However, I insist: do not allow yourself to let the negatives of the place rob you of the real inspirations that are also awaiting you inside! "[The basilica's] obvious deterioration cannot diminish the realities it contains. [You] may feel disappointed at the site of the basilica, but here, more than anywhere else, we must distinguish between the events which happened here and the sights and sounds we must contend with. [You] must use [your] imagination to the full here!"[28] With the proper attitude, and an activated imagination, you can benefit greatly from your experience in this famous and holiest of churches. More will be said about this when we consider the environment, in the time of Jesus, surrounding the tomb itself.

For those with eyes to see, there is much, *much* to see here: "Blessed are your eyes, because they see, and your ears, because they hear. Amen, I say to you, many prophets and righteous people longed to see what you see but did not see it, and to hear what you hear but did not hear it" (Mt 13:16–17).

Before going inside the church, it would be good to discuss first a few items that will help to make sense of what will be seen inside.

Can We Be Sure That This Is the Location of Jesus's Crucifixion, Burial, and Resurrection?
Yes, we can! And this for three reasons.

For one, the "facts . . . of archaeology show that the site is compatible with the topographical data supplied by the gospels."[29] Our Lord was crucified outside of the city on a rock outcrop that resembled a skull (Jn 19:17), and there was a grave nearby (Jn 19:41–42). At the beginning of the first century AD, the site was a disused quarry outside of the city walls, and tombs similar to those found elsewhere[30] and dated to between 100 BC–AD 100 had been cut into the vertical west wall that had been left by the quarry workers.[31] This wall was a piece of rock about fifteen feet in height and was left by the stonecutters because it

---

28   Kilgallen, *New Testament Guide*, 257.

29   Murphy-O'Connor, *The Holy Land*, 49.

30   Such as in the stretch of green grass beside the King David Hotel.

31   Ibid.

was a rock of low quality—possibly broken by an earthquake or fissured during quarrying. This rock stood out in the garden space there (Jn 19:41) and looked like it was a skull rising out of the earth—hence its names *Golgotha*, *Kranion*, and *Calvary*—all of which mean skull. Closing our eyes and imagining this space bereft of the dilapidated exterior or busy interior of the current basilica, we would see two places: ". . . not more than thirty yards apart, with dirt and rock and grass under our feet and the open air all around us. . . . Unprotected, uninhabited, a scroungy garden and former quarry, here was a suitable place for the crucifixion and burial of criminals."[32] To this terrible procedure our crucified Lord was subjected by the acquiescing of Pilate to the near-rioting crowd (Lk 23:24–25:33).

For two, we have the "consistent and uncontested tradition of the Jerusalem community."[33] The faithful of Jerusalem held liturgical celebrations at this site until AD 66, and even when the area was brought within the walls in AD 41–43, it was not built over, but was left as it was at the time of Jesus's death, almost out of reverence for it. As Murphy-O'Connor relates:

> The memory of the site remained, and was probably reinforced by bitterness when Hadrian, in AD 135, filled in the quarry to provide a level base for his Capitoline temple, which was flanked by a shrine honoring Aphrodite. Macarius, bishop of Jerusalem (AD 314–333), was acting on a living tradition when in 325 at the Council of Nicea he petitioned the emperor Constantine (AD 308–337) to demolish the Capitoline temple and to bring to light the tomb of Christ. An eyewitness, Eusebius of Caesarea (AD 260–339), tells us what happened: "At once the work was carried out, and, as layer after layer of the subsoil came into view, the venerable and most holy memorial of the Savior's resurrection, beyond all our hopes, came into view" (*Life of Constantine*, 3:28). Graffiti probably identified the tomb of Christ, as they did the tomb of Peter in the Vatican.[34]

---

[32] Kilgallen, *New Testament Guide*, 258.

[33] Which witness Murphy-O'Connor hails as the "most important argument for the authenticity of this site" (*The Holy Land*, 49).

[34] The graffiti read: "Jesus this is where you were raised" (Murphy-O'Connor, *The Holy Land*, 50).

For three, we have a series of archaeological *felix culpa* moments. The first concerns the constructions of Hadrian. When this emperor rebuilt sections of the city of Jerusalem to be part of his grand, new capital, Aelia Capitolina, he built in the city two temples—one to the god Jupiter and one to the goddess Venus. He built the temple to Jupiter on the very top of the location of the Jewish Temple, thereby preserving the sacred place as a place of worship and prayer, though transforming it into a Roman sacred place.[35] It is likely that Hadrian did the same thing—that is, build a Roman temple on top of a place with a history of devotion—with the temple to Venus, constructing this pagan shrine on top of what was venerated by Christians as a holy place: that of the death and Resurrection of Jesus. Such, at least, can be

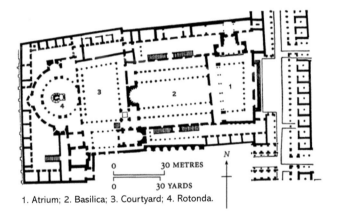

1. Atrium; 2. Basilica; 3. Courtyard; 4. Rotonda.

The Holy Sepulchre. The C4 Constantinian church (after Couäsnon) (p. 51, fig. 12, in Jerome Murphy-O'Connor, *The Holy Land*; used by permission of Oxford University Press).

surmised from the Greek graffiti that the Franciscans found on the walls in the Helena Chapel inside the Holy Sepulcher Church: "We are not here for you, Venus, but for Jesus." Ironically, the intended sacrilege of Hadrian's construction of the temple of Venus instead archaeologically secures the identification of this area as the place of Jesus's death and Resurrection—O happy fault!

---

[35] And thereby fanning the ire that ignited the Bar Kohkbah revolt in 135.

The second archaeological *felix culpa* consists in the destructions, at the hands of various representatives of Islam, of the Constantinian basilica of the Holy Sepulcher. The building—which was comprised of four parts: an atrium, a covered absidal basilica, an open courtyard with the stone of Golgotha in the southeast corner, and a rotunda with the tomb in the middle of it—was set fire by the Persians in 614 but was not completely lost. Then, when the caliph Omar, the successor to Muhammad, came to sign the treaty of capitulation—which transferred Jerusalem from Christian to Muslim control—in 638, he "refused the patriarch's invitation to pray in the Holy Sepulcher, saying, 'If I had prayed in the church it would have been lost to you, for the Believers would have taken it, saying: Omar prayed here.'"[36] Instead, Omar prayed a short distance from the church, and pilgrims can now see, very near to the basilica, the large Mosque of Omar, where Omar prayed instead of inside our basilica. However, Murphy-O'Connor observes:

> Such generosity had unfortunate consequences; had the church become a mosque it would not have been touched by the Fatmid caliph Hakim in 1009. His destruction was systematic; wrecking crews knocked the courses from the walls and attacked the rock tomb of Christ with picks and hammers, stopping only when the debris covered what remained. Eyewitnesses report that they did not succeed in destroying the tomb-chamber completely, despite building a great fire over it.[37]

Notwithstanding the obvious tragedy that this holy site suffered, we should note the work of God's hand thereon and therein. At least the church did not become a mosque with Omar; who knows what would have happened to Calvary and the tomb then? Moreover, the fact that the Fatmid destruction left only the bedrock of Calvary and the foundations of the tomb is something, again, to be celebrated with joy only *touched* by sadness (over the church's destruction), because such incomplete destruction again preserved the integrity of the traditional identification of the location of the Lord's death and Resurrection—of which

---

[36] Murphy-O'Connor, *The Holy Land*, 52.
[37] Ibid.

the conquering Crusaders could be sure as they walked, on July 15, 1099, into the truncated restorations to the basilica undertaken at the turn of the eleventh century.[38]

Why Do We Enter through What Clearly Looks Like a Side Door?

After the destruction by the Fatmids, the Holy Sepulcher was renovated thanks to the gifts of pilgrims and also the aid of Emperor Michael IV Paphlagon (1034–1041). The subsidies were not adequate, though, to repair it completely, and so a good deal of the original building had to be abandoned—namely, the atrium and the nave of the basilica. Only the courtyard and the rotunda remained. The rotunda was made into a church by the insertion of a large apse into its eastern façade.[39] Calvary chapels were cut and dedicated in 1149. A Romanesque church was built over the Constantinian courtyard and was linked to the rotunda between 1163 and 1169 when the apse was destroyed. After that, a bell tower was added in 1170.[40] Current-day pilgrims enter through the side of the link between the Romanesque church and the rotunda, with the chapels of Calvary immediately on the right.

The side, and only, entrance into the Church of the Holy Sepulcher.

---

[38] Ibid., 53.

[39] Ibid., 52–53.

[40] Ibid., 54.

What Kind of Tomb and Burial Did Jesus Receive?

At the end of the Syrian chapel behind the tomb itself, you can see examples of the kind of tomb in which Jesus was buried. These are of the *kokhim* style of tomb and were built before the quarry was incorporated into the city of Jerusalem in AD 41–43[41]—meaning, they were in use, in this spot, during the time of Jesus. Moreover, if you were to visit the very similar tomb recently found behind the King David Hotel, you would see that it had an opening in which a stone was cut like a wheel so that it could be rolled—by a few people, as it was heavy—to open or close the tomb; Mark 16:1–5 comes to mind.

We know that, in the time of Jesus, there was a need to open and close tombs. Family tombs had many people buried inside—not in coffins, but wrapped in towels or linen, and placed on benches. After a few years, when the body of the dead had decomposed, the families would crush the bones and put them in a common jar, placed in the tomb's middle. Such a procedure explains some curious turns of phrases found throughout the Bible that were utilized in order to describe death—for example, in Acts 13:36 Peter, preaching about the resurrection of the dead, speaks of King David in these terms: "Now David, after he had served the will of God in his lifetime, fell asleep, was *gathered to his ancestors*, and did see corruption." The phrase "to be gathered to one's ancestors" literally meant the moment in which the bones of a decomposed body were put into the family urn and, so, became mixed with the bones of his ancestors. Metaphorically, this phrase refers to death.

SCRIPTURE ON SITE:

Mark 16:1-5

It is safe to assume that Jesus's deceased body would have been first laid on the side bench, where the angel sat in Mark 16, and would have been treated according to Hebrew tradition: "They took the body of Jesus and bound it with burial cloths along with the spices, according to the Jewish burial custom" (Jn 19:40). This custom, also in his case, would have ended, had he not arisen, with his bones being gathered and placed in

---

[41] Ibid., 58.

an ancestral jar in the middle of the tomb. Some say that these spices were not intended to preserve the body (as our current practice of embalming similarly does), but rather to catalyze the decomposition process so that the deceased's mortal remains could more quickly be added to those of his forefathers (see Acts 13:36) and so that the burial space—which was at a premium those days—could be freed up. A motivation for such a practice has been surmised whereby, in this way, the Hebrews sought to differentiate themselves from their mortal enemies, the Egyptians, whose mummification procedure sought to *preserve* the deceased's body from corruption.

A family tomb from the ancient city of Beth Shearim. This is the style of tomb in which Jesus was buried.

Why Is the Church So Chaotically Divided among Different Christian Groups?

In short, such is due to the *Status Quo*, a promulgation that established the *order of the house* with regards to the occupation and maintenance of the various parts of the Church of the Holy Sepulcher, causing no little contention over the years.[42] During the time of the Ottoman Empire, fights[43] between the different Christian groups occupying the Sepulcher increased, with entire states getting involved: specifically, France and Russia. In the 1800s, talks began with the Ottoman sultan of the time (Abdul-

---

[42] For an interesting piece on the *Status Quo*, see Sarah Toth Stub, "A 1,000-Year-Old Promise of Peace," BBC Website, November 28, 2016, accessed June 4, 2017, http://www.bbc.com/travel/story/20161121-a-1000-year-old-promise-of-peace.

[43] Tension unfortunately continues to the present day, as seen in the 2008 brawl between Greek and Armenian Orthodox over procession routes.

mecid I), who divided the different chapels among the different groups. In 1853 a treaty was signed called the *Status Quo*, which literally froze the situation inside the Holy Sepulcher, thereby preventing any transfer of property or rights within the church. He did this because Russia, who represented and defended the Greek Orthodox (who at the time did not have a state to their name) threatened to invade Turkey if its Ottoman government, which controlled Jerusalem, granted the request of France to give part of the Greek Orthodox area of the church to the Latin Catholics.[44]

So, thanks to the *Status Quo*, at midnight one night, everything froze: whoever was occupying whatever chapel, that chapel became their chapel, no contest. A common area was established, such that each congregation could celebrate there (for example, in the tomb) during their allotted time slots. However, they must otherwise keep to their own part of the church. No Greek Orthodox priest can go, for example, into the Franciscans's Mary Magdalene Chapel. The groups at times watch each other with cautious suspicion, making the inter-religious tension of this place veritably palpable.

Some of the scruples of this arrangement border on the ridiculous. The actual tomb is divided into centimeters, and each church can polish only its part of it. Continued disagreements surrounding the needed renovations of what was structurally a very unsound tomb edifice finally made progress only recently when the King of Jordan stepped in and agreed to finance its refurbishing. Outside of the church, above the entrance, you will note a ladder near two of the Crusader church's side windows. How did it get up there? Well, a man was cleaning windows in the 1800s, and then the *Status Quo* came into effect one night, meaning that nothing could be changed from how it was at that very time of the accord's promulgation—hence, his ladder had to stay up there, because it was left out overnight when the act was ratified. *Mamma mia*!

Somehow, though, in the twentieth century, the Franciscans slipped enough mechanical pieces past this treaty's re-

---

[44] In the Holy Land, Roman Catholics are called either "Latins" or "Christians." As it is, the latter almost exclusively refers to Catholics. France was the patron of the Franciscans, and, indeed, of the Latin Catholic Church throughout the whole Middle East, as it still is to this day.

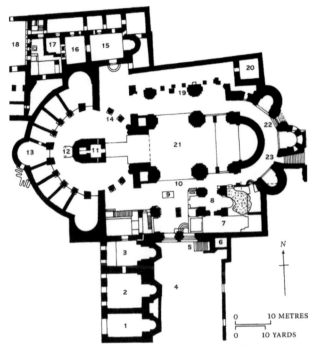

Fig. 14. The Holy Sepulchre. The C12 church (after Corbo). 1–3. C11 chapels; 4. Courtyard; 5. Steps. 6. Chapel of the Franks. 7. Latin Calvary. 8. Greek Calvary (above); Chapel of Adam (below); 9. Stone of Anointing; 10. Greek wall; 11. Tomb of Christ; 12. Coptic chapel; 13. C1 tomb; 14. Tapering columns; 15. Chapel of St Mary Magdalene; 16. Franciscan choir. 17. C11 atrium; 18. C7 room; 19. Byzantine and Crusader columns and piers; 20. Prison of Christ; 21. Greek Orthodox Catholicon; 22. Entrance to medieval monastery; 23. Entrance to Crypt of St Helena.

The Holy Sepulchre: the C12 church (after Corbo) (p. 55, fig. 14, in Jerome Murphy-O'Connor, *The Holy Land*; used by permission of Oxford University Press).

stricting order to be able to construct an impressive pipe organ in their quadrant that blares loudly during the solemn Masses (in which *Missa de Angelis* is always sung) and processions (in which *Vexilla Regis* is always chanted), the latter of which follow, of course, the exact path that they followed in AD 1853 when the *Status Quo* came into effect. Ridiculous, and glorious!

With these preceding discussions having been made, we are ready to move into the church itself. This book will proceed site

The wall behind the "Anointing Slab."

by site in a generally counterclockwise manner—that is, by going around to the right, visiting the different places along the
path that ends at the tomb. If you would like to come back and
pray peacefully at these sites, I would recommend arising very
early and making your way to the church around 4 a.m., when it
opens and is as quiet as it will ever be.

The first item that we encounter inside the church is the
so-called "Anointing Slab," or "Stone of Unction." This rock
bed commemorates the anointing of Jesus before his burial (Jn
19:38–40). Every day, early in the morning, a pious Orthodox
woman anoints the stone with oils that are very similar to, if not
the same as, such oils as were used in the time of Jesus for the
purpose of preparing a body for burial (Jn 12:3, 7). The perfume
is most pleasant, and the witness of many pilgrims who place
their hands on this stone in quiet prayer is very edifying. However, this tradition probably first emerged in the twelfth century,
and this stone only dates from 1810.[45] The lack of historical
plausibility, however, should not obfuscate your appreciation of
the prayerful witness of many people's reverent devotion to the

---

[45] Murphy-O'Connor, *The Holy Land*, 56.

body of Jesus. This tender faith is as pleasing to the soul as the anointing perfume is to smell.

Behind the slab stands a mosaic-laced wall, which has no structural function, save that of blocking the view across the church to the tomb! When the fire of 1808 cracked the great arch above, this wall was built so as to support it, and the Greeks hung icons on it. A recent restoration of the arch has made this wall unnecessary, but the Greeks kept it. Unfortunately, the wall covers the graves of four Crusader kings.[46]

Turning immediately to the right, we see a narrow, old, smooth rock staircase leading up. These stairs lead us up to Calvary, which is divided into two principle parts. The first space that we encounter at the top of the stairs is the Latin Chapel of Calvary. Here is commemorated where Mary, the Mother of God, stood at the foot of the Cross. The mosaic above the altar has the Sorrowful Mother, dressed in her typical deep blue, standing above her son who was nailed (*here!*) to the Cross while it is still on the ground. The composure of Mary's posture is simply stunning: sorrowful though she was at her son's suffering,[47] Mary's faith never wavered, and so there she stood, next to the Cross. The Latin quotation of John 19:25 (*stabat iuxtra*

The Latin altar at Calvary.

---

[46] Ibid.
[47] To what can I compare you—to what can I liken you—
    O daughter of Jerusalem?
    What example can I give in order to comfort you,
    virgin daughter Zion?
    For your breach is as vast as the sea;
    who could heal you? (Lam 2:13, NABRE).

crucem mater eius) lines the arch which leads to the Greek Orthodox chapel in mosaics. The chapel contains the rock in which Jesus's Cross was placed (Jn 19:18). Pilgrims can reach under the Orthodox altar through a disk-shaped hole in the ground, where they can touch the actual, original rock of Calvary—upon which our sins were washed away in the blood of the Lamb!

The Greek Orthodox altar at Calvary. Under the altar rests the rock of Calvary, where Jesus's Cross was fixed into the ground at his crucifixion.

Having descended the stairs, turn left back towards the entrance and find a pair of rooms underneath Calvary. This is called the Chapel of Adam. An ancient tradition has it that Christ died where Adam was buried, and this tradition lies behind a detail of the iconography of the Crucifixion, in which scene you can often find, in the ground underneath the Cross of Jesus, a skull—that is, the skull of Adam, the new version of which Jesus became at his death and Resurrection (2 Cor 5:17). Behind the window in the back of this chapel, you can see not only the rock of Calvary, but also a crack. The crack explains why the Roman quarrymen left this rock untouched, as it was crummy building material.[48]

Down the long corridor, you can find a set of steps that descend into lower rooms. This path leads to the Crypt of St. Helena. On the walls of either side of the second set of steps, you can see a multitude of crosses carved by pilgrims on the walls. In fact, the crypt's walls are the foundations of the nave of the fourth-century basilica. These stairs lead down to the Chapel of the Finding of the Cross, an area that is said to be the cistern in

---

[48] Could this crack have been the result of an earthquake upon the crucifixion of Jesus? Matthew 27:50–51 has: "But Jesus cried out again in a loud voice, and gave up his spirit. And behold, the veil of the sanctuary was torn in two from top to bottom. The earth quaked, rocks were split."

which St. Helena discovered the True Cross[49] and other relics of Jesus's Passion, some of which are kept in the Church of the Holy Cross of Jerusalem in Rome. In these cavernous rooms, you can see how this entire area of ancient Jerusalem indeed used to be a quarry.

Emerging from the stairs, follow the corridor further along toward the area controlled by the Franciscans. There, you will find a chapel dedicated to Mary Magdalene, who met our Lord at the tomb very early on the first day of the week (Jn 20:1). To the left, you will arrive at what is known as the *Aedicula*, which is Latin for a small structure used as a shrine, sitting alone in the center of a large rotunda. This construction houses the empty tomb, out of which Jesus emerged, victoriously arisen from the dead.

The present tomb structure, which was just renovated and re-inforced thanks to the initiative of the King of Jordan, dates only

The *Aedicula* built on top of the tomb in which Jesus was laid.

---

[49] Murphy-O'Connor, *The Holy Land*, 59.

from 1810. A fire in 1808 damaged the last of a series of replicas that replaced the tomb destroyed by Hakim in 1009. The current edifice does not exactly look like the original Constantinian tomb. Constantine's engineers had freed a square tomb-chamber from the rock and shaped the exterior into a circle or polygon, which they covered with marble and decorated with columns. They also created a conical roof out of tapering panels and, at the entrance, built a porch with four columns holding up a gabled roof.[50]

Murphy-O'Connor importantly notes that: "A report made during the reconstructions of 1809 recorded that the floor of the

Wilkinson's reconstruction of the C4 Tomb of Christ (p. 56, fig. 15, in Jerome Murphy-O'Connor, *The Holy Land*; used by permission of Oxford University Press).

tomb-chamber was of rock as were the north and south walls, one or both surviving to a height of over 2 meters. Enough of the burial bench had remained to identify its shape."[51] Such a finding synchs with what has been very recently (Fall of 2016) hailed as a terrific discovery, within the *Aedicula*, of archaeological evidence that the actual bench on which Jesus's body was laid is indeed contained under the altar at which Holy Mass is

---

[50] Ibid., 57.
[51] Ibid., 58.

celebrated within the tomb! What a marvelous thing to know with confidence that, here, "not far from Calvary, the place of ignominy and intense suffering, is the site of the glory and eternal joy, of hope for all of us for everlasting life."[52] This is the site of Jesus's Resurrection; *here*, especially in Holy Mass, we *profess his Resurrection until he comes again*! There is no holier site in the Christian world than this, no holier ground (Ex 3:5) than this.

On a practical note, if you would like to pray within the tomb, I would advise attending a morning Mass there. The Franciscans manage the tomb in the mornings for a few hours around 6:30 a.m. and make Mass available every half hour for pilgrims. When a Mass ends, the priests process out of the tomb, and there is usually a gap of about one minute before the next Mass starts. It is often possible to slip in there between Masses. Otherwise, you could arrive shortly after the church's pitifully complicated door-opening ceremony at 4 a.m., which early hour provides for quieter prayer time. In fact, it is almost worth it to go to see the "ecumenical" door-opening ceremony: a Muslim family[53] unlocks the door from the outside, while from the inside one religious group brings the ladder, another group climbs it to receive the key, and another then unlocks the door. Also, the Franciscans occasionally allow—on the condition that you do *not* fall asleep anywhere—a handful of pilgrims to spend the night in the locked church, which provides several quiet hours to pray in the tomb and on Calvary.

Issues Raised

Issue 1

In his book *Jesus and the Jewish Roots of the Eucharist*, Brant Pitre explains how we have evidence that, in the first century AD, the Passover lambs in the Temple were not only sacrificed, but also were, so to speak, *crucified*—which would, of course, make all the more evocative the preaching of John the Baptist, who pointed out Jesus as *the* Lamb of God who really takes away the sins of the world (Jn 1:29):

---

[52] Kilgallen, *New Testament Guide*, 270.

[53] The Al Husseini family, who were entrusted with the key to this church by Saladin upon his capture of Jerusalem in 1187.

As the Israeli scholar Joseph Tabory has shown, according to the Mishnah, at the time when the Temple still stood, after the sacrifice of the lamb, the Jews would drive "thin smooth staves" of wood through the shoulders of the lamb in order to hang it and skin it (*Pesahim* 5:9). In addition to the first rod, they would also "thrust" a "skewer of pomegranate wood" through the Passover lamb "from its mouth to its buttocks" (*Pesahim* 7:1). As Tabory concludes, "An examination of the rabbinic evidence . . . seems to show that in Jerusalem the Jewish paschal lamb was offered in a manner which resembled crucifixion." This conclusion is supported by the writings of Saint Justin Martyr, a Christian living in the mid-second century AD. In his dialogue with a Jewish rabbi named Trypho, Justin states: "For the lamb, which is roasted, is roasted and dressed up *in the form of a cross*. For one spit is transfixed right through from the lower parts up to the head, and one across the back, to which are attached the legs of the lamb" (Justin Martyr, *Dialogue with Trypho the Jew*, 40).

. . . This is an aspect of the Passover in his day that is neither mentioned in the Bible nor part of the modern-day Jewish Seder, but which has the power to shed light on Jesus's conception of his own fate.

As we will see in a moment, Jesus is going to compare his suffering and death to the death of the Passover lamb. One reason he might have done this is that he expected that the manner of his death would resemble that of the lambs in the Temple. Not only would his lifeblood be poured out; but he, too, would be "crucified," his body transfixed to the wooden beams of a Roman cross, like many other Jews before him (compare Mt 16:24). [54]

Such a fascinating analysis helps to make sense of Jesus's statement and the evangelist's commentary in John 12:32–33: "'And when I am lifted up from the earth, I will draw all men to myself.' He said this indicating the kind of death that he would die." Jesus clearly foresaw not only his own crucifixion, but also, moreover, his crucifixion as the Lamb of God.

---

[54] Brant Pitre, *Jesus and the Jewish Roots of the Eucharist: Unlocking the Secrets of the Last Supper* (New York: Image, 2011), 63–64.

Issue 2

Speaking of seeing Jesus as the Lamb of God, you might ask where in the Gospels can we find such imagery. In his book *The Lamb's Supper*, Scott Hahn collects a series of texts that illuminate the similarities of sacrificial lambs and the events of Jesus's Passion:

- None of Jesus's bones were broken on the Cross, "that the Scripture might be fulfilled" (Jn 19:36). Which Scripture was that? Exodus 12:46, which stipulates the Passover lamb must have no broken bones.

- John relates that the onlookers served Jesus sour wine from a sponge on a hyssop branch (Jn 19:29). Hyssop was the branch prescribed by the Law for the Passover sprinkling of the lamb's blood (Ex 12:22). Thus, this simple action marked the fulfillment of the new and perfect redemption. And Jesus cried out, "It is finished."

- Finally, in speaking of Jesus's garment at the time of the crucifixion, John uses the precise term for the vestments the high priest wore when he offered sacrifices such as the Passover lamb. John makes it clear to us that, *in the new and definitive Passover sacrifice, Jesus is both priest and victim.*[55]

Issue 3

While reading John's account of the Passion, one thing becomes quite clear: "Jesus was in absolute control of everything that happened to him."[56] In John 13:2–3, Jesus, fully aware "that the Father had put everything into his power and that he had come from God and was returning to God," stands up from supper and intentionally puts into motion, via the washing of the disciples's feet, the series of events that will culminate in his death and Resurrection. In John 18:4, Jesus, "knowing everything that was going to happen to him," again takes the initiative, as he "went out and said to [Judas and the band of soldiers]: 'Whom are you

---

[55] Scott W. Hahn, *The Lamb's Supper: The Mass as Heaven on Earth* (New York: Doubleday, 1999), 23.

[56] Kilgallen, *New Testament Guide*, 228.

looking for?'" In fact, in every exchange of this dialogue, Jesus takes the initiative, asking the questions himself, and his power, which he reveals in pronouncing the divine name, "I AM," caused the crowd to turn away and fall to the ground (Jn 18:6). In John 19:28 and 30, Jesus continues to take the initiative at the very moment of death, when we read similar words in the Gospel: "After this, aware that everything was now finished, in order that the scripture might be fulfilled, Jesus said, 'I thirst' . . . When Jesus had taken the wine, he said, 'It is finished.' And bowing his head, he handed over his spirit." Note here the *active* voice of the verb with which Jesus gave up his spirit. This verbal form shows that Jesus, from start to finish of his Passion, was in control. Nothing, not even death, had power over him.

POINTS FOR REFLECTION

- After their pilgrimage to the Holy Land, many people share that one of the things they most remember about the Church of the Holy Sepulcher is its distinctive smell. Almost the entire inside of the basilica is filled with the waft of lingering incense and the anointing nard used to wipe the Stone of Unction. Let these smells, as well as the sounds of the different kinds and languages of chanting, activate your imagination and be another instance of appreciating the incarnational logic of our faith, which is so *real*,[57] so connected not only to sights but also our other senses of smell, hearing, and touch. With this in mind, you might ask yourself, here in this church: "Is the faith real to me? Or is it somehow abstract and distant?" Pray that the faith be made present in a real way not only now, but even after your pilgrimage ends.

- While it is hard in the moment fully to "take in" all that Calvary means and should mean to us, a good place to start is the simple realization that Kilgallen very movingly writes: "When I sit in the Basilica of the Holy Sepulcher and realize that here is the place where my Savior died, the confession of Paul overwhelms me: 'He gave himself for me; while we were still God's enemies, God gave his

---

[57] From the Latin word *res*, meaning *thing/object*.

Son for us.'"[58] Jesus, God-made-man and God's "beloved son" (Mt 17:5), my redeemer and the lover of my soul, died here for me. Wow! For me! Kilgallen is paraphrasing Romans 5:8–10, which is worth reading in full and praying over here on Calvary.

Especially for Seminarians

- The reality of the faith is something that you will be called to present to the faithful in a compelling way on a daily basis in your homilies as a priest. Recall the sights and sounds of the Church of the Holy Sepulcher to aid you in this ministry. "Lord, that I may see!" (Mk 10:51)

SCRIPTURE ON SITE:
Romans 5:8–10

The altar of Mary Magdalene, which commemorates her encountering the risen Jesus near his tomb in the garden area, which area is now the Latin quarters of the Church of the Holy Sepulcher operated by the Franciscans.

---

[58] Kilgallen, *New Testament Guide*, 269.

Victimae Paschali Laudes

Victimae paschali laudes immolent Christiani	To the Paschal Victim praises may Christians offer.
Agnus redemit oves: Christus innocens Patri reconciliavit peccatores.	The Lamb has redeemed the sheep: Christ, innocent, to the Father has reconciled sinners.
Mors et vita duello conflixere mirando: dux vitae mortuus, regnat vivus.	Death and life in battle contended marvelously: the champion of life, having died, yet reigns, alive.
Dic nobis Maria, quid vidisti in via? Sepulcrum Christi viventis, et gloriam vidi resurgentis:	Tell us, Mary, what you have seen on the way The tomb of the living Christ, and the glory of him rising I saw:
Angelicos testes, sudarium, et vestes.	Angelic witnesses, the shroud, the clothing.
Surrexit Christus spes mea: praecedet suos in Galileam.	Christ my hope has arisen: he goes ahead of his own in Galilee.

Scimus Christus surrexisse
a mortuis vere:
tu nobis, victor Rex,
    miserere.
Amen. Alleluia.
	We know that Christ has arisen
	truly from the dead:
	You, Victor King,
	    have mercy on us.
	Amen. Alleluia.

The sculpture-relief of the
Fourth Station of the Cross
along the Via Dolorosa.

ST. ANNE/
BETHESDA

*After this, there was a feast of the Jews, and Jesus went up
to Jerusalem. Now there is in Jerusalem at the Sheep Gate
a pool called in Hebrew Bethesda, with five porticoes. In
these lay a large number of ill, blind, lame, and crippled.
One man was there who had been ill for thirty-eight years.
When Jesus saw him lying there and knew that he had been
ill for a long time, he said to him, "Do you want to be
well?" The sick man answered him, "Sir, I have no one to
put me into the pool when the water is stirred up; while I
am on my way, someone else gets down there before me."
Jesus said to him, "Rise, take up your mat, and walk."
Immediately the man became well, took up his mat, and
walked. Now, that day was a Sabbath.*

(John 5:1–9)

Scriptural Background

Though this place is known to Christians as the place at which
Jesus cured a man who had been ill for thirty-eight years, it has an
important history before the dawn of the new era. In the eighth
century BC, a dam was built here across a shallow valley to capture runoff rainwater. It became known as the *upper pool* de-

scribed in 2 Kings 18:17,[1] as well as Isaiah 7:3 in the same words. Thus controlled, the water flowed south in an open-air, rock-cut channel to the City of David.[2] Toward the end of the third century BC, a second pool was made, probably at the time of the High Priest Simon—"In his time the reservoir was dug, a pool as vast as the sea" (Sir 50:3)—and the channel was transformed into a tunnel. It seems that one of these two pools, at least, was used for ritual purification baths, which all pilgrims travelling to Jerusalem to

Part of the deep, large pool excavated at Bethesda.

SCRIPTURE ON SITE:
John 5:1-8
Acts 21:27–22:29

celebrate the feasts had to undertake before entering the Temple area. Such shows that there used to exist just outside of the Holy City two focal points of ritual purification for pilgrims coming to Jerusalem—that is, one in the north (the pool of Bethesda) and one in the south (the pool of Siloam).

Also, here we find ourselves standing on or nearby where once stood the old Antonia Fortress. There, Paul was arrested—rescued, actually, from the mob who was beating him—and taken into "the compound" of Antonia (Acts 21:34). Having

---

[1] "The king of Assyria sent . . . a great army to King Hezekiah at Jerusalem. They went up and came to Jerusalem, to the conduit of the upper pool on the highway of the fuller's field, where they took their stand."

[2] Murphy-O'Connor, *The Holy Land*, 29.

responded in Greek to the surprise of the cohort commander (Acts 21:37), he silenced the crowds by then addressing them in Hebrew[3] (Acts 21:40), delivering a dramatic defense of linguistic and rhetorical brilliance that finally enraged the people sufficiently enough to demand that he be taken away (Acts 22:22), which action would lead to his eventual sending-off to Rome and martyrdom.

Archaeological History

Between 150 BC and AD 70, a popular healing center developed east of the pools. A number of caves were adapted to serve as small baths whose function seems to have been "religious or medicinal"—the two were, at the time, inseparable: "health was a gift of the gods."[4] Apparently, at special moments of a given day, the springs of water underneath the pools would bubble up through the reservoirs into the baths, and this bubbling was thought to be particularly helpful in the healing process.[5] Such a context would explain the name, in John, of this pool: Bethesda, which means "house of mercy"—from the Aramaic *bet* ("house of") and *hisda'* ("mercy").

After AD 135, when Jerusalem was paganized into Rome's Aelia Capitolina, the sanctuary grew into a temple. Second- and third-century AD votive offerings (like statues) of gratitude for medical favors granted were found in the temple's excavations,[6] and this discovery suggests that the temple was dedicated to Serapis (Asclepius), who was a Greco-Roman deity of healing. The cult of Serapis here was undertaken in this way: a person seeking healing would wash in the pool, drink a potion, spend the night in the nearby cave, and then tell the priest the next day

---

[3] Or perhaps Aramaic. Sometimes, when the Scriptures make reference to Hebrew, they really mean Aramaic. For example, the place of Jesus's crucifixion, John says, is called "in Hebrew *Golgotha*" (Jn 19:17). However, *Golgotha* is an Aramaic word/name. How do we know that? The final letter gives it away; in Aramaic, the definite article comes, attached, at the end of the word, and consists in a simple *a*. (In Hebrew, on the other hand, the definite article comes *before* the noun. It seems that, at the time of the Gospels, "Hebrew" was understood by all to refer, in a general way, to the language(s) that many Jews spoke—Aramaic and Hebrew.)

[4] Murphy-O'Connor, *The Holy Land*, 29.

[5] Kilgallen, *New Testament Guide*, 189.

[6] Murphy-O'Connor, *The Holy Land*, 29.

their dreams, which he would interpret and, in turn, promise eventual healing. Within this cultural milieu of healing, which both preceded and followed upon our Lord's healing of the sick man in John 5, we see again how religions tended to re-use existing devotional sites and even structures. This continuity of devotion, as we have seen at Calvary and as we shall see at Bethlehem, has proven to be very helpful in securing the reliability of Christian claims to the locating of certain important events in the life of our faith.

When Juvenal was Patriarch of Jerusalem (AD 422–458), a large Byzantine basilica (forty-five meters by eighteen meters) was built here, where its ruins are still visible. Its naves were constructed on the old dike and pools, and it was supported by seven arches. The church's choir covered what had been thought to be a healing place. Partly burned by Persians in 614, the Byzantine church was succeeded by a medieval church[7] built on top of its ruined presbyterion. This medieval church incorporated various elements of the Byzantine church into its own form.

Ruins of Byzantine and medieval churches built at Bethesda.

---

7   Dedicated also to the birth of the Virgin Mary, who was thought to have been born near here.

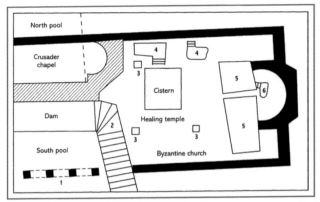

St. Anne's church excavated area (after Duprez). 1: Piers supporting wall of C5 church. 2: Modern steps. 3: Columns of C5 church. 4: Healing baths. 5: Vaulted rooms. 6: Healing bath (p. 10, fig. 8, in Jerome Murphy-O'Connor, *The Holy Land*; used by permission of Oxford University Press).

Sometime between 1131 and 1138 the beautiful Romanesque church of St. Anne was built. Murphy-O'Connor considers it "certainly the loveliest church in the city" and one that offers a view of "Crusader Jerusalem at its best."[8] The church, which is known even still today for its excellent acoustics, was transformed into a Muslim theological school by Saladin in 1192; his inscription is still above the door. Later rulers let this church fall into disarray, and even filled it to the roof with garbage. The Ottoman Turks gave it to France in 1856 as a gesture of gratitude for aid in the Crimean War. France cleaned it up and entrusted it to the care of the White Friars. The church's crypt is built, as the Byzantine tradition goes, on the house of Mary, where she grew up with Sts. Anne and Joachim.[9]

Issues Raised

Issue 1

A reading of John 5 *in situ* creates an excellent opportunity to linger over two textual issues that raise the larger issue of some textual traditions that should at least be familiar to seminari-

---

[8] Ibid.
[9] Ibid., 32.

The interior of the Romanesque church of St. Anne, built just after 1130. A fine example of Crusader architecture, the dimensions of this church were arranged so perfectly that the nave boasts some of the best acoustics in the world.

ans. If we take in hand the Nestle-Aland 28 version of the Greek New Testament and read John 5:1–9, we see indicated a number of interesting things. Firstly, at the word "Bethesda" in verse two of the text, we see a mark (an upside down capital L) that sends us, the reader, down to the critical apparatus, where we see that a number of different variants on the spelling of this place have been attested in different manuscripts. The most familiar reading, "Bethesda," appears in manuscripts[10] that are not the oldest of sources and, hence, are not usually chosen as the *preferred* reading of a given variant in question. Usually, Nestle-Aland chooses the reading of the Codex Vaticanus (B), which fourth-century document contains arguably the best version of the Greek New Testament. Here, though, Vaticanus's spelling ("Bethsaida") is not chosen as the best reading. Rather, Nestle-Aland chose "Bethzatha," which is found in the other codex—Sinaiticus (‭א‬)—of the fourth century, and which spelling the Revised Standard Version retains (while the New American Bible has Bethesda).

In the end, which is the "right" reading of this place's spelling? The answer is: wrong question! We have no original manuscripts of the Greek New Testament, and though the field of bib-

---

[10] Alexandrinus (abbreviated as "A") and Ephraim Syrian Rescript ("C"), both of the fifth century, and Koridethianus ("Θ") of the ninth century.

lical studies known as textual criticism—which undertakes such operations as above, though in a much more involved manner—can explain, with great probability, certain things about given variants,[11] it can end only with proposing what is most likely to be the oldest reading of a given piece of text. In this case, it seems that either "Bethsaida" or "Betzatha" are the best candidates, the variation of the spelling of which depends, I imagine, on a combination of regional dialects's pronunciation and transliteration into Greek of this name's Aramaic roots (*bet* and *hisda'*).

Issue 2

If we look for verse 4 of this chapter, we see that it does not exist! What happened here? It turns out that many later manuscripts contain a text of John 5 that includes, at this point, material

that is not contained within our best manuscripts and codices. The early Church writer Tertullian knew of this textual tradition, which became the majority text. This reading proceeds as such: "For, at the appointed time, an angel (of God) came to the pool and stirred-up the water; whomever was first to go down into the water after its being stirred-up became healed." This verse is retained in some modern translations of the Bible, like the New King James Version.

How do we explain the presence of this longer text in later manuscripts? It could have been, on the part of a scribe, an attempt to recon-

A touching statue of St. Anne teaching the Scriptures to her daughter, Mary.

---

[11] For example, as being the result of harmonization in later manuscripts, scribal error, Hebraicization in Palestinian manuscripts, etc.

cile a difficulty that the story version of the oldest texts had—that is, of the necessity of having *moving* water in a pool[12]—or perhaps to incorporate into the account a local superstition about how healing would here happen. Regardless, now you will know, every time you read this chapter of John, why verse 4 seems to be missing—it is not contained in the earliest and best textual versions of the Greek New Testament and was possibly inserted by later versions for a variety of reasons.

POINTS FOR REFLECTION

- In this place of healing, I cannot help but pause and reflect, in humble gratitude, on the power invested in the hands of a priest. Anointed with holy chrism, priestly hands are consecrated not only to confect and distribute the Eucharist, but also to impart real healing—spiritual as well as physical—on souls in need of God's mercy in their final hours. If the skilled hands of the surgeon are accounted so precious as they are, how too should be the hands of a priest, by means of which the Lord dispenses such graces to his beloved people!

  I remember the distinct moment in which I was given to see how precious are the hands of a priest. It was as I was reading Evelyn Waugh's biography of St. Edmund Campion, S.J. The saint was summoned, with his companions, to the King's Bench, so as to plead to the phony indictment of treason with which they had been charged. When they were called to take the oath, Campion, whose excruciating sufferings on the torture racks had wrangled his limbs, "could not lift his arm, his crippled hands tucked into the cuffs of his gown, whereupon one of his companions drew up the sleeve, kissed his hand, and raised it for him."[13] Wow! What love for the priesthood, expressed in reverence for his anointed hands!

  Let us pause for a moment and reflect on the power of God made real through the holy hands of the priest, and let us give thanks for so grace-filled a gift.

---

[12] See the long-ill man's response to Jesus in v. 7.

[13] Evelyn Waugh, *Edmund Campion: Jesuit and Martyr* (New York: Image, 1962), 172.

Especially for Seminarians

- As (God willing) future priests, it would benefit you
greatly to contemplate already now the gift that you will
receive as your hands are anointed with sacred chrism oil
just after the moment of your ordination as a priest. As
an aid in this consideration, take to prayer the words of
an anonymous poem entitled: "The Beautiful Hands of a
Priest." Spoken from the point of view of the lay faithful,
this piece evokes tender and awe-filled appreciation for
the shepherding that occurs by means of the gentle, sure,
and holy hands of the priest.

The Beautiful Hands of a Priest
We need them in life's early morning,
we need them again at its close;
We feel their warm clasp of friendship,
we seek them when tasting life's woes.
At the altar each day we behold them,
and the hands of a king on his throne
Are not equal to them in their greatness;
their dignity stands all alone;
And when we are tempted and wander
to pathways of shame and sin,
It's the hand of a priest that will absolve us
—not once, but again and again;
And when we are taking life's partner,
other hands may prepare us a feast,
But the hand that will bless and unite us
is the beautiful hand of a priest.
God bless them and keep them all holy
For the Host which their fingers caress;
When can a poor sinner do better
than to ask Him to guide thee and bless?
When the hour of death comes upon us
may our courage and strength be increased.
By seeing raised over us in anointing
the beautiful hands of a priest!

BETHLEHEM

Today in the city of David has been born for you a savior, who is Messiah and Lord.

(Luke 2:11)

Bethlehem's history, especially as it relates to Christianity, extends back into the Book of Genesis. In the region of Bethlehem, the tomb of Rachel was already on display in the days of Jesus.[1] Jacob, erecting a pillar in memory of her, here buried the wife he loved, who died giving birth to their son Benjamin (Gen 35:19–20). So, in Jewish and Christian memory, this place was associated with such biblical themes as love, childbirth, and sadness. But, indeed, a sadness consoled by the promise of prophecy, which Christians understandably see in light of the Nativity of Jesus who, we read in the prophet Micah, would bring *peace*.

A Christian reads Bethlehem and its history in Christological light so readily because of Jesus's family history, in which we find it associated with the story of Ruth. Invited to "bestow a name on Bethlehem" (Ruth 4:11), Ruth and Boaz gave birth to a son and named him Obed, who was the father of Jesse, the father of David (Ruth 4:17),

SCRIPTURE ON SITE:
Micah 5:1-4a

---

[1] A voice was heard in Ramah. . . .
Rachel weeping for her children,
(slaughtered by Herod [See Mt 2:16–18, NABRE]).

from whose mighty lineage sprung Jesus (Mt 1:5–6; Lk 3:32).

Beyond the memory of Mary, whom many suppose was likely a source for Luke in the writing of his Gospel,[2] especially his infancy narrative, which focuses on Mary, who "kept all these things in her heart" (2:19, 51), the earliest recorded indication of this Davidic succession on the part of Jesus comes from Saint Paul, who takes for granted that such is known when he writes "concerning [God's] Son, who was descended from David according to the flesh" (Rom 1:3).

The story of Ruth bespeaks *fidelity* and *kindness*, as can be seen in the following recap of the events of the first chapter (vv.1–17) of the book that bears her name. In the time of the judges, a severe famine broke out throughout the land, and a man from Bethlehem (Elimelech) and his wife (Naomi) took their two sons and left for Moab, which sat in the high hills east of Bethlehem across the Dead Sea. Some time after their arrival, Elimelech died, and the two sons married Moabite women: Orpah and Ruth. After ten years, Naomi's two sons also died, leaving the widow now with only her daughters-in-law. Naomi and her daughters-in-law prepared to go back to Bethlehem from Moab because, we read, "word had reached her there that the Lord had seen to his people's needs and given them food" (v. 6)—the Hebrew word for food being, of course, *leḥem*.[3]

Naomi said to her daughters-in-law: "Go back, each to your mother's house. May the Lord show you the same kindness as you have shown to the deceased and to me" (v. 8). The word used here for *kindness*—*ḥesed* in Hebrew, *eleos* in Greek—points back to God's self-revelation to Moses on Mount Sinai as: "the LORD, the LORD, a God gracious and merciful, slow to anger and abounding in *loving-kindness* and fidelity" (Ex 34:6). Orpah kissed her mother in law goodbye, but Ruth clung to Naomi, and expressed in beautiful, parallel verse the fidelity that Naomi had just praised in her:

---

[2] For an excellent summary of the issue of the sources of the Gospels, see Jimmy Akin, "Where the Evangelists Got Their Information," *Catholic Answers*, accessed June 4, 2017, http://www.catholic.com/magazine/articles/where-the-evangelists-got-their-information.

[3] Hence *Bet-leḥem*'s meaning of "house of bread," because there the Lord provided food for his starving children.

Wherever you go I will go,
wherever you lodge I will lodge.
Your people shall be my people
and your God, my God.

Where you die I will die,
and there be buried. (vv. 16–17, NABRE)

The faithful kindness of Ruth reflects the *ḥesed/eleos* that God professes to have for us.

A painting of the Nativity found inside the round chapel at the Shepherd's Field.

And so, with the history of *ḥesed* already associated with Bethlehem in Old Testament times, we can understand what the angel really meant when he said to the shepherds: "And this will be a sign for you: you will find an infant wrapped in swaddling clothes and lying in a manger" (Lk 2:12). The child Jesus in the lowly manger is the sign, the visible proof, of God the Father's *fidelity* to the promises he made to "raise up, on that day, the fallen *hut* of David" (Amos 9:11). This was understood by Christians to refer to the line of David, whose ruling succession was broken in the Babylonian Exile, following upon the sins of David and his successor kings, but then *restored* in the Christ-child, who was of David's descent. In the words of Scott Hahn's recent title, God is *A Father Who Keeps His Promises*.[4] God promised that the virgin would conceive and bear a son who would be called Emmanuel, which means "with-us-is-God" (Mt 1:23; Is 7:14). Early Christians were quick to read Jesus as the addressee, and hence fulfillment, of the promise about this child that God made to David:

> When your days have been completed and you rest with your ancestors, I will raise up your offspring after you, sprung from your loins, and I will establish his kingdom. He it is who shall build a house for my name, and I will establish his royal throne forever. I will be a father to him, and he shall be a son to me...I will not withdraw my favor from him as I withdrew it from Saul who was before you. Your house and your kingdom are firm forever before me; your throne shall be firmly established forever. (2 Sam 7:12–16)

A fountain of a shepherd and his sheep in the middle of the Shepherds' Field.

---

4   Scott W. Hahn, *A Father Who Keeps His Promises*: *God's Covenant Love in Scripture* (Cincinnati, OH: Servant, 1998).

At Bethlehem on that holy night, God the Father came through on his promise and showed himself to be true to his word.

We could mention a few more scriptural references to Bethlehem that help put this city, and its importance, into context for our pilgrimage purposes. David, as mentioned above, was born here (1 Sam 16:1–13). When Saul's jealousy forced the future king to become an outlaw, David spearheaded an attack on the Philistines (1 Sam 23:5), who then put a garrison in Bethlehem (2 Sam 23:14). Bethlehem was a walled city, and David's grandson Rehoboam (928–911 BC) fortified it to protect the eastern flank of his kingdom (2 Chr 11:6). Presumably, the 123 Bethlehemites listed among those who returned from the exile in the sixth century BC (Ezra 2:21) resettled in their ancient home. An archaeological survey has shown that the town of this period was on the hilltop behind the Church of the Nativity, and that the caves beneath the church were in fact then in use. The Gospels make no mention of a cave, but both St. Justin Martyr, in the second century, and the *Protoevangelium of James* speak of the cave there in which Jesus was born.[5]

SCRIPTURE ON SITE:

Luke 2:1-7 (Holy Family enrolling for census and so coming to Bethlehem)

Luke 2:8-20 (Shepherds)

Matthew 1:18-25 (Birth of Jesus, after the angel and Joseph)

Matthew 2:1-23 (Herod and Magi)

Archaeological History

Bethlehem is first mentioned in the fourteenth century BC when the king of Jerusalem wrote to his Egyptian overlord asking for archers to help him recover a town that had seceded from his jurisdiction.[6]

---

5 Murphy-O'Connor, *The Holy Land*, 230.
6 Ibid.

A segment of the original, mosaic floor from the Constantinian Church of the Nativity, built by the emperor's mother, Helena.

In the year AD 326, the pious empress Helen, mother of Constantine, embarked on a pilgrimage to the Holy Land. Immediately after her arrival, she ordered the construction of basilicas on the sites of three "mystical grottos" (per Eusebius, fourth century AD) revered since the early days of Christianity: the grotto of Jesus's burial at Golgotha, the Cave of the Disciples (Eleona) on the Mount of Olives, and the Cave of the Nativity in Bethlehem.[7]

Such reverence can boast of considerable historical reliability. As seen earlier, the Roman Emperor Hadrian built pagan sanctuaries *on top of* places that were considered loci of Jewish and Christian worship and veneration. As it turns out, he did the same thing at Bethlehem, where he constructed a grove to the god Tammuz-Adonis and a temple to Venus over the grotto of the Nativity. Origen appears to have visited this pagan cult place in the year AD 220, at which time he "was shown what is familiar to everyone in the area. The heathens themselves tell everyone who is willing to listen that in the said grotto, there was born a certain Jesus, whom the Christians revered" (*Contra Celsum* 1.51).[8]

It is indeed one of the wonderful ironies of history that a key piece of evidence in the definite identification of many Christian holy sites is owed to a Roman emperor's attempted destruction and paganization of those sites. Such a "happy fault" displays, again, how the wisdom of God "governs all things well" (Wis

---

[7] Pixner, *Paths of the Messiah*, 11.

[8] Ibid.

8:1⁹). Such *miracles of history*, we could call them, are manifestations of the providence of God, who makes crooked lines straight (Is 45:2).

The first Church of the Nativity was dedicated on May 31, AD 339. Its apse was in the shape of an octagon and was situated directly above the cave of the Nativity, which was accessed by descending stairs.[10] The only visible elements of this church are sections of the mosaic pavement. In 384, Jerome took up residence in Bethlehem, to be joined two years later by Paula and her daughter Eustochium. Together they made Bethlehem an epicenter of monasticism. Within this framework, Jerome wrote extensively; his most notable achievement was a new translation of the Old Testament, the Vulgate.[11] Jerome attests to the existence of caves *adjacent to the main cave*; in one of them he buried Paula, and in another one wanted to be buried himself so that he could be *near* to where Jesus was born—that is, near to where God entered the world.

In 529, the emperor Justinian ordered the small church of Bethlehem to be pulled down and built up again magnificently. This new edifice has remained in use through the present day. The façade at one time was decorated with a

The original tomb of St. Jerome in a grotto adjacent to the grotto in which Jesus was born. The inscription reads: "Formerly the Tomb of St. Jerome, Priest and Doctor of the Church." (The Latin *locus* was a word used especially to describe medium-sized tombs in catacombs, such as those in Rome.)

---

⁹ This verse is the source of the first "O Antiphon," sung when the celebration of Christmas is nigh!

[10] Murphy-O'Connor, *The Holy Land*, 232.

[11] Contrary to a common misconception, Jerome did not translate the Gospels into Latin, but rather utilized, and perhaps only tweaked, the Old Latin version of the New Testament. The Vulgate has remained the authoritative version of the Bible for Catholics since the Council of Trent.

colorful mosaic, which saved the church when, in 614, the Persian invaders destroyed almost all the sanctuaries in the Holy Land—except, perhaps most notably, this one. How this happened is described in a letter from the Jerusalem Synod of 838, which cited this event in order to argue, against the iconoclasts, for the utility of images: "When the Persians, after having sacked all the towns in Syria, reached Bethlehem, they were greatly surprised to discover on its façade a representation of the magi from Persia. Out of reverence and respect for their ancestors, they decided to honor these sages by sparing the church. And this is how it has survived until this day."[12]

Some 200 years later, the country was overrun by Islamic Arabs, again jeopardizing the fate of the church. But their leader, Omar, did something that the Christians did not expect. He decided that the place where their prophet Issa (Jesus) had been born of the Virgin Mariam (Mary) deserved to be protected. Legend has it that he knelt down in the southern apse of the church to pray to Mecca (Eutychius of Alexandria, *Viae regnorum*).[13] The Mosque of Omar, with its minaret rising at the end of the church plaza opposite the basilica,

The remnants of the façade of the Justinian church, with its characteristic low door as its entrance.

[12] Pixner, *Paths of the Messiah*, 13.
[13] Ibid.

commemorates this gesture of the prophet Muhammad's immediate successor, whose prayerful action prompted followers of Islam to preserve the church as a site holy in the history of Islam.

The original church had three entrances, two of which have been bricked up. The central and highest portal of Justinian's church (mid-500s AD) was lowered during the Middle Ages, and the resulting, pointed arch is visible to this day. During the Ottoman era, this arch was further reduced, leaving the present low and narrow opening that can be passed only when the visitor bends his head and knees, though this lowering was likely done so as to prevent horses, and the carts of looters,[14] from entering into the basilica. An observant pilgrim, who sees the world with what George Weigel called a "sacramental imagination,"[15] can interpret the low door as if it wants to caution him: "Lower yourself, you proud one, if you want to approach God, who for your sake came to us as a child." How God came down to us, we are to approach him—humbly!

You will note that there is a rather Italian-looking church just to the left of the Church of the Nativity. This is the Latin Church of St. Catherine, operated by the Franciscans. Here, the Patriarch of Jerusalem celebrates the Vigil Mass of Christmas. Inside and to the right near the front of the church, you can descend a staircase that leads to various grottos that are close to the principal grot-

The courtyard of the Latin Church of St. Catherine, which is immediately next to the Church of the Nativity. The statue in the middle of the courtyard is of St. Jerome.

[14] Murphy-O'Connor, *The Holy Land*, 234.

[15] George Weigel, *Letters to a Young Catholic* (New York: Basic Books, 2015), 86.

to in the main church, now operated by the Greek Orthodox. Jerome's cave is located down here, as well as Paula's burial place.

Before leaving St. Catherine's, try to get into the sacristy in the front-right of the sanctuary. On the far wall above the dresser is easily the most beautiful painting of the Holy Family that I have ever seen. It depicts Joseph standing next to Mary, who, kneeling in the middle and surrounded by a retinue of angels gazing through the aura of light enveloping her, holds her child, Jesus, while looking up in ecstasy. That—*that*—is heaven on earth!

Issues Raised

Issue 1

The use of the word "cling" in Ruth (1:14) is significant and points to something of which I often make use in marriage homilies to talk about both the nature and function of the marriage bond. This word (*dabaq*; Hebrew) is used in Genesis 2:24: "For this reason, a man shall leave his father and mother and cling to his wife, and the two shall become one flesh." This word is also used in Job 41:23 to describe the action of *crocodile scales*. What a perfect image, rooted literally in God's creation, to describe the indissolubility of marriage and the strength of the marriage bond! You see, crocodile scales "cling" so tightly to each other that they are very, very difficult to tear apart, and they also form a protective shield around the crocodile skin, which they hence keep from getting wet. Just like crocodile scales which remain clung together even when great force is applied upon them, so is the marriage bond intended to be permanent, despite the fierce attacks that threaten to pull it apart. Or, in the words of the marriage vows, a couple is to stick together "in good times and in bad," to love and honor each other all the days of their lives. Such fidelity will then act, like crocodile scales, to repel any attack that might assail the two from without or from within.

Issue 2

Kilgallen offers an excellent presentation of the visit of the Magi to the Holy Family in Bethlehem (127–129). He notes that, at the time of Jesus, the heavens were divided into sections—a zodiac arrangement—that corresponded to sections of earth. Moreover, specific planets and stars represented powers and gods, such that, if one celestial body were prominent in a certain part of the heavens, one could *divine* that some kind of phenomenon was imminent in that corresponding part of the earth. Such was the job of the Magi, who were wise men that advised kings by looking to the heavens for revelations about life down here below. Fast-forwarding to more modern times, Kilgallen points out the discovery by Johannes Keppler in 1604 of a strange geographical relationship between Jupiter, Saturn, and Mars, and that this relationship was so unusual that it occurred only every 805 years—in other words, that it occurred in AD 799 and in 6 BC, the latter of which is what scholars think to be just about the year of Jesus's birth.[16]

This phenomenon would have struck magi as a definite sign from the heavens that something of immense importance was being revealed, and when we put these two cosmological considerations together, the concern of the wise men makes much sense, as the revelation they read in the sky told them this: a king, signified by Jupiter, would be born in a western area around Israel in the final days of earth,[17] and this king would be powerful in war, since Mars signified a warrior. In this light, we understand why the wise men came to the king of Israel bearing precious gifts: to win his favor in these urgent hours.[18]

Issue 3

Do yourself a favor and read every single one of Pope Benedict XVI's Christmas Vigil Mass homilies, available on the Vatican's website. They are some of the best homilies I have ever read and heard! See, in particular, his homily from 2006.[19]

Issue 4

The second decree of the fourth session of the Council of Trent affirmed that the Vulgate is the only "authentic" and "approved" Latin version of the Bible, befitting especially use in

---

[16] Kilgallen, *New Testament Guide*, 127.

[17] Pisces, the celestial section in which the planets aligned, corresponded to the area of Israel and signified the end of the world.

[18] Kilgallen, *New Testament Guide*, 128–29.

[19] Pope Benedict XVI, Homily, Midnight Mass, "Solemnity of the Nativity of the Lord," December 24, 2006, accessed June 4, 2017, http://w2.vatican.va/content/benedict-xvi/en/homilies/2006/documents/hf_ben-xvi_hom_20061224_christmas.html.

the liturgy.[20] Although some English translations (like the RSV) which go back to the original languages do, arguably, a better job of translating some passages than does the Vulgate,[21] the Church today retains the liturgical use of the Vulgate. In the United States, our official version of the Bible is the New American Bible (NAB), which is based on the Vulgate, though it also does incorporate advances in linguistic studies of the Bible's original languages.

POINTS FOR REFLECTION

- What do you mean when you say, in prayer: "Our Father?" How is God "Father" to you? Does your image of God include the idea that, like a good father, God is faithful to the covenantal promises that he makes to you?

- Jesus, God-with-us (Emanuel, Mt 1:23), is peace (Mic 5:4a). Where do you find peace? Is Jesus your peace which the world cannot give (Jn 14:27)?

- Have you ever noticed that many Christmas songs are written as lullabies? Think about "Away in a Manger," "What Child Is This?" and "O Little Town of Bethlehem." All express a fond and endearing devotion to the newborn Baby Jesus. Moreover, has it ever hit you just how awesome it is that we Christians believe in a God who chose to come among us as a child? No other religious group believes that their god is a small child. Most peoples in the days of Jesus supposed their god(s) to be mighty and warrior-like, but not Christians, who, in the Christ child, saw God in the gentle and tender love of a baby. Pope Benedict XVI, in his 2008 Christmas Vigil homily, offers a quote that conveys in a truly singular way one of the most beautiful aspects of our faith:

---

[20] See Norman Tanner, *Decrees of the Ecumenical Councils*, vol. 1 (Washington, DC: Georgetown University Press, 1990), 664.

[21] This is due to its own transmission errors and to later advances in the study of Biblical Hebrew.

The medieval theologian William of Saint Thierry once said that God—from the time of Adam—saw that his grandeur provoked resistance in man, that [by him] we felt limited in our own being and threatened in our freedom. Therefore God chose a new way. He became a child. He made himself dependent and weak, in need of our love. Now this God who has become a child says to us: you can no longer fear me, you can only love me.[22]

Wow![23]

- Do you, like Jerome, love to be near to Jesus in prayer? Do you spend quiet hours in front of the tabernacle, or before an altar where Jesus enters the world, again and again, at Holy Mass? Let Jerome be for you both an example to imitate and an intercessor to beseech for you from the child Jesus the grace to desire to be near him.

- How do you exercise humility? Can you see ways in which you can be more self-deferential in your home and in your workplace? Do you recognize and embrace your weaknesses and imperfections, offering them up to God who, in the person of Jesus, became weak for our sake? Turn to Our Lady and ask Mary to give you to share in her humility.

Especially for Seminarians

- In reflecting on God's fatherhood, it is important to remember that you, as a priest, will be called "Father" every day of your life; this appellation should call you to be

---

[22] Pope Benedict XVI, Homily, Midnight Mass, Solemnity of the Nativity of the Lord, December 24, 2008, accessed June 4, 2017, https://w2.vatican.va/content/benedict-xvi/en/homilies/2008/documents/hf_ben-xvi_hom_20081224_christmas.html.

[23] A piece of sacred music that sublimely conveys our wonder over the "Great Mystery" of the Incarnation at Bethlehem is Tomás Luiz de Victoria's *O Magnum Mysterium* (1572), YouTube video, 4:17, accessed June 4, 2017, https://www.youtube.com/watch?v=9xPh-fXY-Ac4.

faithful to the promises that you make—the recitation of the Liturgy of the Hours and to celibacy. How have you been faithful to those promises already, in preparation for Holy Orders?

- Do you exercise the virtue of humility, and in what way? Is there some pride or arrogance in your soul that needs to be uprooted—you who will be called to deny yourself, take up your cross and follow Jesus (Lk 9:23), who, though he was rich, became poor so that through his poverty all might become rich (2 Cor 8:9)? How do you "empty" yourself (Phil 2:7), you who will yourself bend the knee before others in order to wash their feet (Jn 13:1–20)? "Remember, man, you are dust,[24] and unto dust you shall return" (Gen 3:19).

---

[24] In Latin, *humus*, from which we derive *humility*.

EIN KEREM

During those days, Mary set out and traveled to the hill country in haste to a town of Judah, where she entered the house of Zechariah and greeted Elizabeth. When Elizabeth heard Mary's greeting, the infant leaped in her womb, and Elizabeth, filled with the Holy Spirit, cried out in a loud voice and said: "Most blessed are you among women, and blessed is the fruit of your womb."

(Luke 1:39–42)

Scriptural Background

Once the Archangel Gabriel, having announced to Mary the birth of her son, the Messiah, departed, Luke tells us that Mary set out from Nazareth in haste to the hill country, to a town of Judah, to attend to the needs of her cousin, Elizabeth, who had marvelously conceived a son in her old age and was already in the sixth month of pregnancy (Lk 1:36). The Bible does not identify the town to which Mary hastens, but tradition says that it was Ein Kerem, which sits about four miles west of Jerusalem in an indeed very hilly region. Here lived Elizabeth and Zachariah, and later with them their son, John. So, in this place, there occurred the famous events of Luke 1:39–80: the Visitation (vv. 39–45), including Mary's *Magnificat* (vv. 46–56); the birth of John (vv. 57–66), including Zechariah's *Benedictus* (vv. 67–79); and John's permanence "in the desert until the day of his manifestation to Israel" (v. 80).

The Church of the Visitation.

Archeological History

At Ein Kerem, we find two churches: in the town, the Church of St. John the Baptist, and on the outskirts of the town, the Church of the Visitation. The usual route from one church to the other takes the traveler by a spring of water called, since the 1300s, the Fountain of the Vineyard, which is the meaning of the town's name: *ein* ("fountain [of]") *kerem* ("the vineyard").[1] At the Church of St. John the Baptist are commemorated the birth

---

[1] Kilgallen, *New Testament Guide*, 102–3.

of John and his father's inspired hymn. If you descend the stairs to the left of the altar, you will see that John's birthplace is commemorated with a little round disk on the floor; the circumscription reads: "Here the Precursor of the Lord was born." At the Church of the Visitation, the encounter of Mary and Elizabeth and Mary's own hymn of praise are recalled. In the church's lower level, a rock memorializes the second-century legend in which the baby Baptist, with Elizabeth, there escaped the massacre of the Holy Innocents (Mt 2:16), as recounted in the *Protoevangelium of James* 22.3:

> Elizabeth, having heard that they were searching for John, took him and went up into the hill-country, and kept looking where to conceal him. And there was no place of concealment. And Elizabeth, groaning with a loud voice, said: "O mountain of God, receive mother and child." And immediately the mountain was cleft, and received her.[2]

The rock which split open upon Elizabeth's prayers to God for help in hiding her son from the slaughter of the Holy Innocents by King Herod.

Hence the Latin inscription above the rock, in English: "In this rock it was given for Elizabeth and John to hide away."

"Which event(s) actually happened *where*?" you might ask. As it is, that question is incredibly difficult to answer. Murphy-O'Connor seems skeptical not only of the church's locations but also of the location of the Visitation event. About the latter, he writes: "the attractiveness of the site, and the fact that it is equidistant from Jerusalem and Bethlehem, probably explain

[2] Trans. Alexander Walker (1886), rev. and ed. Kevin Knight, accessed June 4, 2017, http://www.newadvent.org/fathers/0847.htm.

the 6th century tradition which placed here [the events of Lk 1:39–80]." Regarding the former, he posits: "Two churches are mentioned in the 12th century when the property apparently belonged to the Augustinian canons who served the Templum Domini (Dome of the Rock). In the post-Crusader period, traditions tended to move from one church to the other and back again depending on which was the more accessible at any given time."[3]

I, personally, would not question the veracity of the region/town—and this, ironically, on Murphy-O'Connor's own information later provided. He mentions that the earliest church on the site of the Church of St. John the Baptist goes back to the fifth century; this fact, I deem, could certainly be a fruit of credible, early-Christian memory. Moreover, on the next page, Murphy-O'Connor mentions the confirmation, on the part of an 1106 visitor to the Church of the Visitation, of the localization there of that second-century legend in which the Baptist escaped

The hill country of Ein Kerem, where Elizabeth and Zechariah lived.

3   Murphy-O'Connor, *The Holy Land*, 169.

the massacre of the children of Bethlehem.[4] The early dates of these traditions lead me to think that, here, we need to be "meek as doves" (Mt 10:6) and give tradition the benefit of the doubt, at least with regard to the likelihood of the events taking place in this town and its vicinity.

However, with regard to where precisely within this town— meaning, at which church's location—these things happened, I think we need to be "cunning as serpents" (Mt 10:6) and take a realistic look at the situation. From what I understood from my early Christian history class, before the tenth century, both the birth of John and the Visitation occurred at the location of the current Church of St. John the Baptist. However, thanks to the work of a certain monk, Daniel, the events came to be separated, geographically. Why this displacement happened, nobody really knows: perhaps it was in order to facilitate pilgrims, given that the site of the house of John was closed to Christians during the centuries in which it was occupied by Muslims, who "used it as a byre,"[5] until the Franciscans recovered it in the second half of the sixteenth century.

In any event, the churches, as well as the views of the hills and valleys, are quite beautiful! The upper Church of the Visitation houses glorious, frescoed tributes—biblical, historical, and doctrinal!—to Mary. Each is an excellent place to take up Mary and Zechariah's hymns in praise to God for his providence and mercy.

SCRIPTURE ON SITE:

Luke 1:39-56 (Visitation of Mary to Elizabeth)

Luke 1:57-80 (Birth of John the Baptist)

---

[4] Ibid., 170.
[5] Ibid., 169.

Issues Raised

Issue 1

A hermit who gave my class a tour of Ein Kerem's surroundings told us that John the Baptist can be seen depicted in art as if he were a figure of "Adam in exile." Just as Adam was given to make a patched loin cloth to cover up his shame as a result of the first sin, John the Baptist is usually clothed in a ratty, tattered cloth, which represents the old sin of Adam that is about to be removed, taken off—or, better, "taken away"—by the "Lamb of God," whom John points out to be Jesus (Jn 1:29), the one who, by his Passion and Resurrection, takes away the sins of the world, restoring to us the dignity from which we had fallen.

Issue 2

Kilgallen expounds on the identification of Mary and Israel. In Christian piety, our Sorrowful Mother is identified, per Lamentations 2:13, with the virgin daughter Zion.[6] In Kilgallen's words:

> In watching how the [Magnificat] psalm develops from Mary's particular glorification to the promise that God will glorify all his people, one realizes that Mary knows her child is not for herself alone. In a sense, she is Israel, the people chosen by God, who are lowly and liable to be forgotten, but now destined, as in the past, to enjoy the blessing of God, this time through Jesus. Mary's psalm is a hymn of encouragement: the lowliness of Israel (indeed enslaved to Rome) should not discourage one from trusting that God will remain faithful to his agreement to protect Israel. Israel should always remember, should never forget, the many times God has intervened on its behalf, for those past interventions are constant proofs that God will intervene again, for he is faithful to his word. Mary's pregnancy is the latest, indeed we believe the most glorious, of God's loving interventions, an ex-

---

[6] We Catholics are used to hearing, especially at the fourth Station of the Cross, "For great as the sea is your *distress*." Perhaps that translation came through the Latin *contritio* here in Lam 2:13; both the Hebrew Masoretic Text and the Greek Septuagint text, on the other hand, convey by this verb in question an action akin to destruction, shattering, bursting, ruin, etc.

pression of God's love rooted in his promise to Abraham: "I will be your God."[7]

POINTS FOR REFLECTION

- The fruit of the Second Joyful Mystery is well chosen: love of neighbor. In this episode, we see Mary, herself having received incredible news, depart in haste not to go tell Elizabeth about her own (indeed earth-shattering, history-changing) news, but rather to help her cousin. She divined from Gabriel's message that Elizabeth could use her help, as she was with child despite being past normal conceiving age (Lk 1:36). Mary's interests were never her own; she never sought her own will, but rather God's (Lk 1:38), and here considered the needs of others before the needs of her own. Moreover, she made personal sacrifice to show such selfless charity to the mother of John the Baptist: the journey to Ein Kerem from Nazareth meant days of walking through rugged and hilly terrain. What altruism in this act of visitation! And yet, how often do we sin against charity toward our neighbor, in particular by falling into selfishness! Here would be a good place to pray not only for humility, but also for a greater charity toward your neighbor. Paul tells the Philippians: "Do nothing out of selfishness or out of vainglory; rather, humbly regard others as more important than yourselves, each looking out not for his own interests, but everyone for those of others" (2:3–4). Do you?

Especially For Seminarians

- Such lines as those above speak particularly to us priests, who should strive to minister zealously with the pastoral charity encompassed in St. John Vianney's famous phrase: "The priest is not a priest for himself, he is a priest for you."[8]

---

7   Kilgallen, *New Testament Guide*, 104.

8   Cited in Pope Benedict XVI, *Letter Proclaiming a Year for Priests* (2009), accessed June 4, 2017, http://w2.vatican.va/content/benedict-xvi/en/letters/2009/documents/hf_ben-xvi_let_20090616_anno-sacerdotale.html#_ftn6 (link to footnote 6).

CLOSING PRAYER

"It is all for your sake, so that as grace extends to more and more people, it may increase thanksgiving, to the glory of God" (2 Corinthians 4:15)

Here at the end of our pilgrimage to the Holy Land, we would do well to pause and offer to the Lord a prayer of thanks for all of the blessings that he has bestowed upon us during our days in these truly sacred places. Let us pray:

"Lord, it is good that we are here" (Matt 17:4). We have been so privileged to experience firsthand the land that you called your home—the hills and valleys, seas and rivers, country sides and cities with which you were so familiar. We turn to you with hearts full of gratitude. In the words of David, your forefather, we give thanks to you with all our hearts, and we promise you that we will tell of all your wonderful deeds (Psalm 9:1) to our friends and families. Let the graces that we have received in our pilgrimage till the soil of our hearts, so that the seeds of faith that you have planted therein may blossom and bear great fruit (Luke 8:8). Please protect and prosper our brothers and sisters in Christian faith who live in the Holy Land. And may Mary of Nazareth, who there welcomed God into her heart and into her home, obtain for us the grace to invite and welcome you her Son, our Savior, into our own lives.

BIBLIOGRAPHY

Akin, Jimmy. "Where the Evangelists Got Their Information." *Catholic Answers*. August 13, 2012. Accessed June 4, 2017. Http://www.catholic.com/magazine/print-edition/where-the-evangelists-got-their-information.

Aquinas, Thomas. *Super Evangelium Sancti Matthaei lectura*. Edited by R. Cai. Turin: Marietti, 1951.

Augustine of Hippo. *The Confessions*. Translated by Maria Boulding. New York: Vintage, 1997.

———. *Contra Faustum*. Translated by Richard Stothert, 1887. Revised and Edited by Kevin Knight, 2009. Http://www.newadvent.org/fathers/1406.htm.

———. *De Doctrina Christiana*. Translated by Edmund Hill. New York: New City Press, 1996.

Benedict XVI, Pope (as Joseph Ratzinger). "Biblical Interpretation in Crisis: The 1988 Erasmus Lecture." *First Things* (April 26, 2008). Accessed June 4, 2017. Https://www.firstthings.com/web-exclusives/2008/04/biblical-interpretation-in-cri.

———. General Audience, March 7, 2007. Accessed June 4, 2017. Https://w2.vatican.va/content/benedict-xvi/en/audiences/2007/documents/hf_ben-xvi_aud_20070307.html.

———"Faith, Reason, and the University: Memories and Reflections" ("The Regensburg Lecture"). September 12, 2006. Accessed June 4, 2017. Https://w2.vatican.va/content/benedictxvi/en/speeches/2006/september/documents/hf_ben-xvi_spe_20060912_university-regensburg.html. German Original: "Glaube, Vernunft und Universität: Errinnerungen und Reflexionen." *Acta Apostolica Sedes* 98, no.10 (October 6, 2006): 728–39.

———. Homily, Midnight Mass: Solemnity of the Nativity of the Lord, December 24, 2006. Accessed June 4, 2017. Http://w2.vatican.va/content/benedict-xvi/en/homilies/2006/documents/hf_ben-xvi_hom_20061224_christmas.html.

———. Homily, Midnight Mass: Solemnity of the Nativity of the Lord, December 24, 2008. Accessed June 4, 2017. Https://w2.vatican.va/content/benedict-xvi/en/homilies/2008/documents/hf_ben-xvi_hom_20081224_christmas.html.

——— (as Joseph Ratzinger). *Jesus of Nazareth: Holy Week; From the Entrance into Jerusalem to the Resurrection*. New York: Image, 2011.

———. *Letter Proclaiming a Year for Priests*. 2009. Accessed June 4, 2017. Http://w2.vatican.va/content/benedict-xvi/en/letters/2009/documents/hf_ben-xvi_let_20090616_anno-sacerdotale.html.

——— (as Joseph Ratzinger). *The Spirit of the Liturgy*. San Francisco: Ignatius Press, 2000.

———. "Travel Companions. A Reflection of Benedict XVI." *L'Osservatore Romano*. October 12, 2016. Accessed June 4, 2017. Http://www.osservatoreromano.va/en/news/travel-companions.

Bergsma, John S., and Scott W. Hahn. "What Laws were 'Not Good'? A Canonical Approach to the Theological Problem of Ezekiel 20:25–26." *Journal of Biblical Literature* 123, no. 2 (2004): 201–18.

Catechism of the Catholic Church. 2nd ed. Washington, DC: United States Catholic Conference, 2000.

Collins, John J., *The Scepter and the Star: The Messiahs of the Dead Sea Scrolls and Other Ancient Literature*. Grand Rapids, MI: Eerdmans, 2010.

Conley, James. "Looking to the East." *Southern Nebraska Register*. November 21, 2014. Accessed June 4, 2017. Http://www.lincolndiocese.org/op-ed/bishop-s-column/3004-looking-to-the-east.

Davies, William D., and Dale C. Allison, *The Gospel According to Saint Matthew: I–VII*. International Critical Commentary. Edinburgh: Bloomsbury T & T Clark, 1997.

Fassberg, Steven. "Which Semitic Language Did Jesus and Other Contemporary Jews Speak?" *Catholic Biblical Quarterly* 74 (2012): 263–80.

Feingold, Lawrence. *Faith Comes from What Is Heard: An Introduction to Fundamental Theology*. Steubenville, OH: Emmaus Academic, 2016.

———. *The Mystery of Israel and the Church: Things Old and New*. Volume 2. Saint Louis, MO: The Miriam Press, 2010.

Flusser, David. *Jewish Sources in Early Christianity*. Jerusalem: Adama Books, 1987.

Francis, Pope. Post-synodal Apostolic Exhortation *Amoris Laetitia*. March 19, 2016.

Grilli, Massimo. *Quale rapporto tra i due Testamenti? Riflessione critica sui modelli ermeneutici classici concernenti l'unità delle Scritutture*. Bologna: EDB, 2007.

Hahn, Scott W. "Abba or Allah: Important Differences between Catholicism and Islam." Lighthouse Catholic Media, 2011.

———. *A Father Who Keeps His Promises: God's Covenant Love in Scripture*. Cincinnati, OH: Servant, 1998.

———. *The Lamb's Supper: The Mass as Heaven on Earth*. New York: Doubleday, 1999.

———. *Understanding "Our Father": Biblical Reflections on the Lord's Prayer*. Steubenville, OH: Emmaus Road, 2002.

Harrison, Brian. "Does Vatican Council II Allow for Errors in Sacred Scripture?" *Living Tradition,* nos. 145–46 (2010). Accessed June 4, 2017. Http://www.rtforum.org/lt/lt145-6.html. Originally in *Divinitas* 52, no. 3 (2009): 279–304.

———. "Restricted Inerrancy and the Hermeneutic of Discontinuity." *Letter and Spirit* 6 [*For the Sake of Our Salvation*] (2010): 225–46.

John Paul II, Pope. Encyclical Letter *Fides et Ratio*. September 14, 1998.

———. Apostolic Letter *Novo Millennio Ineunte*. January 6, 2001.

———. "The Roots of Anti-Judaism in the Christian Environment" (Discourse at the Synagogue of Rome). April, 1986. Accessed June 4, 2017. Http://www.vatican.va/jubilee_2000/magazine/documents/ju_mag_01111997_p-42x_en.html.

Josephus, Flavius. *Antiquities of the Jews*. In *The Works of Josephus: Complete and Unabridged*, 30–650. Translated by William Whitson. Peabody, MA: Hendrickson Publishers, 1987.

———. *Wars of the Jews*. In Whitson, *Works of Josephus*, 651–925.

Kenyon, Kathleen M. *Archaeology of the Holy Land*. London: Ernest Benn Limited, 1965.

Kitchen, Kenneth A. *On the Reliability of the Old Testament*. Grand Rapids, MI: Eerdmans, 2003.

Kilgallen, John J. *A New Testament Guide to the Holy Land*. Chicago: Loyola Press, 1998.

May, Natalie N. "City Gates and Their Functions in Mesopotamia and Ancient Israel." In *The Fabric of Cities: Aspects of Urbanism, Urban Topography and Society in Mesopotamia,*

Greece and Rome, 77–121. Edited by Natalie N. May and Ulrike Steinert. Leiden: Brill, 2014.

Meier, John P. *A Marginal Jew: Rethinking the Historical Jesus.* Volume 1. Anchor Bible Reference Library. New York: Doubleday, 1991.

Murphy-O'Connor, Jerome. *The Holy Land: An Oxford Archaeological Guide from Earliest Times to 1700.* 5th ed. Oxford: Oxford University Press, 2008.

Pacwa, Mitch. *Holy Land Prayer Book.* San Francisco: Ignatius Publications, 2004.

Paul VI, Pope. Homily at Nazareth. January 5, 1964. Accessed June 4, 2017. Https://www.crossroadsinitiative.com/media/articles/lessons-of-nazareth/.

Pitre, Brant. *Jesus and the Jewish Roots of the Eucharist: Unlocking the Secrets of the Last Supper.* New York: Image, 2011.

———. *Jesus and the Last Supper.* Grand Rapids, MI: Eerdmans, 2015.

Pixner, Bargil. *Paths of the Messiah and Sites of the Early Church from Galilee to Jerusalem: Jesus and Jewish Christianity in Light of Archaeological Discoveries.* Edited by Rainer Riesner. Translated by Keith Myrick and Sam and Miriam Randall. San Francisco: Ignatius Press, 2010.

Pontifical Biblical Commission. *The Inspiration and Truth of Sacred Scripture.* Translated by Thomas Esposito, O.Cist, and Stephen Gregg, O.Cist. Collegeville, MN: Liturgical Press, 2014.

———. *The Interpretation of the Bible in the Church.* Boston: St. Paul Books and Media, 1993.

Puhl, Louis J. *The Spiritual Exercises of St. Ignatius: Based on Studies in the Language of the Autograph.* Chicago: Loyola Press, 1951.

Serratelli, Arthur J. "Praying Ad Orientem." *Catholic News Agency.* February 28, 2017. Accessed June 4, 2017. Http://www.catholicnewsagency.com/column/praying-ad-orientem-3713/.

Stub, Sarah T. "A 1,000-Year-Old Promise of Peace." BBC Website. November 28, 2016. Accessed June 4. Http://www.bbc.com/travel/story/20161121-a-1000-year-old-promise-of-peace.

Suarez, Federico. *Mary of Nazareth*. New York: Scepter Publishers, 2003.

Tanner, Norman. *Decrees of the Ecumenical Councils*. Volume 1. Washington, DC: Georgetown University Press, 1990.

Trochu, Abbé François. *The Curé d'Ars*. Translated by Dom Ernest Graf. Charlotte, NC: TAN Books, 2007.

Vanderkam, James C., and Peter Flint, *The Meaning of the Dead Sea Scrolls: Their Significance for Understanding the Bible, Judaism, Jesus, and Christianity*. San Francisco: Harper Collins, 2002.

Vatican Council, First. Dogmatic Constitution *Dei Filius*. 1870.

Vatican Council, Second. Dogmatic Constitution on Divine Revelation, *Dei Verbum*. 1965.

Vermes, Gaza. *The Complete Dead Sea Scrolls in English*. London: Penguin Classics, 2012.

De Victoria, Tomás Luiz. *O Magnum Mysterium*. 1572. YouTube video, 4:17. Accessed June 4, 2017. Https://www.youtube.com/watch?v=9xPh-fXYAc4.

Walker, Alexander, trans., 1886. *Protoevangelium of James*. Revised and edited by Kevin Knight. Accessed June 4, 2017. Http://www.newadvent.org/fathers/0847.htm.

Waugh, Evelyn. *Edmund Campion: Jesuit and Martyr*. New York: Image, 1962.

Weigel, George. *Letters to a Young Catholic*. New York: Basic Books, 2015.